THE
ROAD
HOME

In Praise of *The Road Home*

"Without sugar-coating the difficulties, *The Road Home* is a specific guide for families getting back together with all the messiness and opportunities to try again. Ruben's affection for parents as well as young people shines through this book. It's a life-affirming handbook on families that should be on every parent's bedside table, not just the parents who've had their children in treatment."

—**Anne Lewis**, MA
    Educational Consultant
    www.TeenHelpCenter.net

"*The Road Home* fills a much needed and profoundly missing link in the journey of healing, hope, and wholeness for those navigating the challenging terrain of bringing your child home. Ruben Jimenez's ability to combine his clinical experience, life-long learning, spiritual wisdom, and good old common-sense practicality have created a wonderfully livable and applicable resource for you and your family."

—**LeeAnn Heinbaugh**, MA
    Journeys in Living
    www.JourneysInLiving.com

"With a son on the cusp of returning home from treatment, my husband and I found *The Road Home*. Hallelujah! It was exactly what we had been praying for, a step-by-step guide, complete with all the tools necessary to insure our part in the recovery process was a success. Ruben has given us a newfound confidence in parenting all of our kids."

—**Jacque Connor**

"I read *The Road Home* at the perfect time in our family's process. Our son had just returned home from treatment after nearly two years away. Our therapeutic boarding school prepared us, but the reality of his being home, now a young man, meant that there were many "what now" moments for our family. *The Road Home* provided concrete suggestions as to the next steps to be taken and how to implement a plan that would work for our son and our whole family. Sending your child away is a life changing decision for all involved. After all of the emotional growth and expense, it was a welcome resource to have this book and use it as a guide for this next part of our journey."

—Hallie Rosen

"*The Road Home* provides an invaluable and highly-accessible roadmap for families at a critical, and often times overwhelming, crossroad. Ruben delivers his message with not only wisdom and authority, but frank honesty and humor. His model provides concrete and practical guidance, while fostering in families a greater sense of connection, a more clear understanding of their strengths and values, and the ability to move forward with confidence and clarity."

—Joshua J. Cluff, PsyD
ClearView Psychological Services
Salt Lake City, UT
www.DrJoshuaCluff.com

THE
ROAD
HOME

A Guide for Parents with Teens or
Young Adults Returning from Treatment

Ruben Jimenez
LCSW

ROAD
BOOKS

Published and distributed by:
Road Books
P.O. Box 44
Ojai, CA 93024 USA
Tel: +1 970.426.9227
www.RubenJimenez.com

Contact us for information on author interviews or speaking engagements.

First Edition
Printed in the United States of America

Designed by Kayla Morelli
Cartoon art by Greer Haines Nelson

Publisher's Cataloging-in-Publication Data
Jimenez, Ruben.
    The road home : a guide for parents with teens or young adults returning from treatment / Ruben Jimenez — 1st ed. — Ojai, CA : Road Books, 2014.
    p. : ill. ; cm.
    The Road Home is a guide for parents that provides practical tools, insights, and strategies to help their child translate the gains made in treatment to the real world, while managing their own emotional health and well-being.
    ISBN: 9780990009009
    1. Young adults — Substance use — Prevention. 2. Teenagers — Substance use — Prevention. 3. Parenting. 4. Parents of drug addicts. 5. Parents of alcoholics.

HV4999.Y68 .J56 2014   649.48 — dc23

2013918091

This book is dedicated to my parents.

For my dad, Ruben, who always told me to "Go for it, son." At times I resisted, but I have lived those words in my finer moments. And for my mother, MaryAnn, who taught me to follow my heart and spirit.

I further dedicate this book to the parents, teens, and young adults who were my real university. I humbly thank you for inviting me into your living rooms and your lives—no small matter.

You continue to teach me.

Contents

Foreword · xi

Introduction · xv

1. Parenting in Today's Culture · 1

2. Understanding Your Child · 13

3. Preparing for Your Child's Return · 31

4. Unearthing Your Vision, Values, and Expectations · 51

5. Becoming Confident, Middle-of-the-Road Parents · 79

6. Engaging in Transparent and Loving Communication · 99

7. Embracing the Concept of Rules · 117

8. Crafting Your Family Rules of the Road · 129

9. Adding Truth and Consequences · 191

10. Addressing Mental Health and Addiction · 213

11. Writing the Home Agreement · 245

12. Rolling Out the Welcome Mat · 293

13. Navigating the Reunion · 309

14. Growing Your Child's Inner Adult · 347

15. Dealing with Regression · 375

16. Surviving a Transition in Trouble · 393

17. Paving the Road Ahead · 405

Acknowledgments · 413

Foreword
by Heide Boyden

We have two children, born 18 months apart. I gave birth naturally because I wanted the world to be their oyster, and for them to greet it as clear and clean as possible. I made sure they listened to music and foreign language in the womb. I nursed them and feathered our nest with activity charts and picture books. We chose the best schools to stimulate their keen minds. And then one day our oldest at the age of 14, lashed out at us. He hated us. He turned on us. Our bell jar cracked. Then it shattered when we found out he was using drugs. Not just a little weed now and then, but lots of drugs. All kinds of drugs. Regularly.

When we sent our son, at the tail end of his sophomore year in high school, to wilderness therapy we felt instant relief. That lasted all of two days, and then the loss gutted us. We missed him, not the dysfunction, but who our son truly was. We ached for his soccer games, to witness his clunky young romances; I wanted to cook for him. I envied my friends who still enjoyed family movie nights and worried about catastrophes such a driver's test flunked for a second time. I missed being "normal." Why had we been robbed of something I never thought could be taken away from us—parenting our son?

As our son moved on to a therapeutic boarding school, it was fear that crippled me. What if he was the one kid that couldn't be helped? What if he was an addict? What if it was all my fault? A year sometimes dragged and sometimes flew by and then it was time for our child to come home for a visit, which signaled that within a year he would be coming home for good. The school staff did its best to educate us, but how could we ever help our son the way all those knowledgeable professionals could? Our son spent the last six months in his school's exceptional and unique transitional program, but there wasn't such a program for us—the parents. It became evident that we needed more help to prepare for his return, but there were no books, or Internet sites dedicated to this topic.

Our educational consultant recommended Ruben Jimenez, a veteran wilderness therapist who had recently moved to our community and had set up shop as a family coach. We wasted no time and called him.

Ruben's gentle demeanor and genuine understanding of what we had gone through set the stage for a trusting relationship. Ruben began our work by prompting us to reestablish the ideals and ethics we wanted our children to embrace. He helped us plant our feet firmly on the earth and establish boundaries and a Home Agreement that our son and we could live up to. He taught us, with patience and wit, how to have honest conversations with our kids and one another. During all this, we consistently encouraged Ruben to actually write the book he had in his head but could never quite put on paper. I guess we were convincing because you now hold that book in your hands.

Eventually, with Ruben's guidance and our son's willingness and hard work put forth at his therapeutic school, we welcomed our son home and even ushered him off to college. It hasn't been smooth every step of the way, and yet it hasn't been hell either.

The Road Home has met a great need. It is the single resource out there that helps parents translate what treatment centers do into practical and useful information that can be used effectively at home. Don't stuff this book on your bookshelf. Leave it open on the kitchen table. Sit down and complete the action steps. Use it daily to gain the confidence and know-how it takes to raise and eventually launch your child.

Working with Ruben and subsequently reading and following *The Road Home* has given us back our parenthood. It has made us feel almost "normal" again. That being said, I'm reminded of a quick quote I read on a post-it note once: "Normal—a cycle on the washing machine."

I wish you a very successful and loving homecoming.

Introduction

If you're reading this book, you've already been through the wringer. You have bled, sweated, and wept. Then you became exhausted beyond tears. Many of you have lost years to worry, have lost your health, or have even lost your job or your spouse over this process of helping your child. And now, the weight of helping your child can feel significantly heavy again, because your child is leaving treatment and coming home.

You could not predict your child's journey or control the being you brought into this world. You didn't know your child would have serious issues. Most likely you have felt very alone and completely lost, like your world was out of control. You have watched your child fall apart and you've covered for him through thick and thin. You've sent him to treatment and now you are anticipating his return with mixed emotions. The last thing you need is a book that shames you or sends you on a guilt trip. What you need is a guide, a map that shows you how to successfully move your child back home and out into the world. You need a path—a "road home"—just as much as your child does.

In reading this book, you are about to continue the journey of raising your child, after treatment. When I say "treatment," I refer to a multitude of modalities, including:

- Therapeutic wilderness programs

- Leadership and other programs for kids at risk

- Therapeutic boarding schools

- Therapeutic transitional living

- Residential living and treatment centers

- Drug and alcohol treatment and rehabilitation centers

It's part of my purpose to let you know that you have done the very best you could in parenting a child born with free will into this messy, crazy world. The most important part of my mission is to help you as you navigate this rat race we live in with a teen or young adult in tow. You are now looking for assistance with this child who has had treatment, and that's what I want to give you. To develop trust, I think it's only fair that I let you know a bit more about who I am and what I believe. You can then make an informed decision as to whether or not what I have to offer is for you.

I am a licensed clinical social worker, which means I have psychiatric training. I have had the good fortune to be trained in research-oriented placements and extensive private practice. I've worked in clinical settings and in the wilderness. I chose, in the past, to work primarily in the field of wilderness therapy and the common after-care options—therapeutic boarding schools, residential treatment centers, and drug and alcohol rehabilitation programs. This work taught me a lot about kids and young adults: what they think and what they're up against—their fears, phobias, issues, hopes, and despairs.

While working in wilderness therapy, I asked many educational consultants what needs were not being met for families with children (ages 13 to 17) and young adults (ages 18-28) in treatment. I received the same answers promptly and repeatedly: pre- and post-treatment support, including interventions, the coaching of parents, the mentoring of teen and young adult children, and post-treatment home contract creation and follow-through.

This prompted me to embrace my entrepreneurial spirit and go where I could be most useful. Thus I began my career as a coach for families with children returning home after therapeutic treatment. In the wilderness, I worked at the beginning of a child's journey of healing. Now I work at the end. Since saying farewell to my wilderness career, I have spent countless hours around the country in the living rooms of kids returning home. I have witnessed the challenges. Facing defiance, blame, and regression can be overwhelming—even for me, a seasoned therapist. My clients have helped me gain the wisdom to discern what is healthy human experience and what is pathology or disease.

Through these up-close and real-time experiences families have shared with me, the ideas for this book have been gleaned. The book is intended to be an extension of my service—a resource that provides solutions for all individuals involved in the transition of children and young adults from treatment back to the family.

The information out there for parents who have kids coming home from treatment is overly clinical and obtuse. Parents need better guidance. Most of you are equipped only with a contract that was developed in treatment, often with minimal involvement from you and based on the realities of the therapist and the child in treatment, not on the foundation of your family. Most parents don't know how to translate such a document into something workable at home. That's because you are not, in most cases, clinicians.

Although treatment centers are well intended about the contracts they draw up with their clients, most of those contracts end up in a drawer and never again get referred to, much less enforced. I am not devaluing a contract; in fact the crux of this book is the development of a contract or what I like to call a Home Agreement. But the difference I offer is that a Home Agreement is an extension of who you are. It is actually part of you—what you stand for and believe in, put into words.

The work this book encourages you to do is not driven by treatment. It is only informed by treatment—and driven by *you*. You need the know-how to incorporate your child's continuing treatment goals into the less predictable outside world: home, friends, extended family, school and college, work, community, and the world at large. When your child crosses your threshold once again, you need to be ready to steer your family life with parenting skills based on your values, beliefs, and background . . . your ethos. To navigate this real-world terrain, you'll want a reliable road map and the confidence it takes to get behind the wheel. *The Road Home* is the map that can help bring your child home, with all that it symbolizes—home to you, home to her own true self, and home to her place in the world.

While she heals in treatment, it is an excellent time for you to look at your family system, your marriage, and your personal well-being without wearing blinders or rose-colored glasses. It's the perfect time to take on the work you need to do to help ensure your child's success. *The Road Home* initially provides some theory, but only a chapter or two, and then it dives into practical, can-do information with chapter Action Steps designed to help you:

- Assess your personal life and set up a program to get healthy and strong.

- Rekindle your original visions of a flourishing child and family.

- Determine your family values around which you can build a parenting style and solid home foundation.

- Become confident parents.

- Engage in transparent and loving communication (TLC) to help you develop an authentic relationship with your child.

- Create rules you can enforce.

- Draft a Home Agreement, the heart of the process, in conjunction with your child in treatment and her treatment counselor, with the purpose of continuing your child's positive growth.

- Hold boundaries that support your child's maturation.

- Adjust to life with your child at home and help him launch into the world as a mature and healthy young adult.

Your child is coming home more whole than he has been in a long time. Your dream of seeing him reach for his potential is about to get back on track. And, despite how fearful you are, it is a fact that your child needs to come home and then venture out into the world. Your desire to parent well will never go away, despite your child's age, yet he or she can't be cocooned forever. By the time you've read through this book you will have developed the tools and mindset to manage life with a child such as yours. Perhaps then you can replace the angst you're now experiencing with excitement and anticipation for your child's return.

You can't control what your child will ultimately do. You can, however, influence the environment and conditions surrounding his reentry to home and the world. You have most likely wrestled with guilt, deflected criticism (often from other loved ones), and written letters to your child that drained you and broke your heart. You have heard many dark stories from him about things you hoped he would never have seen or experienced. Most admirably, you have loved him through it all. I would assert that your effort to support his reentry is just as vital as any part of treatment or any action you have taken thus far. It is the most tenuous and important part of the journey.

Keep your eyes and heart open.

I wish you safe and fulfilling travel down the road home.

—*Ruben Jimenez*

THE
ROAD
HOME

1

Parenting in Today's Culture

One fatal error still being routinely made today by treatment professionals is to assume that parents can do what clinicians do, and in the same way. Parents are not, in most instances, clinicians, but you *are* in charge of raising your child. You don't understand pathology, and why should you? You don't have the vocabulary, the training, the countless hours of group therapy under your belt.

You are, however, quite experienced in the history, makeup, and workings of your family. You have your religion or spirituality, your values, and your aspirations. Your culture—what you believe makes up "family"—will be the foundation on which you build and maintain your child's post-treatment gains.

What you need most when your child comes home are parenting skills, complemented by clinical treatment. This book will help you build those skills based upon who you are. As a result, your confidence in your own ability to parent will increase, and you'll be able to let your child know exactly what is expected of him. He will feel safe at home just as he did in treatment, and can continue on a healthy, natural trajectory to adulthood. He will build on the gains already made without your needing to be a psychologist, a licensed clinical social worker, or an addiction counselor.

Coming of Age through the Ages

Before treatment centers existed, before wilderness programs, before state institutions and therapeutic boarding schools, where did youth—not just troubled youth—go to heal and figure out the world in which they lived? Many cultures had their version of treatment within the context of their society. Some native cultures sent their teens on vision quests. The wilderness was not just a metaphor. Wilderness survival was put into practice as youths ventured into the wilds to evolve into their true selves and to come to understand their place in the universe . . . to mature.

I see wilderness therapy and treatment centers as contemporary versions of what humans have used since the dawn of mankind to transition children to adulthood. Your child's distress was a signal, letting you know that it was time for him to wander the wilderness, venture upon an inner journey, and basically gain some time to reflect. It is a powerful gift that you have given in response. I mean, truthfully, how often do any of us get two months to two years to shut out the noise and reflect on our lives?

The Christian culture has for millennia used monasteries to help youth develop depth of character within a scriptural framework. Judaism to this day celebrates rituals centered on the coming of age at 13. Asian culture still uses Buddhist monasteries to foster the development of the young into mature beings.

In southern Nepal, I once visited a Buddhist temple in a refugee camp set up by Sir Edmund Hillary of Mount Everest fame. The chants for the mostly adult congregation were led by 10-year-old monks. Watching these boys giggle while conducting such an important ceremony, I was overwhelmed by how these youths were being guided to maturity. How responsible and yet lighthearted these boys were. They giggled, and yet they could sit obediently, chant with authority, and reflect on their role in the universe.

Children—all children, whether ensconced in Eastern culture or Western—need long moments to gain perspective. They need weeks and months in which to be self-reflective. Maybe that is what treatment has done for your child—provided her with precious time to ignore the outside world's strong, chaotic influences, to gather herself and find her way.

The Elephant in the Room

My pastoral counseling supervisor once said, "To live is to have angst." I agree. To be fully alive, we must acknowledge and respond to that daily knot in our existential gut, but there is something larger looming—the elephant in the room that is crippling us as a society. I'm speaking of a chronic, massive anxiety that overshadows our run-of-the-mill worries and fears.

We live in a time when more is expected of us than ever before, so people tend to jump on board the hamster wheel. Most teens and young adults, at least the ones who I encounter, recognize the insanity of this lifestyle, and they commonly respond to the task before them like this: they freeze. They become rigidly immobile because they're not sure they can meet all the demands of the adult life laid out before them.

With smart phones placing us on call 24/7 to anyone interested in reaching us, with social media contacts appearing more tempting than live friends, we and especially our kids are becoming ever lonelier and more isolated from the world. Virtual reality is replacing real life, and as a result we're seeing a proliferation of new illnesses brought on by panic and melancholia. Like your children, I find this call to be everything to all people in a frenetic life to be overwhelming. Until we learn to respond appropriately, it can make us feel worn out before our time.

I don't know how we'll solve or change this new phenomenon. It might not be possible or even desirable. But, like a traffic cop at the scene of an accident, I can point you in a different direction; I can reroute you. As parents, you need to embrace and model coping skills so your kids don't get derailed, especially post-treatment. And these coping skills I want to offer you are basic: slow down, breathe, and take care of yourself and those close to you.

In fact, the opportunity to slow down is the remediation that occurs in the wilderness. There are no clocks and no plug-ins there. Instead, you tune out to tune in. It is during this quiet, reflective, sit-with-who-you-are-or-might-be time that something crucial happens: young people begin to grow up. They gain the strength and perspective that it takes to meet the expectations and responsibilities that are on the threshold leading to maturity. And maturity promises a future.

Rites of Passage Reinvented

As a culture, we've lost the rites of passage that humans need to mature. Yes, religion still provides a few markers, but overall we no longer have a way of providing loving, communal guidance to our kids. We, as a culture and individually as families, have inadvertently abdicated the responsibility of preparing our children for adulthood. As a result, our very resourceful kids have begun to create their own rites of passage and to invent their own definitions of maturity.

Today, most parents fall back on the age mandated by the Federal Government to consider their children as adults. What's so magical about 18? Why not sooner? Why not 13 or 16, as it has been in many cultures and religions? Some young people, in their restlessness, might be ready before they're 18 to venture from home and gain wisdom from mentors in the world.

Other kids, not so much. Many young adults readily admit that they don't want to grow up and are consciously delaying the process because they're truly scared. On some level, they know they're not prepared for the full responsibilities of adulthood.

Rites of Passage

Ice Age   18th Century   Today

It's an individual journey for each of us. What's important is that parents appropriately push their child to mature, and not hold him back because they can't stand the thought of their baby growing up.

I have only praise for the cultures that still put a reasonable amount of pressure and expectation on teens and young adults to behave beyond their years. Humans want that challenge, and with it we thrive. Unfortunately, the American culture with its grueling pace doesn't provide time to mature, and with its technology and disrupted family systems doesn't provide the experience. While we encourage our kids to follow their bliss, let's also teach them self-reliance, responsible behavior, and a solid work ethic. Today's teens desperately need us to show them when to mature and what maturity looks like. Without this parenting, they wander into adulthood unable to face their fears, work hard, and pay their bills or a fair price for their dreams.

There's No Teacher Like Reality

As a parent, it's very important that you lead and show your child what adulthood looks like, but that doesn't mean you micromanage. Instead, you set boundaries that encourage growth. You can be most helpful as a witness to your child's life, not a control freak, with him also a witness to yours. Witnesses validate experiences and give them a context. When you embrace this role as witness, it allows your child to live life, make choices, and experience the natural consequences of reality while knowing that you are there when it's absolutely necessary. It also allows you to live *your* life—something parents often sacrifice.

> Today's teens desperately need us to show them when to mature and what maturity looks like.

If children are spared reality, they stay entrenched in old, immature patterns. One of the greatest teachers in life is plain old ugly/beautiful reality. There is more desirable change in kids when they must learn to accommodate the world, not the other way around. Life's natural consequences speak to young people in a way that parents, mentors, coaches, therapists, uncles, aunts, priests, and treatment centers cannot. Because what is life? It's reality. How else do these ideas move from theory into practice? How else do they move beyond spirited, philosophical conversations to actions that lead to surviving and even thriving?

Reality is your child getting a job as a waitress and learning how to be pleasant while she has a headache. It's walking to class at the community college. It's paying for his own car insurance. It's having a direct encounter with the world and culture we live in without being saved by loving parents. Reality will mold a narcissistic child into an empathetic young adult quicker than talk therapy.

> Reality will mold a narcissistic child into an empathetic young adult quicker than talk therapy.

When your child discovers that he is not the center of the universe, but just another bumbling human among billions, he will realize that charm gets him little and hard work delivers more. He will learn what sobriety offers and addiction metes out. It's a tough old world, and that is what your child needs to experience . . . sooner rather than later. In order to develop in a healthy way, he needs to encounter reality as a vital part of his journey. The ultimate goal is to make your child ready for the world and capable of shaping it according to his own dreams. By continual interaction with reality, he'll find out who he really is. By experience and achievement, he'll have the opportunity to grow real confidence and self-esteem.

The Gift of Laughter

We often hear that humor is the elixir of life, yet when I walk into a new client's home the tension is often as thick as clabbered milk.

The parents are stressed and holding on to issues so tightly that their fingernails dig into the kitchen table. Parents such as yourself are so accustomed to dealing with the seriousness of your child's situation that it feels sacrilegious or just plain impossible to smile. It might indeed seem twisted to laugh "at a time like this," and yet I do, and I encourage you to join me.

Sometimes worrying and stressing out makes you feel like you're doing something, but this is not the case. Holding tight to any life situation is strangling life. Your home doesn't have to be the gallows, and I know you don't want it to be. People who view life as being so terribly serious get old before their time. They become crippled by negativity . . . paralyzed by their fixations. They lose their innocence.

Your child will come home from treatment happy and doing well, but please know that he'll also be very aware of his challenges and tired of the heaviness and hard psychological work he has benefitted from. He'll want a break from talking about his problems and issues and dealing with consequences. A light, positive environment as he returns home will buoy his spirits. It is up to you to set the attitude for the home. It is ineffective to lead with intense, serious energy that manifests in preaching, lecturing, and micromanaging in a heavy-handed way. Don't become so grown-up and dour that you lose perspective and eventually your child. You do still have a sense of humor. I see it all the time in families that are healing. You can chuckle—even just a little—and with even the least bit of mirth you'll find emotional relief, more clarity for leading your family and a *better perspective.*

Life is full of yin and yang. We need lightness to balance heaviness. If you let it be all heavy, it will pull you down and negatively affect your attitude, relationships, and parenting. Smiles encourage; fear does not. Your child's journey might be a bit heartbreaking, but it has some quality of folly and merrymaking, too. The joy is just as valid as the pain, and deserves as much of the stage. So, like your kid might say, "Lighten up, dude!"

Now that the world in which your child was struggling is before her once again, what you do to back her up will make all the difference in the world. Take heart! It's an unnerving and scary time, but with a little guidance from this book you'll have what it takes to make it profoundly rewarding, too.

2

Understanding Your Child

No doubt the prospect of your child's return has knots in your belly once again. For some time now, you've rested better at night knowing your son or daughter is safe and in good hands.

You probably don't feel that the same is possible when she's under your roof—the place where she sneaked out routinely or got high in the bathroom or used her laptop for things you never dreamed a computer could be used for. As unnerving as the transition might be, in most cases it *is* necessary for your child to return home. Wilderness programs, treatment centers, and therapeutic boarding schools do what they can, but all treatment reaches a point of diminishing returns. Once your teen or young adult has done the necessary work and has grown about as much as can be expected in the treatment environment, she needs to come home, where her growth will continue.

In my view, coming home is the completion of treatment. The exact reasons why children need to come home have yet to be determined, but I speculate that it's a fundamental part of their growth. It makes sense mythologically: the hero returns from the desert to contemplate his recent adventure, to integrate the wisdom he has gained. The child needs to come home and finish childhood before venturing out for the next part of the hero's journey as a young adult.

> As unnerving as the transition might be, in most cases it *is* necessary for your child to return home. Wilderness programs, treatment centers, and therapeutic boarding schools do what they can, but all treatment reaches a point of diminishing returns.

On a pragmatic level, I see kids strongly needing to reconnect with their parents, and vice versa. Home is home. It's the familiar place where teens and young adults get to pet the dog, eat Mom's food, lie on the couch with the family watching a movie, be comfortable, and rest. If a child doesn't complete this part of his journey, it might hold him back from progressing in life. For him, there might always be a sense of unfinished business—no closure on his growing up. Ideally, your home will be the final place for healing before your child steps into the world as an adult.

Rest Assured That Treatment Works

You should feel encouraged to learn that every child I've worked with has changed for the better in treatment. Treatment works. Your child, if nearing the end of her treatment, is probably about as whole as you have ever seen her. She's moving toward maturity, having developed a more adult-like mind and voice, and has integrated her childhood essence within her changing persona. That's more than you could ever have imagined before treatment.

Before   After

Exactly how much change has occurred is the outstanding question. The degree to which your child holds her gains depends on the severity of her issues and the amount and integrity of the work she has done.

During the time of treatment, scores of staff members have worked relentlessly to effect growth and positive change in your child. Yet their ability to do this boiled down to how open your child became, to afford staff the opportunity to help create the necessary change. Treatment provided your child with the containment, assessment, and renewed launch into life she needed to "own" her mental health. Such ownership is crucial, as unresolved mental health issues can be something your daughter or son will live with for a lifetime.

Motivation Is the Key to Success

One of the main variables to treatment success is your child's degree of motivation. Highly motivated kids who do honest work tend to want the same structure and support at home, and they will then succeed. Kids who are less motivated and change to a lesser degree don't want structure and are more defiant.

> The rule of thumb is this: The more real change that happens in treatment, the more real change that will continue to happen at home, given reasonable effort on the part of the parents.

This is an immediate red flag. If your child was consistently stubborn and obstinate in treatment, the return home will be just as rocky. The rule of thumb is this: The more real change that happens in treatment, the more real change that will continue to happen at home, given reasonable effort on the part of the parents.

Keep your child motivated and knowing that the path he began in treatment is well worth it. This flame is fueled in talk therapy, but more importantly it happens through life experience. When your child willingly works toward change and genuinely feels internal rewards such as confidence and joy, he'll maintain his momentum.

My work has been greatly influenced by the theory brought forth in the book *Motivational Interviewing: Preparing People for Change* by William R. Miller and Stephen Rollnick, who suggest that change happens when one has resolved to change. Treatment affords kids the time and coaching they need to explore and resolve their ambivalence toward change, which eventually allows them to indeed change. If a program is savvy enough, the staff facilitates this and then helps your child hold on to gains for the remainder of treatment.

In treatment, some kids heal 99 percent and others 20 percent. No one can really know how honest a child has been, how much he has healed, or how deeply he has traveled on his inner journey until the proof shows up in the pudding at *your* kitchen table.

It is then one of your tasks to learn and follow along with what the treatment staff has been up to, and to emulate a similar process. Parents who push the program to help nail down the "at home" piece contribute greatly to a successful transition. If possible, this work should begin two to three months before your child leaves treatment.

Is It Time to Come Home?

You certainly want to start this journey home with your best foot forward, so what is the first step to mapping out a successful transition? It's making sure your child is actually ready to return. Do not shortchange yourselves. Time and therapeutic treatment are necessary for both you and your child to regain health and normalcy in your lives.

The longer someone gets treatment, the more real and lasting the healing and change will be. Yes, it feels right to miss the hell out of your kid and want him back in the fold, but as with bread in the oven, you don't want to under-bake. You want to knead it, give it the right amount of time to rise, and bake it until it's done. A premature release date, usually the result of a child manipulating parents, jerking the heartstrings, is rarely effective. Believe your treatment program professionals when they say your child is not ready for home. Do not let guilt undermine your parenting when you have your child on the road to health and maturity. Be strong and confident enough to know that you're doing the right thing by keeping your child in treatment. You're gifting him with help that you are not trained to give directly. Sending him to treatment and keeping him there as recommended is good parenting.

> Do not let guilt undermine your parenting when you have your child on the road to health and maturity.

Too often I have heard parents say, "I brought him home too early, and I knew I shouldn't have." Please do not go against your gut. Some more cunning kids will work parents for an early release. They portray life in treatment as being so miserable that their parents cave in. Don't take the bait! Instead, follow your insight and instinct, and gather input from your child's treatment team to truly assess his status before he returns.

If there are green lights everywhere, then cross this intersection. If there are "Caution" and "Men at Work" signs popping up and you can afford to continue treatment, then disappoint your child and keep him in the program or move on to another treatment modality. If signals are mixed, then explore the facts set before you by the treatment team and move forward judiciously. Maybe your child needs to be pressed to sort out his most disconcerting issues before coming home. Most programs customize treatment and will address further issues with your child or extend treatment for a few more months per your request.

Wilderness therapy makes real inroads with kids in trouble, but it's harder to hold on to those inroads if a child goes directly home. If your child is not healed on a significant level and you can afford it, aftercare is highly beneficial and often recommended. If she is belligerent, med-noncompliant, or fully intending to go back to drug addiction, move her into additional or more suitable treatment.

As a general rule, long-standing mental health issues call for longer treatment. Such issues include, but are not limited to, severe mood disorders such as bipolar disorder, psychotic disorders such as schizophrenia, and character issues such as narcissism and borderline personality disorders. When any of these conditions is combined with a chronic alcohol or drug dependency, this is considered a dual diagnosis.

The road to recovery is usually rougher for a kid with bipolar disorder than for one with mild anxiety or depression. For someone with a serious mental health issue, it might take six months just to get the medication right. Most transient issues such as depression, anxiety, and cutting will be mitigated by the time your child comes home.

For the substance abuser, the treatment environment is very supportive and containing. It keeps substance abuse at bay. It's known that the longer someone remains sober, the longer they succeed, and there is something magical about 12 months that is statistically significant. The environment surrounding the home might contain negative influences greater than your child's internal strength. This makes it much more difficult for anyone, especially an addict, to come home and hang on to her gains. Despite high levels of structured support put in place by the Home Agreement, she might find herself heavily triggered to use. And substance abusers who really don't want to stop are some of the toughest to deal with back at home.

These are all examples of when it's especially advisable to keep a child in treatment for as long as possible to achieve the greatest benefit.

If your child has truly exhausted treatment options, or finances or family matters make it a necessity for her to come home earlier than desired, don't throw in the towel. I encourage families in this situation to continue looking for affordable or alternative treatment. Here are a few suggestions:

- Ask the treatment program your child is currently in, or one you are considering, if they can offer you a reduced rate or scholarship.

- Check with your insurance carrier and learn what services and providers they will cover.

- Ask your current at-home therapist or school counselor for affordable possibilities in your community.

- Call your county and state departments of social services and behavioral health.

- Talk with your family spiritual counselor. Some clergy or houses of worship will have recommendations for some kind of help for youth and their families.

- Don't disregard the power of the Internet. You'll be surprised at how many services and support groups are out there. Beware of sites that offer a quick or miraculous fix.

- Reconnect with your educational consultant if you have one and pick her brain.

In any of these scenarios, one factor remains constant: the success of all treatment is determined to a considerable extent by the recipient's willingness to grow and heal. When your child returns, if he holds on to the majority of his change, the future bodes well. It is up to him to apply what he learned in treatment to real life; until he does, his journey is not complete. What you can do is anticipate that growth and provide an environment that will encourage its continuation.

The Lure of Home

Even the kids who like treatment the most will be jonesing to get home. Yes, they made friends, grew up, sobered up, and discovered who they were. Still, the majority view treatment as prison. They are "over" the tight structure and constant supervision they're told is so good for them. They believe they've learned all there is to learn in treatment and that they're ready to take on life. Kids in treatment have been waiting for their liberation since the day they started treatment. Who can blame them? Yes, they've had problems, but these kids usually feel *Now I've dealt with them and I need to go home.* They want to break out of their prison and grab hold of their freedom—yesterday.

During treatment, the draw of home is both fantastical and real. The idea of home fuels kids' imaginations. It is comfort, Camelot, Nirvana, the place of their dreams. In essence, they might feel that *Everything will be ten times better once I get home and see my old friends, have my games back, chill at the beach, and hug my dog.*

> Kids in treatment have been waiting for their liberation since the day they started treatment.

This type of fantasy offers hope during your child's darkest therapeutic moments. Returning home has been the goal, and has served as a very good reason to work hard and make progress. Your young one is so excited to be liberated from the bowels of treatment that she'll say almost anything you want to hear just so she can get home. She thinks it's going to be easy—a well-deserved vacation—and her excitement seems enough to carry the day.

Initially upon her return, she will love the freedom. Sleeping in— in her own bed, in her own room—with her cat, hearing her parents talking downstairs in the kitchen, smelling bacon frying . . . this is the honeymoon period that can last for up to a month, sometimes even longer.

False Bravado

Beneath the bravado displayed by your child lies ambivalence about having left the structure and attention she experienced in treatment. Yes, some of her confidence is real, but a fair amount is pretense. Deep down, she's nervous, because she's unsure of herself in this place that is both familiar and different. Her ultimate fear: she doesn't know if her past dysfunctional behavior will come back.

I have yet to see one kid in my practice admit to her parents that she's scared, and yet every child I've worked with has confessed this to me. Why is this the case? Because kids are concerned that if they show fear or weakness you might construe it as a reason to send them back to treatment.

Now that I've officially ratted on your kid, please take this information to heart. Expect your child to use false confidence and a cavalier attitude as a coping mechanism. No, you don't need to take action; in fact, I recommend that you don't. Simply keep in mind the reason for her uneasiness.

Gone is the safety and consistency of checking in with the therapy group each day. Gone is the therapist who knew your child and could read her like a book and look after every little need. Gone is the mentor/coach who challenged your child and pushed her to be courageous. Gone is the schedule that this child used, albeit sometimes grudgingly, to know when to brush her teeth, eat healthily, exercise, and go to bed. Gone are the extensive supports, crutches, and structure. *Scary* is what that gets down to . . . more so than lions and tigers and bears!

Dealing with Disorientation

Other than false confidence, there's another behavior that many kids exhibit once they get back home. What can be construed as laziness is often the child's way of experiencing a reorientation. Life feels surreal. When your child last lived at home there was major conflict, maybe a drug stupor, and loads of lying and hiding the truth. His last recollection of life at home is one of chaos, fear, and loathing. Now there is quiet, peace, integrity, more noticeable love . . . and pressure. Pressure to communicate honestly, to complete chores, and to follow through on expectations.

In some cases, your child has never experienced ordinary life at home. And now, his parents and siblings have changed—along with expectations of maturity, respect, responsibility, and much more. Who needs an acid trip when you come home and it's all like a strange dream already? Your own transparent communication, appropriate boundaries and expectations, and willingness to follow through will help your child navigate this challenge.

If your child is disoriented in his own home, imagine what it's like for him outside. Most kids at this stage will admit that they *kinda forgot what it's like out there*. Some former friends are not friends anymore. *How does money work again? Oh, the smell of cigarettes . . . of weed wafting through the park. I can have coffee? Wow, she's hot. Movies!—all I want? Social media? Let's connect!*

Talk about bombardment.

More than familial conflicts and the attempts at stretching boundaries, it's these unsettling anxieties creeping up on your kid that raise the most concern in the first few months after reentry. Too often a child's sometimes overwhelming anxieties are overlooked as parents get caught up in the day-to-day spats and give their attention to fires that need to be put out.

When your child leaves treatment, I maintain that "shell shock" accompanies his return. Most of my young clients don't admit to this, and they hide it extremely well. There is almost a sense of shame. I suggest that you look at your child's apparent numbness, laziness, anxiety, or angry flare-ups with this in mind.

> At home, your child is no longer the sole center of attention, and this can be very disheartening and disconcerting.

How unfair it must seem to these kids. They have worked and persuaded and argued that it's time to end treatment and come home. They expected joyous freedom. Instead they feel dread, and it's a gorilla on their back. They think they should be fine and living it up, but instead they squander their freedom . . . lying around, playing games, bored after spending only an hour at the mall when they used to "live there."

They realize that home has changed, yet don't know why, and they keep having impulses to get the hell away—away from everyone—and sometimes to run back to treatment, where they felt safer, surrounded by care, and better understood. At home, your child is no longer the sole center of attention, and this can be very disheartening and disconcerting.

Children Need to Heal—Not Get Fixed

And what about the plans your child made to hang out with his friends when he got back? Well, guess what? Many friends have left, and those who are still around have changed. *They don't understand me* is what I commonly hear from kids who return home. *I could be my real self with Ashley in wilderness.* Suddenly and jarringly, friends from treatment seem more real and true.

While all this is going on inside your child, what do you do? You watch, you listen, and you support, but you do not try to fix it. People don't get fixed; they heal. Healing takes time, time, and more time, and very often it's a solo journey. Even through her hazy, surreal shock, your child will be able to observe those around her. She now possesses the language and tools of treatment, and can use them.

In treatment, she was taught to look at the process of her life, to observe her life and environment with some discernment. When she does so, she'll realize that it is she who has changed, not everyone else. And that's when the healing process at home begins in earnest. Once your child recognizes that she has changed, she'll pin it on treatment. Like it or not, she has taken on a wisdom and knowledge that will never leave her.

Most kids respond to this revelation in both negative and positive ways. They still might make poor choices, but later they will always reflect on how they responded. They'll start to hold themselves accountable and to realize that they have the power of choice. They can decide whom they want to hang with, and will know that their environment matters because it affects their behavior.

They'll begin to determine who's real in their life—such as their parents, cousins, and healthy friends—and they'll see who is on the take and insincere. They'll finally be able to activate free agency in a way they've never experienced. They'll not be reactively on autopilot as they were before treatment, and not grudgingly doing well like during treatment. Post-treatment, they'll be exercising wisdom on their own. This is freedom, the thing they've so been craving.

Expect Some Resentment

Still another feeling resides somewhere inside your child upon his return, and that feeling is resentment. Yes, you have spent untold money and energy and exerted heartfelt emotion, but still your child resents you, on some level, for sending him away. He might trace his resentment to the "goons" who whisked him to wilderness at three in the morning, or to the drudgery of the therapeutic process—it doesn't matter. You did it to him, and he'll harbor ill feelings because of it . . . at least for a while.

> Yes, you have spent untold money and energy and exerted heartfelt emotion, but still your child resents you, on some level, for sending him away.

Most kids don't communicate feeling resentful to their parents, even after they recognize it. It will come at you sideways, looking like irritability, annoyance, and frustration. Let him have this. Don't challenge it. When there is the first bit of conflict in the first month of your child's return, remember that some of that pent-up resentment is displaced by your child into safer conflict such as a dirty-room argument. Let your kid have his frustration, within reason, and validate his feelings.

Oftentimes, anger of this origin might be diffused during family sessions while your child is still at treatment. I suggest that you not wait until the last session at graduation but handle this topic earlier, even if it's over the phone. I encourage parents to do this while the treatment counselor can moderate the discussion, especially if there's discomfort about opening a can of worms. Begin the discussion with something like, "I don't blame you for being sick and tired of all this treatment. Can you tell us what's been good, and what's been not so good?" Or, "Are you still bummed out about the transport service coming to the house?"

Most kids appreciate their parents' acknowledgment that the treatment process hasn't been entirely rosy. After venting some of their anger, they will also admit that great things have happened to them and that they do understand why you did what you did. Many children even say thank you.

Forgive me if it seems I have thus far pointed out many challenges and offered relatively few solutions. The purpose of this chapter has been to let you know what to expect and whom you will most likely encounter when your child first comes home. I want you to have an understanding of who that person is on your doorstep—what he or she might be thinking, and why. You'll find that the rest of this book is dedicated to solutions.

Your teen or young adult child is moving back home. Home should be familiar to him, but familiar can play out not so well. And familiar seems different when one has changed. What your child is mainly doing is moving into a new time in his life. He is going to be establishing a new normal.

I can offer one generalization at this point—one important piece of advice. Whatever your child exudes, be it anger, happiness, frustration, or zombie-on-the-sofa lethargy, be present to listen and validate. Be interested in what your son or daughter has to say. It's still your responsibility, as parents who care and parents who have given it all, to continue working. It's your job now to create an environment that will allow for the progress gained in treatment to continue. And you'll do this with love, open communication, and confident parenting.

Preparing for Your Child's Return

For your child's entire life, you have invested love, countless resources, and 24/7 care. Plus, you've done what you thought you would never have to do. You've sent your child away. No good parent does this easily or thoughtlessly. It goes against your nature to let your child out of your sight, let alone to have him or her leave the safety and heart of your home. Yet you did send your child to treatment, to save his life. This sacrifice was personal on every level.

You have spent untold amounts of money—more than you could afford. You have blitzed through retirement savings, mortgaged your home; you've done anything you could to help your child endure his mental pain and heal. You have invested your heart, soul, wallet, and any vestige of pride. And now you need to invest this one last bit, and that bit is change.

I consistently see both hope and fear in parents when their child is released from the highly structured environs of treatment. And I also see low expectations and lax or unclear rules. When a child has just spent two months to two years growing with structure and with clear-cut consequences, it's unfair to have her come home to the same old same old.

The Parent-Child Relationship

When your child entered treatment, most likely one of the top issues to be dealt with was coded V61.20: Parent-Child Relational Problem. Every child I've worked with in wilderness has had this diagnosis. By the time your child is slotted to return home, this issue should be resolved to the extent possible within your family dynamic. This, of course, leaves room for growth. There is always room for growth.

To enhance your relationship with your child, don't hesitate to ask his treatment therapist for advice. Before your child comes home, learn as many communication skills and deal with as many issues as the therapist suggests. Then clear the air with your child on major issues.

Every treatment program I've worked with follows a detailed programmatic structure and plan. Inherently these plans have a specific sequence and achievable goals. What best sets up your child for success in this momentous transition home is the same—a well-thought-out family plan that culminates in a Home Agreement or, as some call it, a home contract. You need to discover what is true north (the healthiest path to maturity) for your child and map it out as clearly as possible. Without a map, everyone in the family can wander in different directions and the child who has returned can easily get lost in terrain that was once familiar and now seems foreign. A reliable map will provide you and your child with:

1. The lay of the land.

2. The most direct route available to get your child where she should be while still staying on the path set out in treatment.

3. Guardrails to keep her on the right path.

4. Mile markers to help determine how far along your child has come and if she's regressing.

It is ideal if all the obvious family dysfunction has been identified and dealt with, and new patterns initiated and practiced, before a Home Agreement is written. Do as much work as you can, individually and as a family, before your child returns. Work can look like many different things. It can be family therapy or individual therapy, but mostly it means becoming authentic. It means being honest and open with each member of the family and creating an environment conducive to honesty and integrity. It means striving for a family dynamic in which each of you can respectfully work out your inevitable differences. Handling issues at home, while your child is away, shores up the foundation on which to build a future with your child. When he returns to you more whole and healthy than ever, let him return to parents who are also more whole and healthy.

If your child has been away for more than a few months, you have missed out on precious time—informative years—with him or her.

This is a sad but necessary reality. You may need to grieve this lost time, which is a truly personal and often a very private loss. What I can offer to perhaps more favorably reframe the journey thus far is this: Your child will likely come home to you more honest and capable. You won't have to watch her struggle with day-to-day life through several layers of dysfunction. Vulnerable parts of the child you used to know will still show up now and then to be healed and to catch up with the rest of her psychological maturity. You may also be delighted to find that, a few months into the return home, you and your child will share more intimate moments than you ever dreamed possible. I have seen it, many times.

Meet her in the present, and together acknowledge the time lost. She, too, may be grieving her childhood despite all her grumbling to be treated like an adult. Then, as your child allows, accompany her as she moves into the future.

At first, you will have to be the driver, or at the very least the navigator, for your child. I certainly would not allow a child just out of treatment to parent herself in this fast and furious world. Winging it, wishful thinking, and hoping it will be like the good old days will not be your ticket to success. Just as you prepared the nursery for your baby's arrival, it is once again time to prepare for her return—this time as a teen or young adult.

She must be given some driver's education, and as she demonstrates that she can stay on the right side of the road you can, little by little, let her go off on her own for longer and longer periods of time. Progress toward the desired destination is manifested in a child who can live by the expectations set before her without you driving or navigating the car. You might have to remind her now and then of the safest, surest route, but overall she needs to know the right direction and, very importantly, have the intention to go that way. The destination is reached when a mature child takes full responsibility for her life and moves consistently toward health.

Create a Team

You and your child are the key players in this adventure; however, I highly recommend developing a transition team to assist in the whole process of bringing your young one home. The first players to recruit are the members of your child's existing treatment team. Learn as much as you can from the professionals you have worked with during your child's stay in treatment, and adapt the lessons learned to your own personal ethos and family culture. Work closely with them and any other support at home you deem necessary to assist in the process of developing a solid road map.

> Learn as much as you can from the professionals you have worked with during your child's stay in treatment, and adapt the lessons learned to your own personal ethos and family culture.

Support for you might come in many forms: clergy, extended family members, a personal therapist, a marriage counselor, Al-Anon, group therapy, or actively managing your health, relaxation, and personal goals. For your child, support might mean AA or NA meetings; seeing a psychiatrist for medication; having a mentor, life coach, or therapist; and beneficial activities such as school, sports, and employment.

Creating a team might take time and some trial and error. Choose these folks wisely. Who will you want to talk to when the going gets tough? Do you have someone readily available to you? Will your daughter need a drug counselor, one she can truly connect with at home? What about a life coach or educational consultant for college? I urge you to begin this prep work no later than two months before your child comes home, and preferably many months before. Ultimately, I want you to have the confidence and sense of peace that comes with knowing that you can, with your transition team, bring your child back home and have it work. Then, as you see steady, healthy growth in your child and yourself, you can wean your family off this structure as it feels comfortable and appropriate.

Grounded Parents

To take the helm and guide this transition process effectively, you need to stay grounded in the healthiest sense of the word. What I mean by "grounded" is that you should possess an overall sense of how to take care of yourself and how to manage stress with good coping skills. A child's return home can be an incredible stressor to parents. Most likely your child's problems have eroded the foundation you used to have. Marriages and partnerships already rocky might be stressed to the breaking point. Tense divorces might be further agitated.

Time and again I have seen, without fail, quick regression in children who return to homes where chaos reigns. No one wins. And yet I hold out that it doesn't have to be this way. I would like to offer another model. Let your child be a catalyst for you to work together more closely and heal broken relationships. Your child's return could unite you as parents (married or divorced) as never before, or at the very least you could agree to disagree *except* on what it takes to help your child.

Think back to how it was before you sent your child away. He knows how to split you from your significant other, if there is one. He's a pro at it. Just because your child has healed in treatment doesn't mean he won't be tempted to split you again. Yes, your kid now knows unequivocally that he should not play you against one another—that it's dysfunctional—but still he might try.

Teens and young adults play their parents. They just do; it's the nature of the beast. To prepare for this, work to solidify your marriage or partnership with your significant other. Unity between parents is the first boundary you can set up for your child. *My parents are rock solid—they cannot be manipulated.* Your child is accustomed to seeing unified and grounded role models in treatment, and when parents are grounded, too, the continuity allows him to move into a home or homes that are safe, sorted out, and united.

> Unity between parents is the first boundary you can set up for your child.

Right now, you might feel burned out from focusing so much energy on your child in treatment. Even if you don't, after he returns home you'll most likely run into a wall when siblings and spouses get tired of putting so much energy into this one person in the family. Please respect this impulse and do just that: take a vacation from problem solving and figuring out his life. Let him go a bit and get back to your life, your relationships and your health.

Encourage all in your family to do so as well. This gives people permission to feel real exhaustion and resentment—their own natural limitations—and to reserve their psychological energy for themselves. Spending inordinate amounts of energy thinking and worrying does not solve any of your child's issues. If your partner or siblings don't respect your desire to take a break from thinking and problem solving, then create and schedule practical time-outs when no one is allowed to commiserate. Set up some structure to stop those codependent tendencies.

When you stay healthy and grounded, and are enjoying your life, it models to your child how to live. I studied and worked for years to be the professional I am today, but in honesty much of my success in work and life comes from my parents. They modeled, and still do model, a healthy way of living that I am free to consider. They talk openly about their lives, preach little, and authentically live their beliefs. They are direct in their communication, and more importantly they try to hear me and validate my experience. They are grounded people who each have their separate hobbies and interests, and yet my siblings and I know we are greatly loved. I still go back home when I need to rest and nourish my soul.

I tell you this because, although bookstores offer a glut of contemporary parenting books that impress upon moms and dads the need to take care of themselves, I often work with parents who have completely lost sight of this. Becoming and remaining grounded in today's world isn't easy. What does grounded even look and feel like in modern day-to-day life? For each of us it will be different, but this is what I saw my parents do and what I recommend to help keep personal and interpersonal lives healthy:

- Go on dates with your significant other without discussing the kids.

- Attend church or temple or seek a way of becoming more centered. For some that means a hike in nature; for others, meditation.

- Have fun . . . and that means making time for it.

- Get physical exercise, on your own or with your significant other. Try yoga, tennis, surfing, hiking, horseback riding, Argentine tango . . . whatever floats your boat.

- Grow your career.

- Get a physical, get good sleep, and generally make sure you're addressing the needs of your physical body.

- If you need to sort things out mentally or spiritually, find a therapist, life coach, or spiritual guide.

- Find your community. This might be Al-Anon, a book club, or the church social.

- Do what you loved to do when you were younger: paint, grow roses, go fishing, ride motorcycles, complete the *New York Times* crossword puzzle on Sunday, or make a homemade pie. In short, do what you need to do to feel good about your life, independent of what your child needs. Parents who are engaged in a life they love can better parent and better handle the vicissitudes of this road home.

Many of my clients who are parents have their own psychological issues holding them back from becoming grounded. The more common issues are depression, unchecked substance abuse, and pervasive anxiety. People can unravel when they see their child struggling, as it often stirs up their own past and present dysfunction.

Parents often regale me with experiences that mirror their child's. These parents endured their own serious trauma, setbacks, or developmental problems around the same age as their youngster in treatment. Did you have a hard time as a teen or young adult? Was there some trauma such as abuse or violence in your family? Was there loneliness, profound rejection or academic failure, drug and alcohol addictions, suicidal thoughts or self-loathing? If so, take the time now to heal alongside your son or daughter. Give yourself the gift of seeking out the help and guidance you need with counseling, support groups, or therapy. A life coach, lifestyle changes, yoga, meditation, recreation, medication, and addiction recovery are just a few options to consider in your healing process. When you do your own work, you will be more able to effect the change you desire in others.

Reaching out for help and getting healthy is beautiful modeling for your child. Don't keep your work a secret or consider it a sign of weakness. Let him know you see room for improvement in your life and that you, too, are working to change. Share your story and your truth with your child. It will give him reference points and wisdom to pack along on his own journey.

Don't Work Harder Than Your Kid

As you work to be a more grounded and unified individual, so should your child. Be careful you don't fall into a common parental trap: working harder than your child at creating his life. Early in my training, my wise and wonderful counseling supervisors cautioned me to not work harder than my clients. In my profession, heeding this advice is the difference between burnout and a thriving practice with real joy and lightness.

If you're so entrenched in your child's situation that you've lost perspective, the first thing you can do is to stop crucifying yourself, and secondly you must stop giving too much. When parents work harder than their kids, not only does the child resent it but also most likely the parent gets exhausted and resentful, too, which leads to anger and frustration and can escalate conflict and cause regression.

Parents who have embraced this concept of not working harder than their child often say they had an "aha" moment. A light bulb came on and their lives were illuminated: they could clearly see that they had a life of their own to live, regardless of what their son or daughter decided to do. I'm not suggesting that you become ruthless, self-centered, or narcissistic. I'm not asking you to give up on your kid. I'm suggesting that you work to empower yourself and change the flow of energy. Set up a family system that will get your child doing the bulk of the work of creating his life, so you can put some energy into yours.

> Be careful you don't fall into a common parental trap: working harder than your child at creating his life.

When your child was young, he truly needed you for most everything. Now that he's a teenager or young adult, he requires space to separate and obtain many of his needs on his own— from the world, not from you. At this time, the line between parent and child moves and shifts. It is most beneficial if parents realize it's time to let go and allow the child to take responsibility for his own life. Please don't wait for your child to graduate from high school to begin this process.

The Imparentives

When your prodigal child returns, expect good days filled with family barbecues, chores well done, birthday cakes, and heartfelt "I love you-s." But also be prepared for less-than-perfect days when it feels like everything in your world is falling apart. Those days when you feel that your child is still an unfeeling, selfish monster. On those days you might need a boost—a gentle reminder that empowers you to continue.

THE IMPARENTIVES

IT IS IMPERATIVE THAT YOU:

1. GET GROUNDED AND TAKE CARE OF YOURSELF PHYSICALLY, EMOTIONALLY, AND SPIRITUALLY.

2. NOT WORK HARDER THAN YOUR CHILD AT CREATING HIS LIFE.

3. KNOW WHERE YOU END AND YOUR CHILD BEGINS.

4. PARENT FROM YOUR VISION, VALUES AND EXPECTATIONS SO YOU'RE NOT BULLIED INTO GOING AGAINST YOUR GUT.

5. KEEP A LIGHT HEART AND A SENSE OF HUMOR.

6. INSIST THAT YOUR CHILDREN TREAT YOU WITH RESPECT.

7. USE TRANSPARENT AND LOVING COMMUNICATION TO DEVELOP AUTHENTIC RELATIONSHIPS.

8. CREATE CLEAR EXPECTATIONS AND RULES, AND DELIVER APPROPRIATE CONSEQUENCES.

9. REMEMBER THAT YOU ARE THE BOSS, NOT YOUR CHILD.

10. RECOGNIZE WHEN YOU'VE HAD ENOUGH AND ASK FOR HELP.

To download a copy visit www.TheRoadHomeBook.com/downloads.

To assist you on those bleak days, I distilled some of the wisdom I've learned from my clients. I call these bits of wisdom "The Imparentives." They're akin to the Ten Commandments in that they are key tenets that parents can use as guidance. Parents who use the Imparentives remain grounded and are reminded of who they are. They find their backbone. And, most importantly, teens and young adults respect parents who live by the Imparentives.

These might, at first glance, seem so obvious as to be unworthy of mention. Yet I believe they *are* imperative. Most of us know the precepts of the Ten Commandments, but it doesn't hurt to be reminded every now and then.

I've already presented a few of these tenets to you. By the end of this book we will have covered them all. For now, make a copy or download the Imparentives. Post them on the fridge, the bathroom mirror, in your smart phone, next to the computer . . . wherever they will help boost morale. Let the Imparentives inspire you to stay grounded, especially on those days when it seems everything is falling apart—those times when you feel angry, frustrated, ineffective, or just plain sad.

I'll say this yet again. *You* can do this. You can raise and teach your child. You are the best people for the job, because you are the parents.

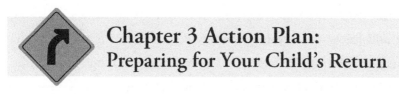

Chapter 3 Action Plan: Preparing for Your Child's Return

(To download blank worksheets, visit www.TheRoadHomeBook.com/downloads.)

#1. Recruiting a Support Team for Your Child

a. Make a list of concerns you have regarding your child's mental health, substance abuse, personality, character, and abilities. What issues related to your child and your family are concerning you? Here are a few examples:

cutting, marijuana, video game addiction, whole family unwilling to talk about anything "bad"

_____

_____

_____

_____

_____

_____

_____

_____

b. Contact your child's treatment team leader and discuss the above. Get the team's input on what supports should continue when your child returns home. Don't forget to consult your child.

c. When you have received feedback from your child's treatment team and know the key issues of concern, search for resources that can help you with those issues. These resources can range from professional therapists, to clergy, to local 12-step programs. Again, here are a few examples.

Child Issue	Contact Name	Contact Info
depression	Mary Max, therapist	###-###-####
academics	Joe Jackson, tutor	###-###-####

#2. Recruiting a Support Team for You and Your Significant Other

a. Are you falling apart? Do you want to work better with your partner? Do you have your own issues to deal with? If so, please think about what you would like to work on and list it here. Examples:

abuse by stepfather, worrying and not sleeping, marriage rocky

_____

_____

b. Make a list of people who can support you, and include contact information. Make sure these people know they're on your list. Examples:

Self Issue	Contact Name	Contact Info
Don't understand addiction	Al-Anon at Presbyterian Church on Wed. night	Rev. Ralph ###-###-####
Overweight and need exercise	Weightwatchers, Tues. night Trainer at gym	###-###-#### (go with Mary) ###-###-#### (Jocelyn)

#3. Getting Grounded

What's missing in your life? Are you content? Do you even have a life outside of your kids? Are you physically healthy? Do you have someplace to go and relax and fill the well?

a. Make a list of some things you want to change in your personal life. Here are some suggestions of possibilities (additional room next page):

exercise three times a week in the morning before work, go on a date night once a week and don't talk about the kids, eat organic food, make it to the farmer's market because it's fun!!

_____

_____

_____

_____

_____

_____

_____

b. Do one thing on this list and practice it for a month. Make it routine.

c. How is your marriage or the relationship with your child's other parent? Does it need help? Is some fence mending necessary or possible? Write down the issues here and, if you can, discuss it with your spouse or ex. Enlist the aid of a counselor if you need to.

_____

_____

_____

_____

_____

_____

_____

_____

_____

_____

#4. Lightening Up

The next time you speak with your child, do so with a light heart. Crack a joke. Put a smile in your voice. And notice: How does this change the interaction with your child, if at all? Make a note of the change here. Can you do this more often?

_____

_____

_____

_____

_____

_____

_____

_____

Unearthing Your Vision, Values, and Expectations

Every single parent with whom I have worked, no matter how jaded, broken, or sad, has still had a flicker of hope in his heart regarding his child. Good! Hope is the spark that can be fueled into a guiding light with which to lead your child home and on into life. You might have felt weary and defeated in the recent past, but now it's ever so important to renew your energy and get back in touch with hope.

The first time I meet with parents, I usually begin our dialogue with the same question. Who did you envision your child would be when she grew up? Can you remember your dreams regarding your child? Have you settled for something other than what you believe she can be?

The fact that your child is in treatment suggests a situation that fell short of your ideal vision. I encourage you to take heart, to be brave—even bold—again. Revive your aspirations and your convictions. Contemplate who it was that you wanted to bring into this world.

Your Vision of Your Child

I would like to clarify up front what I mean about *your* vision of *your* child. I'm not talking about forcing your values down his throat, or you supporting only the career *you* want him to have. I'm talking about you making sure not to abandon the vision of who you're raising, and what you believe he is capable of.

Perhaps you knew without a second thought, when your child was a tyke, that he would be a good soul who could handle the ups and downs of life with grace. Or maybe you fully expected your once-reliable babysitting daughter to use her heart, mind, and natural gifts to better the world. So why not rekindle those dreams?

> Treatment often helps kids remember and renew their unique song for the world.

Treatment often helps kids remember and renew their unique song for the world. Most likely you once again glimpsed this potential in your child during wilderness or other treatment modality. The question is: How can you continue to foster that genuine goodness and potential? It begins with nurturing your vision for your child. Search the archives of your heart, rediscover who you want your child to be, and help him orchestrate that vision into reality.

Reaffirming Your Values

I further encourage you to simultaneously unearth your values. What do you believe in? What are you about as a parent? What is the culture of your family, your underlying philosophy and way of living? Does your home culture reflect your values? If not, it might be prudent to get the two in sync before bringing your son or daughter home. A family culture is the marriage of vision and values, which set the stage for realistic and true expectations. This is a good time in the history of your family to reset the clock, and accurately.

For the past few months, past year, or however long you've been dealing with your child and his treatment, it's safe to assume that you've spent most of the time focused on him and his siblings. That's what good parents do. But now this exercise of resurrecting the vision and values focuses on *you*, not your child. And I mean the individual you first, and the plural you, as parents, second.

Whether you're parenting alone or with another, take a few days to examine your personal values and allow them to be a central point of focus. Contemplate what you value most in life for yourself and your family. What are your beliefs regarding love, honesty, integrity, work, money, and coming of age? Study the world before you and think of the foundational wisdom your child needs to navigate through it with integrity and in health. These basics, vision and values, are the foundation to the road home.

All too often, parents try to accommodate their child's culture and values, or lack of same. In doing this they compromise their own

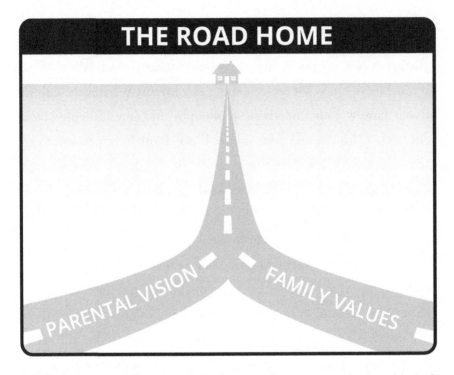

family values, and therefore their dreams. By nature, values and beliefs are visionary and idealistic. They can be either global (your religion) or specific to a certain issue (tobacco use). They set high standards and realistic expectations. If you disregard any of your values regarding the core issues of life, from spirituality to sex to curfew to academic standards, you'll be placing Pandora's box in front of your child. And the lid to that box will be open more than just a crack.

Who Are You?

Take the necessary time and energy to understand what you're all about. Muster the courage and chutzpah to be bold. After all, you're the leader of your tribe—the pack of humans you call family. You can't lead if you don't know what you feel strongly about: which values are black-and-white and nonnegotiable, in contrast with where you can afford to let things go and feel comfortable with gray and fuzzy.

You might be surprised to discover that some things you used to believe no longer hold true. Don't fear this change. Work with it and rediscover who you are. Your child needs to know and feel in his bones what you believe life is about, both generally and specifically. Make it explicit. That's what the next chapters will be all about: the creation of rules, expectations, and family boundaries based on your truth, and how to firmly establish and maintain them in your home.

Generational Guidance

I love the unique nature of each family. Families have history. Families share DNA. Families have issues. Families have ethnicity. Add religion, socioeconomic background, the parents' take on life and view of the world, the individuality of neighborhoods, schools, friends and mentors, and a family hierarchal structure and you can see that these infinite variables create many different kinds of families. A family in Salt Lake City, Utah, is thematically different from one in New York City or the Louisiana bayou. Just as each of us has a unique fingerprint, each family has its unique culture.

Heritage deserves to be passed on from generation to generation. It does matter what belief system you hold dear, whether it is that of an atheist or an Evangelical Christian. It does matter what your roots are—whether you were raised in a refugee camp, grew up on a Midwest farm or a ranch in Wyoming, or are a recent immigrant from Mexico. It does matter that you roast a turkey on Thanksgiving or make tamales for Christmas. Your culture matters, and I encourage you to celebrate it. Be who you are.

Knowing where and whom you come from can help explain situations in the present. Treatment professionals might have asked you or your child if depression or addiction ran in the family, because such information can shed light on a current situation. It's also good to appreciate the riches of your familial past: the story of how Uncle Mathias came north via the underground railroad, or how your grandmother worked two jobs to put your father through med school. Pass on your heritage in these stories. Celebrate your family's uniqueness with your sons and daughters. This history will anchor your child, as she becomes part of something bigger than her present-day issues. Let the work your daughter is doing, her heroine's journey, become part of the family oral tradition. This will give meaning and purpose—context—to her life. It will create a pride in her name and raise the bar of what is cherished and carried forward in your tradition.

> Let the work your daughter is doing, her heroine's journey, become part of the family oral tradition.

How Does Adoption Fit In?

It hasn't gone unnoticed by my colleagues or myself that a disproportionate number of teens and young adults in treatment are adopted.

With regard to adoption, many of us use words such as *attachment* and *abandonment*, and I hope we use them cautiously, because too many parents are already full of needless angst for their children, based on compassion, because those children were adopted.

If your child in treatment was adopted, what will help him enormously are solid, predictable parenting and a relationship with you that cannot be manipulated. If he can still maneuver you and play off your compassion about what he has gone through, he'll feel less grounded in his relationships. Parents who offer clear expectations, along with empathy for their child's feelings and needs, offer stability to any child, and this is very much so, where an adopted child is concerned.

When I work with clients who are adopted, I do make some allowance for that fact. My understanding and empathy are enhanced, but my approach to creating emotional stability—my rules and structure—remain the same as they would for any of my young clients. With adopted clients, my job is to provide constant trustworthiness and stability so they can be more safely themselves and get on with their development the best they know how. There is no doubt in my mind that adopted children have a different journey, and that in their teens and twenties they will go through a special and necessary process of discovering what they're about.

Trusting What We Know

The culture we live in likes to tell us to be this way or that way. I recommend that you not assimilate the external messages of pop culture. You'll be a more effective parent if you go inside for answers instead.

When you tune in and reflect on what's important to you, you might very well hear a familiar voice: the internal voice that you consult when you're looking for guidance. I learned early in my pastoral counseling training that this voice with which we talk to ourselves (self-talk) is an amalgamation of influences from our past—the wisdom of our parents, mentors, teachers, relatives, close friends, coaches, clergy, and counselors. Yes, we each have our own distinct and unique voice, but we have borrowed from others to create it.

> I recommend that you not assimilate the external messages of pop culture. You'll be a more effective parent if you go inside for answers instead.

We begin developing our voice when we're young, and continue doing so into adulthood. Clients often say to me, "I heard your voice in my head all week." Or they share with me that, when they're trying to determine what to do, they ask themselves, *What would Ruben say?* I am merely a short-term hired hand, and if what *I* say matters, how about the pastor or rabbi who has led your congregation for ten years? Or the football coach who kicked your butt in a good way all through high school? What about the aunt or godfather who served in the Armed Forces and taught you to honor your country? The voice you hear today is an amalgamation of many. We've integrated all these folks into our lives, and their values manifest in how we talk to ourselves, what we say to others, and how we live.

Take a moment and think of some authority figures from your earlier life. What might they say to you right now? What guidance can they offer? You might be surprised to discover that not all of these familiar voices are positive. Keep looking; sort through those voices from your past. I recommend that you continue to listen to the healthy influences, but jettison the toxic messages that no longer serve you or your family. Let go of the negative and bring to your awareness the good that you want to pass on to your child.

What you have to say to your children, and ultimately teach them, is of utmost importance, as is the way in which you say it. Your voice matters, both in content and in delivery. If your voice is wishy-washy, hesitant, and unsure, grow the needed confidence so your child knows beyond a doubt who you are and where you're coming from. Enhance your voice. Make it clear and impactful so that it can indelibly imprint on your child's psyche as a messenger of wisdom, courage, and health.

Don't Let the Past Spoil Today

Some parents repeatedly beat themselves up for having failed their child. The thought is that, if they hadn't failed, their child wouldn't be in treatment. Let's not spend any more time there. Instead, look at what can be done now, in real time, today. And if you really are feeling too unsure of yourself to truly parent with conviction, try out this age-old advice: "Fake it until you make it." I'm serious.

While your child was in treatment, her well-being was most likely controlled 80 percent by the treatment center and 20 percent by you (if you were lucky). Well, the ratio is just about to shift. It is now time for parenting more than it's time for therapy. You know your family best, even though you might not believe it, and you know what is best for your child. I want you to be empowered, and to feel as confident as parents as I do as a therapist and family coach. By taking a hard look at who you are and embracing what you're about, you will be able to affirm your right to parent. It might feel like you're rusty, but you are capable—in fact, the *most* capable person to take on this task.

Create Expectations for Now and for the Future

Once you've reconnected with your vision of who you want your child to be and your values, it's time to create the expectations you have for him. Start by sharing your vision and values with your significant other. Create a safe atmosphere within which to do so. This means a place where you both feel at ease and will not be interrupted, at a time when you can focus on the task before you. Most often, parents agree on the lion's share of issues as they discover that they have values in common, which is very likely part of what brought them together in the past.

Disagreements might arise when you attempt to incorporate your values into the expectations you have of your child. For example, probably you both agree that honesty is an important value, and yet one of you might think a white lie now and then is fine while the other thinks *any* lie is intolerable *always*. Because this type of discussion might stir up deep emotion, make a point to hear each other out completely when a contentious issue arises.

Honor each other's viewpoints and concerns. Each of you is revealing your most closely held values, and if you can respect the person in front of you while practicing healthy listening and reflection, you'll be able to collaborate in the creation of a solid set of expectations. An expectation is an achievable benchmark regarding character and behavior that you set before your child—and you *expect* him to *achieve* that benchmark.

If a major difference exists between you and your significant other over a vital issue such as honesty, take a time out, for days even, to reflect on how you can find common ground. Who knows, you might reconvene and come up with a value statement that goes something like this: "We are honest people; we say what we mean. When there's conflict, we muster the courage to say to each other in a transparent, nonviolent way what we really think and feel. We don't manipulate each other. We can dialogue about anything in our family. We can be ourselves."

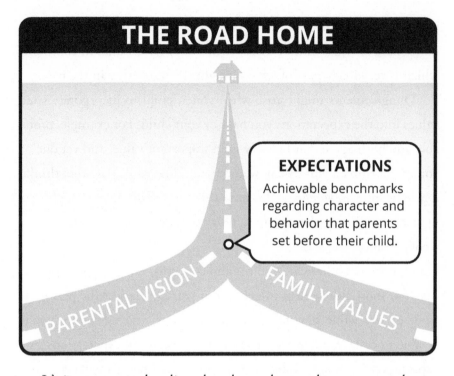

It's important to be aligned on key values and to agree on the expectations that you put into a Home Agreement. If you don't, your child might divide and conquer through manipulation. Within the families I counsel, it's not uncommon for me to discover that the one or two values that are points of contention between the parents are the exact same areas in which the child struggles. I would suggest that your child might already know this.

Closing the Great Divide

One of the greatest challenges in my current practice is helping parents, whether married or divorced, find common ground when they don't share the same values and family culture. Even in very congenial families, it's natural to have tension over some issues. When there is hostility between partners it's difficult to make a Home Agreement work, day in and day out.

It takes a tremendous amount of energy on the part of parents, especially if they're divorced and in two different homes, to create cohesiveness. And yet, take hope: if you are divorced, or see things differently than your spouse, you can still find equilibrium. To start, though, you have to believe and agree that this is the time to put all resentments aside or, better yet, heal them if possible. To do this, adaptation is required.

In split households, most often each parent has a Home Agreement to cover what goes on under his or her roof. The job here is to streamline and coordinate the two—how in-sync can they become? I often find that parents who think they're light years apart in

> What gets in the way of compromise is that the divided parents differ in the way they want to lay out the day-to-day rules, consequences, and other particulars.

their beliefs actually share some key values and a family culture. Even in hostile divorces, the parents share love for the child, and hopes for his college success or life fulfillment. What gets in the way of compromise is that the divided parents differ in the way they want to lay out the day-to-day rules, consequences, and other particulars.

If within the two Home Agreements specific rules and consequences can be made the same, or close to it, this will reduce headaches for all. For example, a no-smoking rule with the same consequence can exist in each home. Chores might be different at each residence, but requirements for outside employment can be the same. If disrespect occurs (and please be precise about what constitutes that in your households), the consequence should be the same in both homes and consistently enforced.

I often hear parents say, "My child is a master manipulator. He would make a great attorney." Your child easily accomplishes this when parenting is inconsistent between the parents. Your child, the lawyer, will discover the loopholes and work them to his advantage. Treatment teams shut down this insidious game of manipulation by working together, and as a result your child self-corrected. Why? Because his maladaptive communication and behavior didn't get his needs met.

Try to work with your partner for consistency. It will be healthier for your child and will make your lives easier. The truth is, if one home is permissive with pot and one is not, then that child will go back to smoking in no time at all. Consistency and congruency within a household or between two households is the desired modus operandi.

That being said, I am a realist; it's not uncommon for me to work with two parents who are not on speaking terms. Separation, divorce, and irreconcilable differences can lead to very hostile situations where former partners and spouses will not, and actually cannot, speak to each other. If this is your situation, try to develop Home Agreements that are relatively the same in spirit, and communicate the basics of what is going on via email or text. Do coordinate consequences, especially over high-profile issues such as drugs and academics. I'm not trying to sound Pollyanna-like, but I frequently see strained parental relationships heal somewhat when both individuals engage in the process of creating a Home Agreement. This labor of love for a child in common can heal, or at least put a bandage on, old wounds.

Clear Expectations

Married or not, shared and clear parental expectations are the foundation for a child's successful transition back home. But how do you get there? Let's say both parents agree that a strong work ethic is imperative. It's very important to you, a cornerstone belief, and you want your son or daughter to embrace this vision combined with a value. It breaks downs like this:

> **Vision:** That our child will be a hard worker like his grandparents and like us.
>
> **Value:** A work ethic leads to a more fulfilling job and life.
>
> **Expectation:** We expect our child to work hard and pay his own way in the world.

This expectation clearly doesn't tolerate a child who behaves like an entitled slacker. It is also reasonable and, with any luck, realistic in light of your child's capabilities. Just writing down such an expectation should make you feel good, because it's an extension of you, of your ancestors. Your child needs to know this expectation and, at least while under the family roof, live it. And you need to hold her accountable. Set expectations that are real, but not easy. In treatment your child was often expected to do things she never thought she could do. Then when she accomplished them she felt good, maybe better than she had in her entire life. So set the bar high for expectations.

The Happiness Trap

One of the possible pitfalls in placing expectations before your child is choosing expectations that don't go deep enough. If they are shallow, they won't make a real impact.

I often hear parents say, "I just want my child to be happy" or "I just want him to find something he's passionate about." While I agree in spirit with these statements, their broad and nonspecific nature can lead young people to feel entitled, that life will just go their way. A child might then lack the drive to be creative and innovative, or to work toward his goals.

Also, statements such as these can easily be turned against the parents: "Smoking weed makes me happy, so get off my back." I wish I had a dollar for every teen who told his parents, "I'm going to play my guitar and become a rock star because that's my passion. It's what makes me happy." How many parents have been caught in a bind when this "passion" is the reason their child drops out of high school or chooses not to go to college? So be careful what you expect, and base each expectation on a value.

> Be careful what you expect, and base each expectation on a value.

Yes, your child has been unhappy and it hurt you. You saw him spiral down into the dark. Happiness, however, comes and goes all through life. It is not a constant state of existence. Contentment and peace can be, so a more attainable vision and sensible value on which to build an expectation might be:

> **Vision:** I see my child content no matter what his station in life might be. I want him to experience a full life, filled with more joyous moments than sad or dark ones.
>
> **Value:** I believe self-worth, peace of mind, and success come from working toward a better future.
>
> **Expectation:** My son will exercise his own intention, ability, and creativity to attain a life that is content and fulfilling.

Some kids who are told to find their passion, especially early in life, might indeed find it. Most of us, however, have to work hard at it, and then we have to work even harder to hold on to it, because passion is fluid. It moves. It doesn't hold still. To follow one's heart is important, but while following bliss one must also expect to pay the price for success and achievement. The nature of life is that moments are not always blissful. One must have the fortitude to endure drudgery every now and then.

I shall never forget watching my brother suture a grapefruit, hour after hour. He had to practice relentlessly to follow his passion of becoming a surgeon. It wasn't that he had a knack for orthopedic surgery that made his dream come true; it was his persistence in working unflaggingly through the mundane learning process. If kids don't hear about this reality of life, they'll assume that following their passion is going to be easy. My personal and professional experiences have taught me that, if you follow your bliss, you will also need courage, humility, fortitude, tenacity, a work ethic, and a capacity for drudgery.

To hope that your child will be happy or that she'll do something she's passionate about are vague, anemic visions that will frustrate the child trying to attain these goals. Give your kid a more pragmatic approach to life that can lead to happy moments and a steady life purpose, earned by honest sweat and elbow grease. Reward is sweeter when you've had to toil a bit to achieve it.

Creating Suitable Expectations

Here is another example of how to create expectations for your child. Most parents want to model for their children the moderate use of alcohol. Everyone envisions a child without alcohol dependency. Some parents follow a European model in which kids are gradually introduced to alcohol under parental supervision. Others don't want their children experimenting with alcohol until they're of legal drinking age—if at all.

> It is absolutely okay to be countercultural and therefore true to your ideals.

At one time you might have felt comfortable with the thought that your child would, like you did as a teen, sneak a few beers from the fridge in the garage. Then, you were accepting of this form of curiosity and experimentation. Now, not so much. Your child might be unable to drink in moderation because of addictive tendencies. Let her current situation inform your beliefs today, and then clearly let her know what you believe and what you expect of her.

> **Vision:** We see our children healthy in mind and spirit.
>
> **Value:** We believe in keeping our bodies and minds healthy and treating them with respect.
>
> **Expectation:** We expect our daughter to live life with a clear mind and healthy body. We expect her to be sober and substance-free until she is 18, or better yet 21.

Another area in life that can be fraught with tension is sexuality. This topic deserves attention, as parents tend to compromise their values concerning sexuality. It is absolutely okay to be countercultural and therefore true to your ideals. In this area, I recommend that you err on the side of caution. In other words, have tougher expectations if you fear your child will make poor choices when given too much freedom.

An expectation regarding sexuality that parents might come up with is: "We believe that you deserve to be with someone who respects you and cares for you. We expect you to hold off on engaging in sexual activity until after graduating from high school." Based on religious and spiritual values, some parents might say, "We expect you to wait for marriage before you engage in sexual activity." Others parents believe sexual activity is acceptable in high school. An expectation from them might be: "We understand that you're experimenting with your sexuality. We expect you to be responsible, to be in a committed, caring relationship, and to take the necessary health precautions before having sex."

Any one of these expectations will work. The purpose is to address the main, emergent issues relevant to your child's life after you're certain of your own values. Let your children clearly know what values you hold dear, because even if they choose to miss the mark you've set, they'll know they've missed the mark and will hear your voice somewhere in their conscience.

> The big-picture goal is to use your values to raise your children and to incorporate generational wisdom into their lives as they mature.

Yes, your child will grumble, grouse, and openly rebel at times. Yet very often those same kids return to the values of their parents later in life, for it is part of their heritage—your legacy. The big-picture goal is to use your values to raise your children and to incorporate generational wisdom into their lives as they mature. You are the carriers of this wisdom, since you have listened, lived, and learned.

Be very deliberate in passing down your values and beliefs and laying out your expectations, as they will create long-term ramifications for future generations. When you are conscious of who you are and intentionally specific in communicating it, you affect your family for good and for health. Let your sons and daughters know what a fulfilling life looks like within the tribal culture of your family; let it become part of their bones, sinews, and psyches. Let it become tradition.

In my family, I grew up hearing "Sweet dreams, God bless," every night. When I visit my parents' home, this tradition of love continues. I like to think that someone a hundred or two hundred years ago initiated this custom in some quaint European village. A parent who deeply loved his children intentionally formalized that feeling in a simple statement with which to end the day. And now, exponentially, hundreds of kids have heard that most endearing statement and continue to be comforted by it. Your children inherit a lot from you, whether from tradition, unconscious patterns, or conscious and intentional wisdom.

Don't believe for a minute that you can't breathe instruction, just as you breathed life, into the child who is your special gift to the world, to yourself, and to himself. Guide this unique individual. Don't leave it up to peers.

You are an essential ingredient in your child's life, so never give up instilling your vision and nurturing your hopes for him. He needs to know what you expect of him. He needs wisdom . . . *your* wisdom. It's a rich part of your journey and your child's.

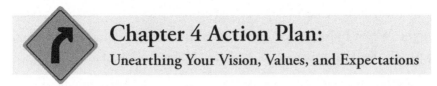

Chapter 4 Action Plan:
Unearthing Your Vision, Values, and Expectations

(To download blank worksheets, visit www.TheRoadHomeBook.com/downloads.)

#1. Vision Quest

Take a moment to answer the following questions. The purpose is to rekindle the vision and dreams you had for your child from the get-go—before troubles, before grief, before treatment.

a. When you were cradling your child as a baby in your arms, what did you hope and expect for her? Example:

I always envisioned that my child would develop her talents and gifts and offer them to the world. Her good effort and service would reward her with a fulfilled life.

_____

_____

_____

_____

_____

_____

_____

_____

b. What kind of person did you hope your child would become? Example:

I hoped my child would always be close to his family and to his faith and would pass that faith down to his own children.

_____

_____

_____

_____

_____

_____

_____

_____

c. Who do you want your child to be? Example:

I want my daughter to follow her heart and be fearless and not let anyone tell her what she should do with her life (except for us—her parents).

_____

_____

_____

_____

_____

_____

_____

#2. Vision Statement

Write a Vision Statement for your child's return from treatment. Example:

I envision my child to be an active participant in a life based on doing the right thing. Because I value honesty, charity, and service, I hope my daughter finds a fulfilling life by helping others and contributing to all of humanity.

_____

_____

_____

_____

#3. Voices

Think back to your childhood. Who were the people who taught you? Who do you remember? Whose voices can you hear? Write the names here. Are all of the voices positive, or are there some negative ones? Can you separate them out? Circle the names that reinforce your values and your family. Let go of the negative ones. Cross those names out, because it's the positive ones that are part of your legacy.

_____

_____

_____

_____

_____

_____

#4. Values

What did those positive voices teach you? Here, to spark your thinking, is a list of characteristics and issues based on values: honesty, integrity, fortitude, a work ethic, fairness, tolerance, obedience, love, loyalty, freedom of speech, health, school, character, sexuality, spirituality, and respect.

a. Make a list of values you cherish:

_____

_____

_____

b. Can you write out two or three value statements that you would like to pass on to your kids? Here is an example:

We value staying healthy and honoring our bodies. We eat healthful foods and stay away from too much sugar and caffeine. We don't abuse alcohol, drugs, or tobacco. Athletics are an enjoyable way to stay healthy. Exercise of all kinds is good for us and keeps us on an even keel.

_____

_____

_____

_____

_____

_____

_____

#5. Expectations

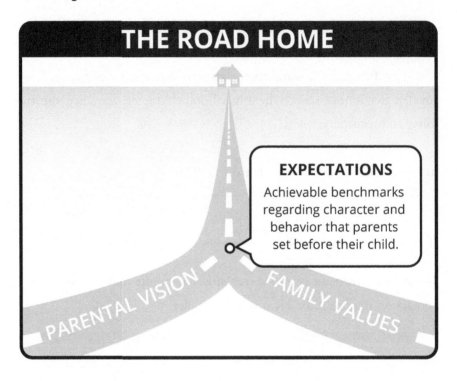

THE ROAD HOME

EXPECTATIONS
Achievable benchmarks regarding character and behavior that parents set before their child.

PARENTAL VISION

FAMILY VALUES

Use the vision you have for your child, plus one of your values, to write a realistic expectation. Borrowing from the sample value statement in Action Step #4b, such an expectation might be:

We honor our bodies and want to take care of them. We expect our daughter to stay away from alcohol, drugs, and tobacco despite peer pressure. Piercings and tattoos go against our belief in honoring the body. We hope our daughter will exercise for her entire life, choose healthful food options, and take good care of her body.

_____

_____

_____

_____

_____

_____

_____

Bonus Step

Are you curious about your child's values? Why not write her a letter, make a phone call, or start up a face-to-face conversation to ask what in life is important to her? What characteristics in others does she value? Perhaps you can see where you and your child are the same and where you're different. Does your child have values that you omitted and now see as important? Write them down, and when you're ready, address them.

_____

_____

_____

_____

_____

_____

_____

_____

5

Becoming Confident,
Middle-of-the-Road Parents

Without putting parents too much on the spot, I like to ask, "How have you changed while your child has been in treatment? Have you allowed yourself to learn and grow from this experience?"

Some parents are incredibly proactive while their children are in treatment. They don't stand still and voraciously learn and absorb all they can. They meet with therapists, coaches, clergy and other family members to work out the kinks in their own personal lives. This bodes well for the family. Parents who are willing to look at their own baggage and parenting style meet with greater success, which translates into success for the child.

Far less effective is the attitude, "The kid has to get his act together and do the changing." This is the situation where I have my work cut out for me, because how willing and invested in change family members are will often depend on the family component of the treatment program. Let this book prompt and guide you into doing the necessary work to effect positive change all the way around.

Part of why your child went into treatment was because she could not find a way to be genuine about her experience—her life—as she truly wanted to be. Perhaps she felt her words fell on deaf ears, or that she wasn't good enough. While your child is still in treatment, listen to the truth that springs forth. Your child's truth, your acceptance of that truth, and the wisdom from therapists and counselors can be successfully channeled into an integrative healing process. With this regained health comes the safety for all family members to be truly themselves and equally respected within the family. When nurtured, this healthy form of familial relationship can sustain a family for generations.

I discovered that most of the young people who show up at wilderness therapy are a warning sign for the dysfunction and wounding of an entire family. Although they communicated their distress in an unhealthy fashion, these kids are very often the *truthsayers*. If you can set aside your child's past poor behavior and take time to listen to what she says about your family, you'll discover that her words hold some honest assessment.

Now that your child is able to speak her truth in a more healthy way, due to treatment, please listen. Listen and your child will help you identify your family's emotional issues and your weaknesses as parents. Sometimes our children are our teachers.

So often I've heard a kid say in a family therapy session, "Dad, you're so easy to manipulate," or "Mom, you didn't have a clue that I was using x-y-and-z drugs." Have you heard this, too, or something like it? If not, I respectfully ask you to hone your listening skills, because this kind of information is crucial. It will help you to address the areas where you need to change your parenting style. And, if you don't make the needed changes, history might repeat itself sooner than you think.

Middle-of-the-Road Parenting

There are a lot of books and seminars on the topic of parenting. I apologize for adding to the plethora of advice, but I subscribe to a rather simple model and would like for you to consider it. I have chosen it after watching and modeling it in my work for a number of years.

If you view parenting styles on a continuum, such as the one that follows, parenting from the middle has proven most effective. I call this middle-of-the-road parenting. When you combine it with a confident parenting style, you will find that you have a lot of fuel in your parental gas tank.

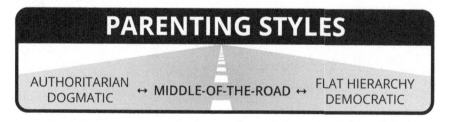

PARENTING STYLES

AUTHORITARIAN DOGMATIC ↔ MIDDLE-OF-THE-ROAD ↔ FLAT HIERARCHY DEMOCRATIC

Stereotypical 1950s-type parents are rooted in the more authoritarian side of the spectrum. They sound something like this: "Do as I say, not as I do. Do whatever I say. Don't question me. Children are to be seen, not heard. Do this! Do that! Do only what I say." Their approach is quite dictatorial, and back in the day was often accompanied by a swift swat on the backside. This is a rather traditional approach that can engender fear and awe. Respect is meant to be the theme, but this type of parenting can be devoid of empathy, causing serious rebellion in the teen or young adult and creating relationship rifts that can last a lifetime.

It can be argued that the social movements of the 1960s were in reaction to this control and enforced conformity. Those counterculture-era kids grew up, and shifted to the other side of the spectrum when it came to parenting. As a result, today's parents are very concerned about self-esteem, not squashing a child's spirit, and lifting the child up close to her dreams.

This type of parent might say things like, "Do whatever makes you happy. Well, Johnny, what do you think your curfew should be? I'll clean your room; you just do your homework. Well, I did that when I was a kid, so I guess it's okay if it's just a little pot or a couple of drinks here at home. He didn't want to go to school, so I let him stay home when he wanted to."

Repeat: Your child is not your equal.

Parents who are overly concerned for their child's comfort carry out this type of parenting. They over-empower their child to the point that he or she is the tail wagging the dog.

Perhaps in your own home you allowed endless debate, so that your child came to consider herself your peer and equal? She is not! Repeat: Your child is not your equal. By not maintaining a hierarchy in the home, you have relinquished your power, allowing your child to drain you, like kryptonite robbing Superman of his ability to fight evil.

I have witnessed democratic parenting so permissive that it has backfired: the child ends up acting spoiled and precocious, and feeling unhappy when life doesn't give her everything she wants. A child kept comfortable never gets to develop real self-esteem by achievement and good action, and this is the antithesis of what you intend. Until your child reaches adulthood by your definition, you are the boss and you're in charge. This doesn't mean you should become a despotic dictator, but it does mean that you must govern your household with clear and decisive authority. You must establish the ground rules and mete out consequences as needed.

Most treatment centers balance these two approaches. Therapists and counselors borrow firmness from the more authoritarian parenting style, as it sets up a useful power differential. Yet the more recent parenting style of empathy and empowerment is also embraced to build a strong sense of self in the child.

Parenting Anew

Before your child left, she probably gutted your parenting style. She knew how to divide and conquer, and how to pressure you into getting what she wanted. She played each of you like a violin. Kids might struggle in life, but they don't seem to have a problem when it comes to manipulation. They know how to mess with your mind . . . and very often your heart.

Your child honed these skills, and felt she had to manipulate, to survive. She basically trashed your power as parents. Then she went to treatment, and now she's used to authority figures who do not get played. Treatment has taught her that she cannot manipulate all adults.

> Then she went to treatment, and now she's used to authority figures who do not get played.

Take advantage of this. Tighten up your parenting style and develop confidence in the expectations and rules you set. Your child will grow to respect them, after an initial phase at home when she'll test the waters to see what she can still get away with. Become confident parents before your child returns—so confident that you feel it in your bones, and so will she. So confident that you don't let environmental and peer influences dictate how you run your home.

I spend hundreds of hours helping parents cut through the confusion and ambiguity that comes along with parenting today. If you feel lost as a parent, I'll bet money that you feel lost in other areas of your life. Unless you're a sociopath (which you're not, because sociopaths wouldn't read this book or strive to help their child), you can and probably *should* rely on yourself much more than you do. You know what you believe in, what it means to be a good human being. This is the gift you have to pass on to the next generation. So take the opportunity your child is giving you to stop doubting yourself.

In this generation of parents, I see too much self-doubt and an overly democratic flat hierarchy created in the home. It appears that, in an effort to raise children's self esteem, many parents have overpraised, overindulged, undermined the work ethic, and admittedly created precocious, arrogant young people. Many of the parents with whom I work admit that they regret giving their children too much leeway. They wish their kids would do their chores, give more value to what it takes to acquire material things, and appreciate their parents' efforts on their behalf.

Confident parenting is all about knowing who you are and what you want from and for your kids. It's being strong enough to not be intimidated by your children. Kids need leadership, and are always watching to see if you're up to the task. From what I understand about the wolf genus, wolves check regularly to see if the alpha is still alpha, and I would say the same stands true for teens and young adults. The pack rests and feels safe when each member is sure of his role in the family system. Your child should be certain that he is safe *and* that he is not the alpha.

Be Present to Parent

Contemporary lifestyles are often fraught with exhaustion and stress. Most of us supposedly civilized humans live in a rat race, no doubt about it. When people are so busy trying to survive, they might miss out on the most important parts of life, such as a fulfilling relationship and raising good people. The temptation is great to check out at the end of a hectic day, but I urge you to hang in there just a little bit longer.

Take the time to care for yourself, and also spend quality time—and a good quantity of time—with your child. If you can do these two things, which might take some priority shifting, you're doing what I call "being present." No, this doesn't translate into making yourself available for every basketball game or dishing up three homemade meals each day. When you're present for your child, it means you're taking care of yourself and are therefore healthy enough to be available physically, mentally, and emotionally for your child, so he or she can come forth and be authentic.

Your child just spent months, maybe years, in a place where the adults almost always had time to listen, validate, normalize, and contextualize because it's what they do. In short, these folks were present for a relationship with your child. I suggest that, for the time he lives under your roof, you work diligently at being available for a relationship with him. Your being present will strengthen him, because you'll be clear-headed enough to assess and then say or do the right thing to keep him traveling along the road to health and not regression.

Different Parenting Styles

I have yet to see two partners with identical parenting techniques. If each of you has your own approach and style, compromise and collaborate on how to raise your kids, while creating the Home Agreement. This gives you an opportunity to work out your differences about the family culture and how it plays out practically. As I suggested earlier, in the case of divorce you might need to create two Home Agreements, one for each household. If each Home Agreement has rules specific to each parent's house, this can still be successful provided the rules and expectations around key issues such as work, friends, education, and sobriety are the same.

In many households it's typical for inherent personality traits to cause dissension. One parent is more lax in monitoring and dishing out consequences than the other, or one parent values regular communication and the other does not. While working on your Home Agreement, discuss these differences, keeping in mind that seldom is one way the only effective way.

Discuss openly why you do what you do, and listen to your partner talk about his or her motives. Figure out how you can meet in the middle. You might both agree that your child should work to earn spending money, but when you get down to concrete rules you disagree on how much and when. When such a difference becomes apparent, search for the middle ground. Agree that your son should hold a job over the summer but spend the rest of the year working on his studies. When finding this compromise, be careful not to water down your expectations.

Emotions That Sabotage Parenting

Many parents feel bad about the reality their children must deal with. Some kids have mental health issues, have experienced trauma, lost their innocence way too early and have seen more than their fair share of suffering and even death. Parents naturally want to take away this pain.

If your child is depressed or addicted and you can see the genetic line from grandparents on down, sympathy can give rise to codependence pretty fast. Parents should know that they're not responsible for the seeming unfairness of genetics or environmental stressors beyond their control. We all have to do our best with the hand we've been dealt, including your child. Since she is not excluded from this reality, your child needs to figure out what he can control and what he can achieve, given who he is. Certainly your empathy is needed, but codependency springing from grief and guilt will hold him back.

> Excessive guilt can translate into codependency.

Excessive guilt can translate into codependency. When my nephew struggled with cancer from ages five to eight, compassion and empathy helped, but there was no room for guilt or extended grief. If my brother had stopped treatment for his son because the chemotherapy was so extremely painful, my nephew and godson would not have graduated from high school and lived to pursue his dreams. Sometimes the medicine is very bitter to take, but is exactly what is needed.

Parenting skills such as boundary setting and holding your child accountable can be impeded by either one of two distinct types of fear. The first is rooted in the past and accompanied by guilt. It goes something like this: "As a parent, I made giant mistakes in the past, and I'm afraid I'll just continue to screw up." This fear is the main reason for the parental work offered in this book. When you do all that you can to care for yourself and to live by your heartfelt values, your success as a parent becomes much more likely.

You will not help your child while nursing intrinsic self-doubt. It's one thing to be honest and to step back with an analytical mind to assess your motives and actions; it's altogether another to let the fear of making mistakes stop you from being the parent your child needs. Gather humble courage and take some risks. Trust your parenting and be willing to fumble. If the staff at your child's treatment center were overly reticent, your child would not have gotten better. Your intentions are sound, so even if you make a mistake the outcome will still be okay. You're human, just as your child is. When you make a mistake, learn from it. Even better, let your kid learn from it.

The second impeding fear that parents often voice is this: "If I hold boundaries and don't compromise, then it's my fault if my child regresses." An example of this is curfew. If you tell your son he must be home by 11 and he disagrees, the fear is that he'll become defiant and angry, go out anyway, and do something dangerous such as relapse into drugs or promiscuous sex. Let's break this thought pattern down.

When you lay out a boundary, there's no guarantee that your child is going to like it and comply, even though it seems cut and dried to you and is based on a very heartfelt value. Whether you're fearful about it or not, this defiant outcome is a possibility. Your child always has personal volition, and can defy what you lay out for him. What's of utmost importance is that you not waffle on your core beliefs. When you're intimidated, your child can smell your fear a mile away. Kids take advantage of this to push harder for what they want . . . manipulation escalation at its finest!

If your child regresses as a result of a boundary, so be it. Don't let obstinacy leave you at a standstill. Instead, follow through with necessary and appropriate consequences, which will be discussed at length in Chapter 9. Suffice it to say, for now, that you must hold your child accountable to the expectations you put before him. If your rules and expectations are realistic and were made with clarity, you have nothing to fear except not following through.

> If your rules and expectations are realistic and were made with clarity, you have nothing to fear except not following through.

Confident parents are reasonable and not dogmatic. In the past, when your child was taking full advantage of you and maybe even jeopardizing his safety and the safety of the family, you were likely moved to anger. You had a right to be angry. And yet, sometimes parents make a decision, a rule, and a consequence out of displaced anger. I encourage parents to work on defusing their hot buttons. Doing so allows you to maintain a level of mindfulness so that your child doesn't become the target after a bad day at work or because of marital strife. This comes back to caring for yourself and possessing self-awareness. When you're healthy and balanced, you have what it takes to listen to your child and, when warranted, deliberate like a wise judge.

Parent Firmly and Fairly

Parents seem to know intellectually that being the patriarch or matriarch of the family is not a popularity contest, and yet their parenting often demonstrates otherwise. It sometimes appears that parents are trying to get personal needs met by their children. I'm not sure this is effective, any more than is parenting gingerly for fear of angering your child. If you parent with firmness and fairness, your child will get angry for the right reasons. It's appropriate for her to get upset and frustrated if you won't let her hang out with that best friend who is on the red light list and leading her astray. Your child *will* get mad or upset when you say no to her smoking pot. Don't expect a thank-you. Be who you are, stand firm with your values guiding you, and let the chips fall where they may.

Avoid the trap of wanting to always be your kid's best friend. This sounds like a pretty simple guideline, but there's more to it. Is not a parent's disciplining of a child an act of friendship? Is not a pastor also a friend, or a favorite professor? It's the type of friendship that matters.

Parents can never be bffs (best friends forever), on equal footing with their child. It's not possible. There will always be a power differential, no matter how diligently parents work to flatten it. Yes, you are fellow travelers on Earth, but you gave your child life. You fed her, kissed her bumps on the head, enrolled her in school, taught her to drive, and corrected her countless times. Even when your child turns fifty, she might need you to parent and not just be a friend. Some days when you indulge in that mani-pedi with your daughter or watch the big game with your son, you feel more like a friend, but the truth is, you're still parenting at the same time.

No one takes the place of a parent. Parents do what no other authority figure can do for a child. Yoda, or any other esteemed mentor, might help raise your child and be a necessary person in your child's life, but he's not you. He is not a mother or a father. Even Yoda didn't change diapers or hold a steady job to put a roof over someone's head for 18-plus years. You are unique and you are special. Your child needs you, even though she'll spend a good portion of her growing-up years pushing you away.

You, parenting with confidence, are the exact right person to show your child how to live . . . and how to die. She needs you throughout life to always be there as a parent, and to be her best friend only at moments. As she matures and succeeds, she'll either grow closer to those who parented her confidently and responsibly or move away from those who didn't discipline and protect her. So, for now or lifelong? It's for you to decide when you most want your child as your friend.

> Kids need you throughout life to always be there as a parent, and to be a best friend only at moments.

Lead and Your Child Will Learn

Successful families have leadership. Successful organizations have leadership. Even successful flat-hierarchy systems have leadership. Call it what you want; your child flourished in treatment because someone in charge was thoughtful, consistent, and facilitating. Someone showed leadership and doled out consequences. Therapeutic environments provide this because it works. Therapists listen to their clients—your children—and hear their stories, but they don't let the kids run the place. Doting, overly democratic parents very often get taken advantage of; you might already have learned this the hard way.

Make your values both attainable and realistic, and expect your child to live up to them. Sound boundaries, benevolent leadership that's firm and fair, and the reinforcement of noteworthy behavior with *proportionate* positive feedback will propel your child to mature. You can expect resistance, but in the long run your child might actually reciprocate with affection.

Parental love can be firm and compassionate at the same time. You've heard the term "tough love," as it gets bandied about a lot. If tough-love parenting allows a young person to experience the full ramifications of his decisions, then I am a proponent. Don't save your child from feeling the sting that results from making a bad choice . . . he needs that information to grow up. Here again, let your values tell you when it's time to step in to keep your child out of dysfunction and protect him from threats to his existence. The goal is for the parents to be the paramount influence on a child—not the dysfunctional red-flag peers who would lead him down a dark and dangerous alley.

No One Deserves to Be Spoiled Rotten

Spoiling is an inside job. A peach or avocado might look good on the outside, but if it's actually spoiled it'll be black and rotten from the inside out.

When I talk to parents about spoiling or entitlement, they think mostly about the material stuff, like indulging their child in too many scoops of ice cream. This is not what I'm referring to (although, does your child really need three pairs of designer jeans, with no contemplation of the price tags?). What I'm alluding to is something deeper. It has to do with character.

Overindulging in praise or material goods and empowering someone who has not earned empowerment will result in character flaws. The same result occurs if you go to the other extreme and deprive someone of an adequate material life, appropriate praise, and earned empowerment. A poverty of affection or food might lead to the same result as an overabundance: character flaws such as criminal tendencies. Markedly, both examples have less to do with economics and more to do with parental influence. Be present to teach your child, through your actions and words, that she is important, and so are others. Raise someone who takes care of herself and respects others. Be there to guide a young person who is not arrogant or manipulative or abusive. Give your child room to play, but also show her what self-control is all about. It's not about getting everything you want and "me, me, me." In mythology, it would be represented as a balance between the qualities of the gods Dionysus and Apollo—between indulging in the joyful fruits of life and carrying out one's duty.

It can be especially hard for parents to refrain from spoiling a kid who's been in treatment. That's because they think their child has suffered there. The opposite is true. When and where else does your child have someone to care for him in every way? When your child is nervous, someone is there. When he has a headache, someone is there. Most programs take the kids out on fun adventures every other day. Yes, your child likens treatment to prison, but it is not.

When your child returns, go ahead and indulge him a little, but steer clear of giving too many Disney experiences. Instead, learn how to *be* together as a family. Although he might not admit it, what your child really craves is to simply hang around home—with you.

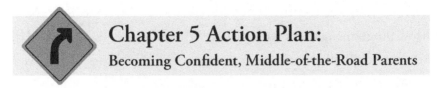

Chapter 5 Action Plan:
Becoming Confident, Middle-of-the-Road Parents

(To download blank worksheets, visit www.TheRoadHomeBook.com/downloads.)

#1. Parenting Styles

Reflect on your parenting style. Mark where you think you are on the spectrum.

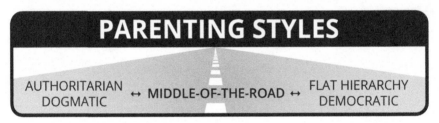

Has your parenting style been working for you? Would you like to move more to the middle of the road? Can you be more effective doing it differently? Are there things that you do that diminish your role as parents? For example, do you need to listen more? To hold your temper in check? Do you need to stick to your guns and do what you say you are going to do? Does your own upbringing make you less effective as a parent? Make a list of what you know is ineffective and how you might change it. I've provided an example:

I want to stop going behind my husband's back and giving in to the kids. I will talk to my husband and make sure we agree on our approach so I don't feel compelled to stray from the plan.

_____

_____

_____

_____

_____

#2. Parental Self-reflection

Give yourself the gift of self-reflection. What can you implement immediately and practice so that you can be a more effective parent? Can you hash out your own childhood with a counselor or maybe a member of your family? Can you role-play "doing what you say you're going to do" with your partner? Can you be honest with yourself and your therapist and explore why you sometimes get so angry that your automatic response is to yell at your child? Make a list of what you can change here.

_____

_____

_____

_____

_____

#3. Take Action

Take action on one of the items you listed above. Add it to your "things to do" list . . . right at the top and then accomplish it. Congrats! Next, tackle number two . . . then three . . .

Engaging in Transparent and Loving Communication

D ialogue . . . transparency . . . dialogue . . . transparency . . .
dialogue . . . need I say more? Anybody who has worked with
me knows this is my mantra. If you communicate transparently (no
lies, no hidden agendas, and from the heart) with all the folks in your
life, you have everything. If you and your family members can safely
communicate and be truly yourselves while doing so, you'll have what
it takes to work through any difficulty. As much as this book is about
the Home Agreement and you parenting your child coming home, it is
equally about you creating and maintaining through communication a
bedrock relationship with your child.

In treatment, whether wilderness, a residential treatment center,
aftercare, or a therapeutic boarding school, professionals spend most of
their energy teaching kids how to possess integrity within their being

and their environment. Transparent and loving communication, what I like to call TLC, is the heart and soul of this process. All the individual and group therapy you and your child have experienced has been practice in being authentic. To live authentically is joyful, healthy, and rejuvenating; most likely it's included somewhere in your values. TLC has never failed me once in my work with teens or young adults. They appreciate being heard and given a genuine voice.

Set up your family culture now to embrace TLC. It is a way of showing respect to any person, not only the child returning from treatment. It's the footing for healthy dialogue, safety, and intimacy, and ultimately to strong relationships. It allows for empathy and real solutions that will last. The trust created allows for even greater TLC; it's self-perpetuating. This doesn't mean that everyone in your family must know everything about you. We all need our privacy, individual boundaries, and personal mysteries. It does mean, though, that your child can be his true self in your presence and be honest in an open dialogue about what's going on in his life. If you can talk to your child about what matters most and he feels safe and answers truthfully, then most issues and problems can be explored, experienced, and eventually resolved.

> If you can talk to your child about what matters most and he feels safe and answers truthfully, then most issues and problems can be explored, experienced, and eventually resolved.

TRANSPARENT & LOVING COMMUNUCATION (TLC)

- IS HONEST AND OPEN ABOUT THOUGHTS, FEELINGS, AND MOTIVATIONS.

- IS DELIVERED WITH LOVE.

- ENGAGES EFFECTIVE LISTENING AND DE-ESCALATION TECHNIQUES LEARNED IN TREATMENT.

- LETS PARTICIPANTS FEEL HEARD AND VALIDATED.

- IS NEVER AGGRESSIVE OR MANIPULATIVE.

- CREATES A SAFE ENVIRONMENT FOR PARTICIPANTS TO BE AUTHENTICALLY THEMSELVES.

- IS GUIDED TO SUCCESS BY THE PARENT.

TLC in Practice

Communicating with transparency sounds pretty easy, but in fact it's a tall order. It takes conscious effort, for it can be arduous and sometimes messy. We all struggle to achieve this type of communication—so much so that we might think we're not cut out for it. On the contrary! Transparent communication isn't reserved only for priests, mystics, and enlightened gurus. Communicating openly is something we can all do, albeit with a modicum of courage, because communicating with transparency means that you tell those you love who you really are.

Some families have passed this form of communicating from generation to generation, so it might be easier for them to be truly themselves in each other's presence. Most of us, however, fumble when putting the idea into action. Past events and some family cultures (even Western culture) have taught us to be less than open. For those of us not used to speaking with transparency, TLC feels dangerous. When it's new to us, being vulnerable, honest and direct can be disorienting and anxiety provoking.

Transparent communication is a learned style. Your child learned it with staff and peers in treatment. Carry that momentum into the family room. Address TLC in your Home Agreement. Perhaps you've had time to practice (with one another or extended-family members) the communication skills that aid in TLC. If not, ask your child to help, as he is now an expert. You might want to pick up Krissy Pozatek's book, *The Parallel Process: Growing Alongside Your Adolescent or Young Adult Child in Treatment*. The author does an excellent job of coaching parents in effective and healthy communication skills.

Other techniques to use are nonviolent de-escalation and reflective and active listening, both of which your child's treatment team has most likely coached you. You might have heard of "I feel" statements. They're very useful, yet families tend not to use them at home because they say they don't feel natural. Experiment with the tools you've been given, to see what works and doesn't work for you.

For the first few months after your child returns, you might choose to have weekly family meetings where you can practice speaking openly. As communication is enhanced and the family culture becomes more open and honest, structured meetings can be reduced in frequency to twice per month, and can eventually be scheduled only as needed. The desire is for transparency to become a daily experience and fairly effortless.

In wilderness, I learned so much about my students and was able to build TLC relationships simply by sharing meals around the campfire. In your home, it might not be possible to eat together every day, but when you do all sit down for a meal you'll most likely experience some TLC. There is something magical about breaking bread together. This type of "communion" is natural, and can be just as therapeutic as a scheduled family meeting—oftentimes more, because your child's defenses are down. During formal family meetings there might be posturing and protecting. When you're grilling in the backyard or going for an ice cream you might meet with more bare-bones honesty.

Your child will have the basics for TLC in her repertoire of skills when she returns home. You may not, and yet I have found that one of the most effective tools you can have as a confident and skilled parent is TLC. Don't let fear of failure stop you from practicing this tool for real, with your kid as often as you can. Here's an example.

Transparency and Love (TLC) at Work

In the kitchen, a mother pours a glass of iced tea for herself and one for her 17-year-old son, who has just sauntered in.

Mom: We need to have a talk. Here *(hands him the tea)*. So you probably know that you failed your drug test. It was positive for THC.

Son: Okay . . . *(big sigh and he sits)* Yeah, it was on Saturday. I just smoked once, though. A guy offered it to me when I was walking home from work and I didn't say no. I just felt like it.

Mom: So you've only done it once—which is a slip from our agreement. Is that what you're saying?

Son: Yeah, it was once. I'm sorry.

Mom: Mr. Hanson next door says he saw you smoking last week in the backyard.

Son: No, I didn't!

Mom: I believe Mr. Hanson. We've been friends since you were a baby. He saw you. Do you want to say anything else? I'm pretty sure there's some lying going on, so I'm going to consequence you for dishonesty as well as the slip.

Son: *(long pause, thinking)* Okay, yeah. I've been smoking for a while. About three weeks, I think.

Mom: Okay. How much are you smoking? And shoot straight with me. I'm not joking around here. I want the facts.

Son: I guess every day. Sometimes twice.

Mom: *(calmly)* I appreciate you being honest with me about this. Thank you, it means a lot. But I'm worried that you've gone back to using. This is significant, and I'm also concerned that you lied. Do you have anything to say about either issue? Using or why you lied?

Son: I don't want to talk about why I'm using. But I'll stop, because I don't want to go back to treatment. And I'm sorry I lied and I won't lie again. I promise.

Mom: I hear that you don't want to talk about it, but we need to in the next couple of days to get more details about why. For now there'll be a consequence. Like we discussed in the Home Agreement, honesty and sobriety were core to your coming home. These are both major violations.

Son: What consequence are you talking about? I forget.

Mom: Well, for substances we'll increase the random drug testing to two times a week, and you need to go back to Marijuana Anonymous twice a week. For dishonesty, the cell phone is mine for two weeks.

Son: But I hate MA, Mom! It's irrelevant.

Mom: And it's what we agreed upon. No negotiating—as we also agreed.

Son: How long do I have to go?

Mom: Until I see a month of clean drug tests. And I have a major concern about your ability to lie so quickly. I'm going to watch to see if you can find more integrity. Honesty is the family policy. Right?

Son: Mom, I haven't lied about anything else, just the weed.

Mom: Okay, and I want to believe you, but I need to see the proof in your behavior. Do you understand what's just happened here? How serious this is?

Son: Okay! Okay! I get it.

The above dialogue shows complete transparency on the part of the mother. Her willingness to be open about her feelings and tough with her consequences shows genuine love for her son, and models how he should communicate back to her. The son in this scenario was able to respond in an overall positive way. Notice how the mother didn't jockey for a total solution to the problem or overnight abstinence. This clear, definitive, response on the part of the mom helped to keep the situation honest, and escalation didn't occur. She used true TLC.

The Pros and Cons of Therapeutic Talk

A good treatment facility will introduce communication strategies to help you maintain an effective, ongoing dialogue with your child. If your son or daughter has gained an appreciation for the communication tools of therapy, use them as often as you can. Active listening, reflective listening, de-escalation techniques, and "I feel" statements can be highly effective. These are all ingredients that can help create TLC.

But here's the caveat: your child will come home tired of therapy and might resent you dropping into the therapeutic talk she learned *ad nauseam*. She's craving normalcy as defined by what was familiar to her when growing up. If she resists therapy talk, drop into a healthy pattern of communication that's more natural to your family. Kids very often appreciate their parents being "real" instead of resorting to artificial constructs, even though these are effective. I'm not in any way suggesting that the therapeutic tools your family has learned during the journey thus far are ineffective. The contrary is true. What I am suggesting is that it's wise to use a tool when it will not be rejected. If your child is vocal about wanting a "normal" life and to be talked to "normally," indulge her. Pull out the tools when they'll be accepted and not turned against you. Transparent and loving communication can at first feel like therapeutic talk. And yet, once you get the hang of it and learn how to use it to really understand your child and be understood, it will feel more like "normal."

Never underestimate your child's ability to use therapeutic talk and other such tools to manipulate and frustrate you into giving him exactly what he wants. He's just spent up to five hours a day learning human behavior and the art of communication, and has practiced it daily. Don't be surprised if you hear something like, "Hey, Mom, I'm going to call you out, and you need to bust an 'I feel' statement." This very well could catch you off guard and overwhelm you.

He has also become adept at sparring psychologically with savvy staff members. Who you'll now have on your doorstep is a Jedi master. If he chooses the dark side, he'll attempt to control you, so stand ready and let TLC be your light saber.

So Tough to Say "No!"

I'd like to share a simple, effective secret that I've learned by working with families— particularly teens and young adults. I say what I mean and I say it once. I am fair and reasonable most of the time, and on topics of great importance and value I do not negotiate. When a teen asks me a question, my yes or no is exactly that. With parents, it tends to not be so black-and-white.

When parents are clear about their values, and stand firm regarding what is nonnegotiable, good things start to happen. Especially if they don't allow their child to come back at them multiple times to negotiate and manipulate. You've heard it before in a different campaign, but I'll borrow it here: "Just say no" to those things you feel really strongly about. Don't doubt yourself. Don't go against your gut. You know what's right for your family, because you are the parent. If something *is* negotiable in your eyes, don't start with "no," as that waters down your word. Only use "no" when you mean it, and then don't flinch.

Shut Down Manipulation with TLC

Transparent communication and confident parenting can be quickly undermined by manipulation on the part of children. You most likely

Ahhhh . . . which pawn shall I manipulate today?

know that your child is a master manipulator. She knows how to beat you at your own arguments, always seeming to be two steps ahead of you. She's astute, and can divide the parental unit and get you and your partner arguing before you know it. It's true: all kids manipulate on some level, whether they've been to treatment or not, to control their environment. No biggie, *but* here's the catch.

As your child matures, you typically request that she give up childish manipulation and be honest and have integrity. This immediately creates internal conflict for the maturing child. She's being asked to give up a skill that served her well in order to take on adult qualities that most often will not reward her (at least in the short term) with what she wants. This looks to the kid like a really bad deal. It rests upon your shoulders to show your child that it's worthwhile to be honest and have integrity.

Your child very likely dealt with this topic in treatment. That doesn't mean she'll come home full of integrity, with no desire to get what she wants. If your child continues to manipulate after she returns, and you allow it, you'll very soon be demoted from the designation of "parent." If it feels like you're being bamboozled, disrespected, split from your co-parent, or frustrated through arguments, you are most likely being manipulated.

When this happens, do what we therapists do: call the child on the carpet the moment you recognize the manipulation. For example, say: "You seem to be working me over the coals about going to Disneyland and not accepting my decision. What's up? You know you're not accepting my decision. So what's going on here?"

> If you give in to manipulation, you're saying to your child that it works, and this will be a detour down a road you don't want to take.

Explore your child's manipulation with her, and validate and normalize the experience. Reflect what you hear. Let her know you understand her feelings, *but* do not change your mind. Let your child know that, just because you're listening, it doesn't mean you're going to give her what she wants. If you give in to manipulation, you're saying to your child that it works, and this will be a detour down a road you don't want to take.

Here is a sample conversation between a father and daughter in which the father successfully shuts down his child's manipulation:

Shutting Down Manipulation with TLC

> **Daughter:** But, Dad, his parents are going to be there and I'll sleep with all the other kids in the living room.
>
> **Dad:** No. You know very well what it says in our Home Agreement. No sleepovers at a boy's house.
>
> **Daughter:** So if it was Mandy's house it would be okay? It's just that it's at his house?
>
> **Dad:** Yep, that's right.
>
> **Daughter:** Well, that's stupid. What you're really saying is that you don't trust me. You *never* trust me.
>
> **Dad:** *(calmly reflecting back and controlling the process)* You sound really frustrated. What's going on?
>
> **Daughter:** Yeah, I'm frustrated. Everyone is going to spend the night and I can't because you sent me to treatment and I have to follow these f---ing rules.
>
> **Dad:** Hey, young lady, watch your language. And, yes, I hear you're really angry about having a Home Agreement and rules. But they're there, and we're going to follow them.

Daughter: Well, Mom said she'd consider it.

Dad: Well, I said no. No sleepovers at boys' houses—and that's where it stands. But I want to talk about how you're manipulating—

Daughter: *(interrupts)* Well, I don't want to!

Dad: Please don't interrupt me again; I'm not done talking. The way you're asking for this is not okay. First, you know it's against the rules, and second, you're trying to split your mom and me on this issue and you're being argumentative. This manipulation is not going to work. Accept my answer, which is a clear "no," or there'll be a consequence for manipulation and disrespect. So, please, let's talk this through in a constructive way.

Daughter: *(sighs, rolls her eyes, crosses her arms, but plunks down on the sofa to talk)* Okay, let's talk.

Transparent and loving communication is the heart and soul of my profession. I use it with proficiency, and yet in my personal life I have made hundreds of mistakes at it. It is hard to always be "on" with the people you live with day in and day out, and yet I think it's truly worthwhile to try. The key is to practice TLC, mistake after mistake. Use it in all your important personal relationships and see what happens.

Chapter 6 Action Plan:
Engaging in Transparent & Loving Communication

(To download blank worksheets, visit www.TheRoadHomeBook.com/downloads.)

#1. Action Statement

Reread the main components of transparent and loving communication:

TRANSPARENT & LOVING COMMUNUCATION (TLC)

· IS HONEST AND OPEN ABOUT THOUGHTS, FEELINGS, AND MOTIVATIONS.

· IS DELIVERED WITH LOVE.

· ENGAGES EFFECTIVE LISTENING AND DE-ESCALATION TECHNIQUES LEARNED IN TREATMENT.

· LETS PARTICIPANTS FEEL HEARD AND VALIDATED.

· IS NEVER AGGRESSIVE OR MANIPULATIVE.

· CREATES A SAFE ENVIRONMENT FOR PARTICIPANTS TO BE AUTHENTICALLY THEMSELVES.

· IS GUIDED TO SUCCESS BY THE PARENT.

Is there one that intrigues you the most? One that you know for sure you could improve in your own communication? Write an action statement here. For example:

I am going to listen to my child and mirror back what he says without comment, so he knows that I really understand what he is saying.

_____

_____

_____

_____

#2. Practice Makes Perfect

Whenever you find yourself conversing with another and the conversation feels sticky or tense, try dropping into TLC. Be honest, open, and reflective. Use learned communication skills. Afterwards, write what was difficult for you. Where do you need more practice? Remember that the more you are proactive, the better you'll be able to communicate effectively with your child who's home from treatment.

_____

_____

_____

_____

_____

_____

_____

_____

#3. Reflect

Next time a sticky issue arises when you and your child are talking, whether in person or on the phone, try guiding the conversation with TLC. If you make a mistake or totally mess up, you still get an A for effort. Afterward, reflect on what occurred. How did the TLC feel to you? How might you and your child have been even more transparent and loving?

_____

_____

_____

_____

_____

_____

_____

_____

_____

_____

_____

_____

_____

_____

_____

_____

Embracing the Concept of Rules

While your child was in treatment, you were probably inundated with information regarding the importance of rules. Treatment is all about rules: lights out, chore lists, dress codes, mandatory therapy times, and exercise and diet routines. Rules are the basic boundaries set around communication, navigating issues, and interacting with others. They are expectations and goals. Rules are the guardrails on the sides of the road, put in place to make life understandable, manageable, and safe. Rules are also the bricks that will be used to build your Home Agreement.

Let's imagine the path home as an uphill (or downhill, for that matter) mountain road with lots of switchbacks, blind spots, and passages too narrow for more than one car to pass through at a time. That could be a hazardous journey. So the highway department puts up guardrails, and signs, maybe even mirrors, to help the driver navigate. They enforce a speed limit. With these boundaries in place, drivers can be more confident and comfortable, which makes them feel more capable of handling whatever hazards might lie ahead.

Megan, 17, wonders, "Will I ever make it?"
She will with Rules of the Road to guide her.

When you feel safe, you become more yourself. Your child just spent months or years in the safety of treatment, and that is mainly why he healed. Things were predictable, and thus he could stop being so fearful. He didn't have to talk so much jive. He could enjoy life and plan his dreams. He could be who he truly is. This needs to continue at home, and that means you must become the highway maintenance crew and highway patrol.

Most likely your child challenged whatever rules you had in place before treatment. Heads up. When he returns, he'll still challenge rules that don't make sense to him and that keep him from getting what he wants. Don't waste a moment getting down on yourself for raising a child who was and might still be a rebel and who thinks for himself. Just stay aware that a freethinking, analytical person is able to wrap your mind in knots.

During your child's treatment, you might have developed 20/20 hindsight and wished you had enforced rules or been more stalwart on certain issues. Good awareness. Use it now to correct past mistakes and to earnestly change. Learn from your treatment professionals. Become bold and brave. Take some calculated risks, and tighten up the family ship to stop the leaks.

Craft Rules of the Road that are homegrown from your vision and values, and heavily informed by the healthy limitations placed upon your child in treatment. Your family rules need to be an extension of you, not just reflections of another parent's or professional's opinion. If your Rules of the Road are practical guidelines rooted in your family

> Don't waste a moment getting down on yourself for raising a child who was and might still be a rebel and who thinks for himself. Just stay aware that a freethinking, analytical person is able to wrap your mind in knots.

culture and values, they will make sense and have longevity. They will work for your kid and they will work for you.

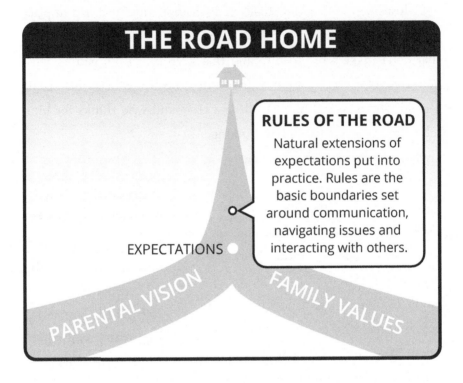

THE ROAD HOME

RULES OF THE ROAD

Natural extensions of expectations put into practice. Rules are the basic boundaries set around communication, navigating issues and interacting with others.

EXPECTATIONS

PARENTAL VISION

FAMILY VALUES

Rules, also called boundaries, are expectations brought down to earth and implemented in the day-to-day business of life. If higher education is an expectation within your family, then grades matter, as does research for college and SAT prep. Thus the boundary of a minimum GPA that is reasonable for your child's ability is put before the child, and she is rewarded proportionately for the effort she puts forth. College exploratory trips are scheduled. You discuss with your child what you will pay for and what she is expected to pay. The Rules of the

Road, when they're homegrown out of a family value system, seem less like rules. They become "just what we do in our family."

Rules Are for Parents, Too!

When your child comes home, having in place succinct rules based on your values will also help prevent you from slipping into previously dysfunctional parenting styles. Boundaries are there so you can know when to and what justice to offer.

When your kid acts up and you're at a loss for what action to take, refer to the Home Agreement and remind yourself of what you agreed to do. Your child's health, as well as your own, rides on you standing behind your expectations with loving strength. This is the continuation of your work as a family.

> The Rules of the Road, when they're homegrown out of a family value system, seem less like rules. They become "just what we do in our family."

Upon her return, your child will deliberately explore boundaries. All you need to do is let her know, each time she pushes against a limit, that it is very real and enforced. She will learn that, if she chooses to frustrate you and consistently break a rule or rules, her choices created the new situation that is effectively limiting her freedom. Enforced rules send the clear message that you are the parent—a loving individual who is fair, reasonable, and a person of your word.

And guess what? Rules grown from the family culture will not be a surprise to your child. For the most part she already knows these rules, because in her gut she knows what your family is all about. The difference with a Home Agreement today, as opposed to before treatment, is that now these rules are clearly laid out as expectations, leaving no wiggle room. These are rules your child can adhere to if she chooses, while still being who she is, maintaining her unique voice without whining, manipulating, or railroading you or others.

Taking On the Issues

When kids come home from treatment, very often there has been a history of rules being enforced haphazardly and a habit of manipulation on the part of the child. If recurring problems are the difficulty, Rules of the Road need to evolve from these issues. In this case, I still urge you to let each issue harken back to your vision and your values.

Any one issue for which a rule needs to be created will have a continuum of possibilities. For example, if your child was addicted to Internet games, you could decide to never again let him own a computer (one end of the spectrum), or you could let him use a communal computer placed in the family room and allow him to play video games for an hour every other day. Or you could just say, "He's 18, he has to manage his own life," and let him play all he wants so long as he pays for the computer and games and supports himself with a job. Among all these possibilities, what's crucial is for the rule created to be an extension of what you believe in and the expectation high enough for your child to reach his full potential. The following chart lists some of the possible issues for which you may want to write rules.

THE ROAD HOME

POSSIBLE ISSUES

Communication & Attitude   Dishonesty

Laziness & Lack of Motivation

Hygiene, Exercise, Diet & Sleep   Piercing & Tattoos

Smoking, Drinking or Drug Use   Cutting   Eating Disorders

Peers   Dating, Love & Sex   Curfew   Money

Counseling, Therapy & Medication   Spirituality & Faith

Chores & Work Ethic   Education & Academics   Technology

Pornography   Video Gaming   Cars & Driving

If you search, you can discover a family value or belief that relates to each of these issues. You can also glean a natural extension of that value—an expectation, and from that expectation a rule can be created.

In the next chapter we'll look more closely at the issues around which you and your child might need some Rules of the Road. We will also take some time to look at mental health and addiction before we actually learn how to craft the Home Agreement.

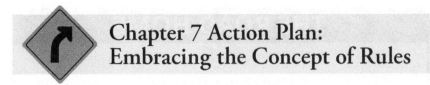

Chapter 7 Action Plan: Embracing the Concept of Rules

(To download blank worksheets, visit www.TheRoadHomeBook.com/downloads.)

#1. Identifying Issues

Look over this list of possible issues and circle those that have impacted your family. With which ones did your child in treatment most struggle? Which created anxiety and fear in you?

THE ROAD HOME

POSSIBLE ISSUES

Communication & Attitude   Dishonesty

Laziness & Lack of Motivation

Hygiene, Exercise, Diet & Sleep   Piercing & Tattoos

Smoking, Drinking or Drug Use   Cutting   Eating Disorders

Peers   Dating, Love & Sex   Curfew   Money

Counseling, Therapy & Medication   Spirituality & Faith

Chores & Work Ethic   Education & Academics   Technology

Pornography   Video Gaming   Cars & Driving

#2. Issues and Action Steps

Are there issues you haven't addressed in earlier Action Steps? Make a list of them here:

_____

_____

_____

_____

_____

_____

_____

_____

_____

_____

_____

_____

_____

_____

_____

_____

_____

_____

_____

_____

_____

_____

_____

#3. Visions, Values and Expectations

For each of the issues you listed on step 2, write out what vision, value and expectation is connected to the issue. I'll give a couple of examples to get you started.

Issue	Vision	Value	Expectation
Gets angry easily and yells at parents.	We see a child who has a positive attitude toward life and is kind and respectful.	We value kindness and respect in all people. We want to treat others as we want to be treated.	We expect you to regulate your emotions and not yell or get aggressive. Please have respect and kindness when you communicate to all.
Smokes weed.	We see a child who gets through life on his own volition and is not dependent upon any substances.	We believe in keeping our mind, heart, and body clean and healthy. We do not believe in abusing drugs or alcohol.	We expect you to be sober.

Issue	Vision	Value	Expectation

Crafting Your Family Rules
of the Road

I n the last chapter, the concept of rules being a natural extension of your expectations was introduced. Let's now delve into many of the issues you might wish to address as you create your family's Rules of the Road.

Crafting rules that you can enforce is the next stopping point on the way to getting your child home. But let me apologize up front for the length of this chapter. It is a whopper, but it had to be in order to address the many issues . . . or roadblocks . . . you and your child might encounter. Please feel free to skip reading any section that you know wholeheartedly does not apply to you and your child. I grant you full permission to do so.

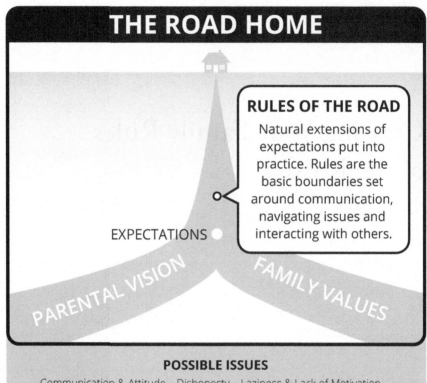

THE ROAD HOME

RULES OF THE ROAD

Natural extensions of expectations put into practice. Rules are the basic boundaries set around communication, navigating issues and interacting with others.

EXPECTATIONS

PARENTAL VISION

FAMILY VALUES

POSSIBLE ISSUES

Communication & Attitude   Dishonesty   Laziness & Lack of Motivation
Hygiene, Exercise, Diet & Sleep   Piercing & Tattoos   Smoking, Drinking or Drug Use
Cutting   Eating Disorders   Peers   Dating, Love & Sex   Curfew   Money
Counseling, Therapy & Medication   Spirituality & Faith   Chores & Work Ethic
Education & Academics   Technology   Pornography   Video Gaming   Cars & Driving

The Attitude Roadblock

The way your child relates with you, in both action and communication, is one of the most important areas to focus on in the Home Agreement.

Very likely your daughter went to treatment partly due to her disrespect and defiance. A good treatment program will put an end to this behavior, because if it went unchecked it could lead to antisocial traits and more serious misconduct. Your child's treatment team spent great effort to curb this displaced attitude and to teach coping and communication skills that offer more effective ways for your child to get reasonable needs met. Despite all that therapy, training, and money well spent, when your child comes home she will most likely be triggered by the past and tempted to test the waters. Rudeness, defiance, manipulation, and a plain old crappy attitude might result.

> The way your child relates with you, in both action and communication, is one of the most important areas to focus on in the Home Agreement.

Here's where having done your work comes in handy. Do not employ maladaptive communication and feed your child's temper. Simply stated, don't be guilty of modeling poor communication. When both parents model transparent and loving communication (TLC) through open dialogue after open dialogue, the road to a successful transition and relationship will be built. If one parent doesn't do the work, the road will be more precarious.

It is critically important to make transparent and loving communication a centerpiece in the Home Agreement. Envision how you want to talk to one another and incorporate your values. For instance: "We believe in communicating in a healthy way by respecting each individual. This means we don't interrupt each other. When there is conflict, we use reflective listening skills and 'I feel' statements. We grant each other the space and time to de-escalate if we're upset."

If these communication concepts are foreign to you, then I highly recommend that you ask your personal therapist or your child's treatment counselor to help guide you in coming to understand some of these valuable techniques.

Just to help a little bit, here is an example of an issue concerning communication and how you can develop a value-based rule:

Issue: Tempers get in the way of our communicating. Yelling and shouting makes it hard to be heard.

Vision: To have a home where we can say what we mean without yelling, and as a result no one feels fearful and we gain true understanding of one another.

Value: Love is the basis of our home. We should have compassion for one another and be able to freely talk and express ourselves.

Expectation: That we respect one another and hear one another out. That if we are very angry we excuse ourselves, which is allowed, and we cool down.

Rule: First, we respect one another's thoughts and feelings and hear each other out. If a viewpoint makes us angry to the point of yelling then we are allowed a cooling off period of 24 hours if needed. But, we always come back to the conversation and handle the issue.

Physical Intimidation

When I was a wilderness therapist, many of the adolescent boys in my care had physically intimidated a parent, and some had actually hurt their mom or dad. Before treatment, your child might have postured physically to manipulate you. This act of aggression should never be tolerated.

With treatment, your child now knows that such aggressive behavior is completely unacceptable. He has learned skills so as to not use physical intimidation as a tool to manipulate and to not ever let things escalate to such an extreme.

If you think there's a chance that your child might bully again, then clearly put it in writing that aggressive behavior of any kind will not be tolerated, and that if it is exhibited there will be significant consequences. If you think physical intimidation is a real probability, consider not bringing your child home until there is no longer such a threat.

If your child has exhibited aggressive behavior in the past, here is an example of how you might come up with a rule about it:

Issue: Aggressive behavior and communication.

Vision: In our family we want to be able to speak openly and honestly to one another, expressing what we really feel, without fear of being physically intimidated or hurt.

> **Value:** We value transparent and loving communication in our family, so that each of us can express who he or she really is and be appreciated for being that person.
>
> **Expectation:** In our family we expect open dialogue that allows each of us to get out our feelings and concerns without feeling fearful or intimidated.
>
> **Rule:** Because we care for one another, we speak with loving and open communication, taking into consideration what the others feel and allowing them to speak freely. To foster open communication, we have a weekly family meeting to discuss issues that concern us. Aggressive communication is not tolerated.

Lying and Stealing

The most common, maladaptive forms of regression that I see exhibited when a child returns home are lying and stealing. Lying suggests that your child has not completely accepted or understood the idea of integrity. Not all kids who go to treatment buy into the full philosophy of healthy behavior. Instead, they go through the motions, and when they return home they slip into their old deceptive ways.

Lies matter. Every family I have worked with has rightly written in their Home Agreement that honesty and trust are at the core of their domestic life.

When your child lies by omission—leaving out pertinent information to deceive, or lies by commission—states an out-and-out fabrication of the truth to deceive, it is critically important to mete out a consequence. This is particularly true for lies around major themes in your Home Agreement about drugs, relationships, curfew, and the like.

> Lying suggests that your child has not completely accepted or understood the idea of integrity.

We'll talk a lot about consequences in the next chapter. For now it's sufficient to understand that for a consequence to be effective, it has to matter to your child. This means inhibiting freedom. Taking away your child's cell phone might not mean anything if he doesn't use his phone. How impacted is he by your consequence? It's possible that you're not attaching a strong enough consequence to your rule and are not getting your child's attention. If he keeps lying and you take away something, such as the privilege of going out on weekends for an entire month, it's not to punish him but to get his full attention.

Just as important as delivering an effective consequence is engaging your son or daughter in a safe, open dialogue about why he thinks he needs to lie. Remind him that honesty is the expectation and that there is a consequence for dishonesty. Let him know that you can be told the truth, that you will listen and reflect and not shame him. This calm manner might be hard to maintain, but to keep the dialogue open and therefore transparent it's important for you to make your best effort. Ask him *why* is he doing what he's doing? What's his rationalization? You may even want to ask him what an appropriate and effective consequence would be.

For kids who shun earning money the old-fashioned way, stealing becomes a quick way to get the cash they want. If stealing has been an issue in the past, then watch for it when your child returns. If a young person is going to choose to be dishonest in this way, and he is creative and smart, it can happen long before you catch it. Know how much cash you have on hand, and notice if your ATM card is not where you always keep it. Diligently check those bank and credit card statements.

Stealing can be a sign of worse things to come, like avoiding honest work or accessing drugs. If your child steals, it might be because he doesn't want to get a job or earn more money doing extra chores or it might be because he wants to buy things beyond his means, such as video games or drugs.

It's important to deal with theft decisively. If you don't, it can lead to felonious behavior and legal consequences. Plus, it's expensive. I have seen thousands stolen from parents or siblings, whether in cash, jewelry, credit purchases, or ATM withdrawals.

Address lying and stealing in your Home Agreement. Here is an example of how you might do so:

Issue: Honesty.

Vision: We see our children as honest individuals, living a life of integrity.

Value: Honesty in all aspects of life is something we value greatly, as individuals and as a family.

> **Expectation:** In our family, honesty and integrity are very important, so lying, cheating, stealing, and illegal activities are not what we do.
>
> **Rule:** Lying and stealing have happened in the past. We want to be clear that these are not acceptable or tolerated in our household ever.

Even if you have openly discussed the importance of honest behavior and have included rules and expectations in the Home Agreement about dishonest behaviors such as lying and stealing, do watch your child closely upon his return. Further, have a TLC discussion with him to make sure you know what his reason was for either of these offenses. Listen to him, and then speak your mind. Let him know why such actions are against your values and why you want him to stay on the straight and narrow.

Laziness and Lack of Motivation

Laziness is probably the hottest potato parents try to grasp when nudging their ambivalent child out into the world. This issue can cause a lot of angst. You allowed your child some downtime upon his return, but now you're not seeing the motivation you would like to see. He seems lazy, and only wants to play video games. Or your daughter only wants to lie on the sofa and watch reruns of some teen melodrama.

It's okay to allow your child a few weeks of rest, but then insist that the activities agreed to in the Home Agreement kick in. When laziness makes an appearance, try not to get too caught up in analyzing why she is being lazy. Instead, reinstate your values. Remind your child how a productive life and the pursuit of excellence is what your family is about. Follow through with consequences. Treatment program staff members know that an active, purpose-filled lifestyle (not busy, mindless, rat race stuff) is what makes us healthy. Even retired people know that lethargy and boredom can be the death of them. The same is true for all of us.

After the honeymoon phase, and if consistent consequences are not having an impact, this question often arises: "Is my kid lazy, or is there something more, namely a mental health issue, going on?" The answer to this is not cut and dried. It can be either one or a combo of the two.

Often, within the families I serve, a pronounced anxiety disorder masks as laziness. An anxious kid becomes avoidant, and this inhibits her desire to get a job. Her anxiety might serve as a reason to do nothing, and this translates into her seeming unmotivated or lazy. It is also true, however, that the opposite can happen. Consistently, young adults confess that, much of the time, at least initially, they really are lazy. Ironically, this choice can be the gateway to old pathology, such as lethargy, depressive episodes, or increased anxiety due to avoidant behavior. Bluntly stated, giving in to laziness can trigger regression.

If the stress of life gets the best of your child, he might hole up in your home in an avoidant way. This can get serious if he can't bring himself to venture out into the world and face life's daily challenges. The only real way for anyone to get past this anxiety is to push through, systematically step out, and do the things that one is so afraid of. I often see this scenario played out when it comes time for the young person to go for a job interview.

This hurdle needs to be jumped. Don't allow your child to pull a Howard Hughes reclusive reaction to life. When parents insist that their child engage in at least one aspect of active life, a positive domino effect occurs. It doesn't seem to matter if the first domino is attending and engaging in school, holding down a job, or getting involved in AA or an intramural sport. Here's how you might address this issue:

> **Issue:** My child is unmotivated and doesn't want to do any work at all. He's content being a couch potato.
>
> **Vision:** I see my child living a well-balanced life where he works, plays, gives back and rests in appropriate proportions.
>
> **Value:** Life is fullest when we engage in it.
>
> **Expectation:** I expect my child to live a balanced life that contains work, play, helping others, resting, and relaxing. I do not expect my child to be lazy and unproductive.
>
> **Rule:** I expect you to exercise three times weekly, to do your chores and to maintain a 3.0 at school. In the summer you can work up to 20 hours a week or help me by babysitting your younger sister.

Movement off the couch and onto the playing field of life is the ticket. But, if taking baby steps doesn't work and your child exhibits serious anxiety symptoms such as panic attacks, he might need further professional support.

A Healthy Body, Mind, and Spirit

When it comes to the health of your child, if all you had to worry about was how much sugar she's eating, health wouldn't need its own section in this chapter. The plain truth is that most kids—whether in treatment, out of treatment, or never needing treatment—take their health for granted, be it physical, mental, or spiritual, and this breeds anxiety for parents.

> Movement off the couch and onto the playing field of life is the ticket.

Related to both health and appearance for many parents is the topic of tattoos and body piercings, both rampant in today's culture. All parents have their own beliefs about these practices. Regardless of where you fall on that continuum, eventually there's a boundary that delineates what's acceptable in your family. In the case of piercings and tattoos, the health of and respect for one's body, more than what the neighbors think, is most likely the underlying issue.

I personally have lived through the body-piercing issue with my parents. In 1986, piercings were rare in my Utah Catholic High School. A piercing had many connotations, most of them negative. It was never stated in my family, but it was clear that piercings were not allowed for the males. Being the rascal teen I was, I decided to get my ear pierced for my junior prom. My girlfriend supported this by telling me I would be sexy with it. That's all it took. I was off to the department store for my piercing.

That night I sported a tuxedo and was making my exit through the kitchen, saying goodbye to my parents while holding my head at an angle for obvious cloaking reasons. And then all hell broke loose. It was the worst fight of my life with my parents, and we did not have many (maybe five max).

That night imprinted hard in my mind. Suffice it to say, I had pushed their values to the limit and they held firm. I did not go to the prom with an earring. I took it out.

Ironically, but true to TLC, one of the things that would have helped my cause is if I had asked permission first. My parents are open-minded, and might have allowed the earring if we'd had an honest and open discussion beforehand.

About a week later, my parents and I were raking leaves in the front yard. They stopped and leaned on their rakes, and Mom said, "Ruben, we decided if you want to pierce your ear, it is okay."

I appreciated those words, as it took a lot of love and reasonableness on their part. But I had gone against their will and been sneaky. I should have asked. When I was 22 years old, I did, at long last, get my ear pierced. And now, many years after that, I am still their only son with piercings . . . and body art, too. We laugh about it all.

In many longer-term treatment programs, tattoos and piercings are usually not allowed. Holes close up. Many kids can't wait to get out and get their "individuality" back. That's when piercings and tattoos can become a very important and heavy issue. Deal with this straightforwardly in the Home Agreement. Break it down like this:

Issue: Body health: piercings and tattoos.

Vision: We see our children healthy and sound in mind, body, and soul.

Value: Your body is sacred.

Expectation: We brought you into this world, and hope you will always take good care of yourself. We expect you to respect and honor your body.

Rule: Under our roof there will be only ear piercings (female), and no other piercings or tattoos. When you are paying for your own home and lifestyle, you can choose otherwise, but we do hope you will continue to respect your body.

This is simply an example, a guideline for you to follow. There are several shades of gray for beliefs around this issue. What matters is that you decide what's right for your child based on who you are.

Caring for the Body

Other health issues that come up in the first month of a child's return are sleep, diet, hygiene, and exercise.

For sleep, the interfering culprit is technology—the great temptation that can seduce kids into getting lazy while they think they're doing something just because there's a remote in hand. We all need sleep to perform to our best ability, and kids who are still on their laptop or smartphone late at night are disrupting their patterns of sleep and waking.

The same is true of diet. If healthful eating is important to you, make clear the expectations you have concerning food. You may choose to limit your son or daughter's soda intake to one diet cola a day. Or you can choose to allow none, but then don't have the fridge stocked up on root beer. If you want to eat all organic, do so in your own home, but realistically it's hard to control what your child eats elsewhere, especially older teens and young adults. What you can control is what you stock in the cupboards and the fridge housed beneath your roof.

Most kids with poor hygiene (a behavioral issue) get this resolved in treatment and might need little reminding upon their return. It's still worth stating clearly in the Home Agreement what is expected; for example, clean clothes, daily showers, morning and evening brushing of the teeth, and the like.

I regularly see families plagued by the topic of exercise for months after a kid comes home. Downtime is needed for readjustment, but once the dust settles it's time for your child to take on a healthful lifestyle. Most likely he followed an extremely active routine in treatment. Maintain this momentum by being very clear about what's expected, and mete out consequences if you're not seeing follow-through.

Boys often get into team sports and weight training while in treatment, and many young women seem to resonate with yoga and sports like hiking, skiing, and paddle boarding. The practice of yoga, especially, offers a venue for healthy growth. It gives many people a way to slow down, be mindful of life, and be more intentional in thoughts and actions. If there is a flicker of interest in your child regarding any of these fitness activities, help ignite the fire.

In your Home Agreement, don't hesitate to state expectations and rules concerning health issues. This can include curfews and bedtimes, technology limitations, and exercise schedules. Just be prepared to follow through with a consequence if your child doesn't follow the rules.

Smoking, Drinking, and Drugs

Since the use of tobacco is adverse to good health, most parents don't want their children to smoke or chew. For teens, the rules about using tobacco go without saying, but for young adults tobacco presents another issue. Most parents recognize that they can't continue to control all aspects of their young adults' lives, and that part of letting them grow up is letting them make their own choices. Later in this book I'll go more into the specific nuances and differences of parenting young adults vs. teens.

If you do allow smoking, please require that your child pay for cigarettes out of his own earnings, and not light up on your property if you find smoking offensive.

It seems that young men and women find cigarette smoking appealing in equal numbers, whereas young men who have been in treatment miss marijuana more than the young women do. Watch for the recurrence of marijuana abuse if this has been an issue for your child. If your son knows he is being subjected to drug tests, he might start using synthetic cannabis-oriented drugs such as K2 or Spice (purchased at smoke shops), which might not be detected by over-the-counter drug tests and can be quite strong intoxicants. Thus be on the lookout for small packets labeled "incense" or "herbals." Does he smell like smoke? If you do his laundry, do you find a lighter in his pants pocket?

When it comes to such substances as alcohol and drugs, most of my young clients have struggled in this area, so covering this in the Home Agreement becomes crucial. If your child has an addiction or engages in substance abuse, this is the biggest risk factor for his continued health. It becomes the priority issue, because addiction affects everything else: your child's physical well-being, the ranking and sequence of issues being worked on, and, very importantly, the possibility of transparent and loving communication. Addiction is a game changer, and therefore it takes priority over all other issues in treatment programs.

> Addiction is a game changer, and therefore it takes priority over all other issues in treatment programs.

Please be incredibly conscientious about monitoring and managing sobriety and recovery. A lot of parents think that somehow treatment dealt with this issue indefinitely, but substance issues might never go away, especially if addiction is clearly there. This means your child will need to learn to take full responsibility and manage this illness for his or her entire lifetime. He or she will need to know what triggers the addiction and develop healthy coping techniques.

To address substances in the Home Agreement, begin with your child's specific problem. Then check in on what you believe about this

problem. Most likely you are clear on your values concerning substances. You want your child to grow into a healthy adult, free of tobacco, alcohol, or drug abuse. Ask your child's treatment counselor what is the safest approach for your child—will she ever be able to enjoy a casual glass of wine, or is abstinence best?

Perhaps your child's treatment counselor will assist your child in creating a relapse prevention plan (RPP). If so, let this comprehensive plan inform the boundaries used to write rules in the Home Agreement. Create a framework to manage your child's diagnosis in a very conservative way. This might include tighter boundaries than you feel comfortable with and providing your child outside support related to addiction. Let's look at a specific issue: smoking weed.

Issue: Smoking weed daily is the reason our son went into treatment.

Vision: We see our son free of substances and enjoying life without dependency upon them.

Value: We believe we should take excellent care of our bodies and not put bad things into them. We believe marijuana is not good for the body and it is also illegal in our state.

Expectation: We expect our children to not use marijuana.

Rule: Because marijuana smoking had such a detrimental effect on our entire family, the use of all drugs including marijuana, tobacco and alcohol is not allowed while we financially support you. When you're 21 and of legal drinking age, we expect you to be responsible about this adult privilege.

Drug and alcohol abuse are pandemic in our culture. These substances are inexpensive and easy to find. It's impossible to keep your child protected from them 24/7. The best you can do is have an ongoing honest dialogue with your child regarding substances, one that might go on for many years. You can set up safeguards specific to certain environmental factors—triggers such as people, places, and events that could lead to relapse—and you can hold your child accountable to continued recovery measures such as AA meetings and random drug testing. That is about all you can do . . . and that's a lot. Substance abuse and addiction deserve books of their own, and there are many out there. In Chapter 10, I'll address addiction in a little more depth.

Cutting

The act of cutting is a serious red flag, signaling that your child is distressed and needs more help. Because change can cause anxiety, cutting might come back into play after your child leaves treatment. If this form of self-injury is a past issue for your child, please monitor her carefully as she is being integrated back into home life. Keep a close eye on the areas of the body that are often targeted: arms, wrists, bellies, and inner thighs.

This problem is particularly common among girls, but boys do it, too. Before your child returns, ask her and the program counselor what suggested supports would help your child if cutting begins again. Often your daughter will have a good idea of what she needs to continue healing this issue post-treatment. It might be prudent to include a consequence of increased support in the Home Agreement if this issue has the potential to resurface once your child is home.

Eating Disorders

Eating disorders such as anorexia, bulimia, and binge eating are life-threatening illnesses that people might struggle with for years. Those so afflicted deserve compassion, as well as parental diligence in addressing symptoms when they arise. If your daughter has an eating disorder, consult her program therapist and reread your child's neuropsychological testing report (if one was written) to refresh yourself on how the disorder manifests. If your daughter's therapist deems it appropriate, have a frank conversation about the eating disorder on one of your calls or visits before she returns home.

Until your child has sufficiently handled this disorder, it would be wise not to bring her home. If, after a good stint in a therapeutic environment, there is still a likelihood of this issue coming back, then include a few well-thought-out sentences in the Home Agreement to address it.

> **Issue:** Health.
>
> **Vision:** We envision children who are mentally, spiritually, and physically healthy.
>
> **Value:** We value the body, mind, and spirit God has given us, therefore we do our best to maintain them and keep them healthy.
>
> **Expectation:** We expect our children to be honest with us and tell us if they are having trouble staying healthy.
>
> **Rule:** If you feel that it's getting too hard for you to manage your eating disorder, we want you to let us know. We will then work together to give you the support you need, whether it be from within the family or with an outside physician or therapist.

Like the issue of cutting, an eating disorder can play out very secretively, so watch carefully for the symptoms already identified by your child and her therapist.

Sometimes the stress of coping with life back home can open the door to a relapse. If the eating disorder does appear, have a sit-down TLC meeting and address the thoughts, feelings, and possible reasons behind it. Listen to your child's concerns about the disorder and how she feels she can best cope with it in her new environment. Some families find help employing supportive consequence that offer coping skills, such as the practice of yoga, which includes body awareness and acceptance in its focus.

Although I chose to use the feminine pronoun throughout this section, and it *is* most commonly females who deal with eating disorders, it bears mentioning that young men in increasing numbers are having problems with this as well.

Peer Power

Friends matter—a lot! So much so that some kids and young adults would never have needed to go to treatment had they chosen peers more wisely. When your child comes home, you will have created an environment for success. What peers will populate that environment?

Like many other treatment professionals, I recommend creating a traffic-light rating system for your child's friends, with green, yellow, and red lights.

Consult your child and his treatment team to determine who is safe. Who truly deserves a green light, who is a maybe, and who is a definite no? Unfortunately, it's been my experience that most teens and young adults want questionable characters, who should be red-lighted, to be given the go-ahead.

PEER RATING SYSTEM

GREEN ↔ YELLOW ↔ RED

Peers with high levels of dysfunction pose the greatest threat to your child. If your child is underage, you can firmly draw the line. With young adults, you might not have such power but you can at least control who steps into your home. In both cases, know your boundaries about who is an acceptable friend, make rules regarding these friends, and make the rules clear to your child.

Build in consequences. For example, if your child chooses to go to the old pot-smokers' den, populated with red-light friends, and to hit the reggae fest—clearly in violation of his Relapse Prevention Plan and the Home Agreement—you have the right to withhold use of the car.

Therapeutic programs cover relationships at great length, so you can know that healthy and unhealthy peer influences have been discussed with your child both one-on-one and in group therapy. Most programs are built around a positive peer culture, and that helped your child get better. A positive peer environment encourages and rewards authenticity and develops a healthy, mature lifestyle and coping skills. At home, you have much less control over the peer environment, and unfortunately there are negative influences out there.

Keep your eyes and ears open and be willing to talk about this issue. Discussions shouldn't be too difficult to enter into, as your child will push the friends boundary regularly. Welcome the conversation. With TLC, you can both explain how you feel. Hear and understand your child, but in determining who is a red light and who is a green, you should rely on your wisdom and your gut and act accordingly.

Dating, Love, Sex, and More

You can't dodge the issue of sexuality at this point in your child's life. Love and sexuality are rich experiences that are on your kid's radar. If your child has been in treatment for over a year, he most likely has been thinking a lot about sex and relationship. This is an area where you really need to know where you stand. If you have ambivalence around the topic of sex and therefore avoid discussing it with your child, it sends a muddy signal. Your kid doesn't know where you or he stands. He doesn't know the family ethos.

Why not take a deep breath and look at your own beliefs regarding love and sex? Again, what did you envision for your child around relationship and sexuality? Perspectives here are widely diverse from family to family, so your concern is for *your* family. What do you hope your child will do with his sexuality, with the way he shows his love? Take that vision and extend it into a realistic scenario around rules of engagement. The basic tenet here is to not tolerate activity under your roof that goes against your values.

In my interactions with post-treatment kids, I observe teen girls and young women consistently sabotaging their lives for love. Too many times I have seen a toxic romantic relationship, post-treatment, steadily strangle all of a young woman's gains and healthy goals. Schoolwork, home life, and healthy habits all get sacrificed in the name of love.

Please make your expectations known to your child, and state them overtly in the Home Agreement. For example, many parents insist on meeting and approving friends, including who one dates. In some cases, when sexual promiscuity has been a past problem, parents ask their daughter to be on birth control even before she comes back home.

If your child has a history of promiscuity or sex addiction, then when addressing this issue in the Home Agreement you will need to have several discussions with his or her treatment counselor. As with drug or alcohol addiction, your child might have developed a Relapse Prevention Plan. If so, use it to aid you in creating solid boundaries that can be enforced.

This generation of young people is interested in exploring their sexual identity in a way that is open-minded. The idea of being LGBTQ (Lesbian, Gay, Bisexual, Transgender, or Queer and/or Questioning) is on the radar culturally and on the minds of teens and young adults. Many parents today do understand and are open to discussion of sexual/gender identity. Willingness to listen as a parent and reflect back, even if you don't agree with your child's beliefs, can save the child a life of confusion and depression, or even prevent an early death by suicide. For some parents this might be difficult, but try to discuss this issue in a loving way that encourages your child to be who he or she is—even if it's in conflict with who you are.

Curfew

Curfews are important. Your child had them for as long as he was in treatment. Long before he comes home, bring up the issue and spell out the rule in the Home Agreement.

When you bring it up while your child is in treatment, it's very likely that he'll agree to whatever curfew you want, because he wants to get home more than anything. Encourage him to have open dialogue with you; don't let it remain superficial. You and he need to be very transparent about this. What are the reasons for you to want a curfew, and what are the real reasons that he doesn't want one? Hash this one out with his treatment counselor if you need the additional support.

Curfew is probably one of the first boundaries your child will test or want changed when he returns. Very often it will seem, in the eyes of your child, as if it should be no big deal to stretch the curfew. For young adults this struggle has a lot to do with autonomy. When a teen turns 18 he wants to be treated like an adult and make his own rules. He wants adult freedoms, and curfew is about the same to him as leg irons. Also, the argument over curfew might be less about curfew and more about testing your rules and resolve as parents. If you don't hold the line here, within reason, then curfew will become the pothole in the road and your entire Home Agreement can quickly go flat and become ineffective.

Most parents do flex and negotiate the curfew if things are going well and their child is demonstrating responsibility and adherence to rules. I would suggest that it's prudent to wait at least a month to "give" on the curfew time, and then do so rarely.

What time should curfew be? It depends on many factors: the time of year, the child's age, the peers the child chooses, and what the child has done in the past. Most parents have a different curfew for weekends and summertime than during school weeks. Young adults usually have later curfews. Again, do what is right for you and for what you want your child to do and be about. While you decide, please keep this in mind: You can expect even the most liberal curfew to be pushed. So why not start on the conservative side?

Here's an example of creating a rule concerning curfew and peers.

Issue: Friends and curfew.

Vision: We see our kids having respectful, loving friendships with both males and females.

Value: We value honest, meaningful relationships and want to have them with our children and with others.

Expectation: We expect our kids to choose healthy, ethical friends and to have meaningful friendships and romantic relationships.

Rule: We expect you to have mostly green-light friends and a few yellow-light. To help you transition back home, we will hold a school night curfew of 10 P.M. and a weekend curfew of 11 P.M. Green-light and yellow-light friends, both male and

female, are welcome to the house. We ask that you not have
friends of the opposite gender in your bedroom. Same-gender
sleepovers will be approved on a case-by-case basis.

Now, parents of a 20-year-old young adult living at home after
treatment may choose to deal with curfew differently.

Issue: Curfew.

Vision: We see our son managing his time wisely.

Value: We value his not being out late when it is more likely
that things could go wrong.

Expectation: We expect our son to manage his life responsibly
and put himself in safe places at safe times of the day, to not be
out late so he is too tired to work the next day and to not be in
dangerous places at dangerous times to reduce chances of drug
relapse and/or legal problems.

Rule: There is no curfew. We ask that you use good judgment.
If you start having problems due to staying up late, whether
it be employment, legal, or other functional issues, then we
will institute the following: While you're living at home we'll
expect you to be back at home by 1:00 A.M. during the week
(Sunday through Thursday) and by 2:00 A.M. on Friday
and Saturday.

Counseling and Therapy

With regard to continuing counseling or therapy, be open to the recommendations made by your child's program. They know where your child is psychologically, because she has told them things you might never know. These clinicians know how dark or deep your child runs, so take their advice, and yet at the same time discuss with them your family culture and where you're coming from. The next life steps for your child should integrate what the expert counselors know and what you, the expert parents, know. Work with your child's program to decide on the right level of ongoing therapeutic support, and integrate that expectation into the Home Agreement.

Most kids, excited to be coming home, are open to a support system, but they need you to do the legwork of finding the right resources. This is an action item that should not become subject to failure because of procrastination. It truly is very hard to find a home therapist who understands the nuances of wilderness and aftercare. Ask your educational consultant, if you have one, to recommend someone local. Otherwise, ask friends, doctors, teachers and clergy to recommend therapists and counselors. Then interview top choices. Take the time to find a professional who can best service your family and provide a shortcut by knowing the road you've already traveled.

When you've found a therapist, whether it's someone new or one your child has seen in the past, share with her your Home Agreement and any psychological testing reports. Provide as much collateral information as you can, so she can familiarize herself with the journey your family has taken thus far. Set up calls for your child's treatment counselor to talk with the new therapist, to update her on what your child and you have gone through. The more information shared, the better. And, of course, let your child in on your recommendations for a new therapist.

You might want to have two or three possibilities. If your child makes a visit home from treatment on a pass, have him or her meet the therapist to ensure that the mix will work. Cross this bridge early on the journey back home, so that you can enjoy the peace of mind that comes with having backup.

Medication

While your child is in treatment, you have a wonderful opportunity to get meds dialed in. Treatment affords professionals the lengthy amount of time needed to observe your child and solidly assess whether medication is indeed needed and, if so, which one(s). Also, once there is a new baseline the treatment team has the time to carefully observe and adjust medications, often in a very collaborative process with your son or daughter.

By the time your child comes home, if medication is still indicated she will most likely take it on her own, because she knows that it really does help. In this case, medication is an easy transitional issue, yet it doesn't hurt to spell out expectations in the Home Agreement, after a dialogue with her and her counselor, about the best approach for medication and compliance. I always like to remind parents that it is the teen's responsibility to take her meds, not yours.

If down deep she doesn't want the meds or doesn't want to tolerate negative side effects, then you might see noncompliance. I do see this occasionally, and when I do, TLC once again opens the door to resolution. Listen to what your child is telling you. She might have good reasons for not taking medication. Problem-solve this issue together. This might mean visiting the psychiatrist, discussing the situation, and redialing the meds.

The situations I see more difficulty with are psychotic illnesses and bipolar disorder. In these cases, meds have side effects that can make it challenging for the child to comply. This is when not giving up takes a concerted effort by the entire treatment team back home. Usually, with tenacity comes a solution that can work for all concerned. This topic is discussed a bit more in Chapter 10.

If meds are refused and are clearly indicated, you might need to rethink keeping your child at home. This is more true for severe mental illness than it is for such issues as ADHD, mild anxiety, or mild depression.

Spirituality and Faith

If your form of spirituality or faith involves a committed practice and you want to carry out the practice as a family, please put that in your Home Agreement. Churches, synagogues, and other such supports offer stability as well as activities that are inspiring for you and your child. It is from these places that much of our ethos and family culture is gleaned. Even for those parents who don't subscribe to a structured belief system, it's worth taking the time to convey to your child whatever gives you peace and fulfillment. If you find beauty and solace in the arts, are politically active, or are an avid outdoors person, you can build these activities into your child's lifestyle.

Your child might have forgotten how important these rituals and mores are to your family. Reintroduce your values regarding hiking on weekends, attending church on Sunday, or making it to the annual Native American pow-wow. Create expectations for your children from your beliefs, as in this example:

> **Issue:** Our faith.
>
> **Vision:** We see our children living fulfilling lives as Christians.
>
> **Value:** We are Christian, and we believe in worshiping as a community. Attending church on Sunday as a family is important to us.
>
> **Expectation:** We expect you to live your life with Christian values.
>
> **Rule:** Although we don't insist that you attend church weekly, we ask that you follow the basic rules of the Ten Commandments and other Christian teachings, go to church on major holidays, and respect our faith.

Upon your child's return, expect him to have a different viewpoint on his faith now that he has done some very serious and deep analytical work. Please listen without shutting him down. TLC will serve you greatly in this area. It will also allow your child to think on his own and mature. Your child is exploring what is going to work for him throughout his adult life, and in the process he needs to respect your belief system and where you and he come from.

Chores

Chores are old-fashioned, but extremely important. They're the playground on which to teach the next generation your values and the beginning of a work ethic. Chores can help put entitlement where it belongs—in the trashcan.

In treatment, your child cooked, cleaned, shared responsibilities with her surrogate family, and had minimal technology or material goods. She developed resourcefulness and a commitment to others. She learned to clean up after herself and her housemates. Why not keep these habits alive when she returns? In fact, feel free to increase whatever chores she used to have and give only an allowance that's truly deserved.

When I was ten years old, I was in charge of folding socks for the whole family (five kids and our parents). I also vacuumed the stairs on two staircases. This happened every Saturday morning like clockwork. I didn't question it, as it was habitual . . . inherent in our family culture. I knew that I was contributing to the daily life of my family, and I felt self-esteem and added stature from helping to run our home. I wasn't an angelic child, and I didn't always want to fold socks. Yet, as I grew up, I looked forward to more important jobs. Soon I wanted to do such things for my family as fixing faucets, painting fences, and eventually building fences. Most treatment professionals know that the best way for a person to gain self-esteem is for him or her to do something meaningful and productive.

Developmentally, humans tend to connect with achievement processes when in their early teens. Thus, at that age, the number and difficulty of household chores should be increased. Babysitting, lawn mowing, and academic diligence take off as the internal reward system kicks in. With or without an attached allowance, it feels good for the child to achieve through work, and thus a cycle of work begins.

Let your child contribute to the running of your household. If you have too much hired help, your kid might learn that (1) others do the work and (2) hired help is necessary to the functioning of a family. I've seen too many cases where a 20-year-old has never done chores and can't hold down a job! This is not a pleasant scenario for anyone involved.

> Most treatment professionals know that the best way for a person to gain self-esteem is for him or her to do something meaningful and productive.

Give your child work to do. At the very least have her clean up after herself, and that means she does her own laundry, washes her own dishes, and cleans her own room. Better yet, have her also work for the community—the family. That means she cooks a meal one night a week, carries in groceries without being asked, and cuts the grass. If this has been a problem in the past, address it in the Home Agreement.

> **Issue:** Not doing chores and lying about them being done.
>
> **Vision:** We see all family members willingly contributing to the well-being and running of the household we share.
>
> **Value:** Completing chores is valuable in that it contributes to a work ethic and benefits the entire family by creating a more efficient and clean home. Lying is not something we accept in our family. We will address this issue further.
>
> **Expectation:** Chores should be completed regularly, well, on time, and without whining.
>
> **Rule:** Your responsibilities to the household are to take out the trash every Wednesday night in time for pick up, to clean your room on Saturdays, do your own laundry and to load and unload the dishwasher whenever it is needed.

Expecting your child to complete chores congruent with your family culture helps the family and simultaneously provides your child with a feeling of self-worth. It truly is a win-win. Expect more from your child, and don't pay her much mind if she gripes. If it sounds like whining, it is.

The Work Ethic

It's not completely clear to me what is happening culturally when it comes to kids who were raised to think they simply should not have to work. Evidently many parents are neglecting to teach a work ethic early enough. This doesn't seem to have much to do with the socioeconomics of particular families. Rather, there seems to be a movement that promotes allowing children to enjoy their childhood a little too long. Work and the enjoyment of childhood can coexist. They have for many, many years, in our society and others.

Work should start while we're young. If your child has been treated like a prince or princess and has not contributed, you're in trouble. Work is a vitamin for the soul of a developing young adult. It not only teaches your child that he is important; it also teaches him to have fortitude and to carry out duties regardless of his mood. For teens, holding down a job is a healthy outlet, a social opportunity, a source of real pride and self-esteem, an opportunity to practice money management, and a way to mature under the tutelage of authority figures other than one's parents. At work, your child will learn to respect and live within a group structure. Work might also provide the positive peer culture that treatment centers value.

> Work is a vitamin for the soul of a developing young adult.

The Real World of Work

Work outside of the home seems like a great opportunity for freedom, which is what your kid says she wants. Yet, for some, it appears to be a painful prospect—the idea of leaving the comfort and indulgences of home. It suggests the death of the warm-and-fuzzy protective childhood, where the child was nurtured and comforted by you. Work looks

scary because it demarcates adulthood. Once that threshold has been crossed, there's no going back. To her, the message might seem to be, *If I work, I have to grow up.*

Many of my teen and young-adult clients have, at some point in our journeys together, confessed that they don't want to grow up . . . and, if they're honest, they'll admit that they feel this way well into their twenties. Many kids want to be respected and treated like an adult, but they don't see the benefits of acting like one.

To foster within your child an appreciation for work, clearly spell out this area of responsibility in the family values stated within your Home Agreement. Discuss it openly while she is still in treatment. While writing the Home Agreement, create specific expectations for work: chores, an afterschool job, and attendance at school or college.

At times, depending upon your family culture, your child's age, a possible pathology, or if your child is going to be in college full-time, a job might not be the issue at hand. If this is the case, still be sure to explicitly state what your child's "work" looks like. For instance: "Your job is to go to school and get good grades," or "Your job is to be a contributing member of the family, helping our household run efficiently."

I see great reward in requiring young people to work and earn their own money. If you see no progress once your child comes home, remind him of his commitment to work. If you let this issue go unaddressed, passive resistance to working might take hold in your child. Don't let yourself create an environment so cushy that there is little incentive for him to face his fears regarding work and growing up. Why would he want to put himself in the position of spending time filling out applications, attending a nerve-racking interview, and making sure his uniform is washed and ironed? Why would he do any of this if he has money in his pocket and a costly wardrobe lining his closet? It's extremely helpful if you, as parents, exert a tandem effort to restrict money, within reason, while coaching job-hunting skills as needed.

The Consequences of Money

Money. It *can* be the root of some evil when it replaces relationship. It makes me sad to see a child-parent relationship be mostly about the child getting money for her own pleasure. When parents start to be valued solely for the cash they can hand over, this is not a relationship. If your child sees you as a candy store, it's because you have *become* the candy store.

Take stock for a minute. How much money have you spent on treatment to date? How much did wilderness cost? That RTC? In treatment at a therapeutic boarding school your child probably even experienced expensive adventures that many families can't easily afford. Most likely your child has always enjoyed a good standard of living. Do you think she understands this—the value of the money you've spent? I don't know; do you?

If you realize that your child feels entitled or expects everything to simply be there for her, give real consideration to cutting back on indulging her. Teach her that money— all money in your family—had to be earned at some time by someone who worked hard and was smart about it. Instead of readily handing over that twenty for the movie or filling up your kid's gas tank, put chores and a job on your child's to-do list. This means decreasing indulgences and increasing earned privileges—a maturation process that rewards work. Let character, relationship, and achievement be her fortune.

> Let character, relationship, and achievement be her fortune.

Each family has its own beliefs around what money represents and how it should be used. Money is value-laden, so be diligent in defining what it means to you, and then communicate that to your family. One good way to help your child value money and still do things for her is to separate money spent on family activities and money spent on individual pursuits. For example, when you all go out as a family to celebrate a birthday, parents can pick up the bill. When your child is out with her BFFs or on a date, she pays for it with her own cash.

There's the family pot of gold that parents can spend on the family, and then there's the kid's earned pot of gold that she can use to pay for her own gas, music, fast food, technology purchases, and the latest style of jeans. When you stop footing the bill, it empowers your child and fosters maturity. As she comes to understand the value of money— how much things cost—she'll be more motivated to earn her allowance or keep her job, because otherwise she'll have to do without.

> **Issue:** Money.
>
> **Vision:** Our vision was to have our children be well provided for, but for them to be grateful and not feel entitled.
>
> **Value:** We want our children to understand that money comes from hard work and "doesn't grow on trees" in our back yard.
>
> **Expectation:** That our children be thankful for all that we have provided and be willing to work for their own money, knowing we will always be there to support them emotionally.
>
> **Rule:** We will pay for your college education. We will also pay for your car, car insurance, cell phone, and school and art supplies, but we expect you to get a part time job during the school year and a full-time summer job and pay for all your incidentals.

Be aware that well-meaning relatives and friends can sabotage your child's motivation to earn money through work. There's nothing like two hundred dollars from an uncle or a thousand from Grandpa to undermine what you're doing. Please ask friends and relatives not to give money for birthdays and holidays, at least not during your child's first year out of treatment. If they do it anyway, you might want to encourage your child to save the money (in an account you have access to) or to spend it quickly on something positive. Too often kids will hoard gift money and budget it out over months so they don't have to do chores or get a job. Believe me on this one.

Life Skills for Earning Money

While your child was in treatment, she might have missed learning some life skills regarding gaining employment and managing money. Not all programs address these issues as they're facing weightier problems such as addiction, defiance, mental illness, academic difficulties, and the like. When your child comes home, assess where she is with these skills and determine what behavior is age-appropriate for her. If she's 23 years old and hasn't yet worked outside of the home or opened a checking account, she has some serious catching up to do.

Most young people returning from treatment do not have practical knowledge regarding preparing a resume, job searching, filling out applications, and interviewing, nor do they understand the tenacity needed to get a job during a recession. And most often those who do get a job don't know how to handle money.

When your child comes home, reach out to her and help her navigate these areas of life. The real world is different from any program, and your child needs your reassurance, as she is probably frightened, anxious, or at the very least nervous about her ability to manage money and a job. Things to consider teaching your child about are budgeting, tithing, savings and checking accounts, rainy day money, recreational money, debit and credit cards, and even April 15—tax time. Share your knowledge and model to her the how of money.

The Allowance

An allowance is a workable system until a child is about 17. If maturity is on schedule, the allowance should then dwindle to nothing as chores become unpaid routines. When older teens and young adults start to work outside the home, allowances become superfluous. The acceptable exception is when a family is highly motivated to see their child complete his higher education. In that situation, parents sometimes elect to cover all costs and provide an allowance. This is done with the understanding that school is the child's job and academic studies take priority. It might also be prudent to have the child work over the summer, or one night a week, to earn spending money to cover entertainment such as a movie or a run through the drive-through.

When your child returns, and especially if he's still a young teen, you might feel that an allowance is still in order until he's more settled. It is, as long as he actually contributes something to the household for it. Remember that you don't want to lose the gains made in treatment. Recall what treatment did, or what system was in place in your family of origin. Consider what other families are doing regarding allowances. Find a scenario that matches your philosophy, or is pretty darn close, and adopt it.

Education and Academics

A solid academic plan will help support your child's success in life, so do address it in your Home Agreement. You probably have, by now, a realistic idea of your child's academic potential. While he was in treatment, or possibly before, testing to reveal any cognitive difficulties such as processing speed or working-memory issues was likely completed. If you sense your child might have academic liabilities and he has not been tested, you might want to access professional services at his school or consult with an independent psychologist. Then proceed accordingly. If liabilities are discovered, put in place accommodations for your child such as an ILP (independent learning plan) or tutoring for difficult subjects. Sometimes a child with learning differences is better accommodated in an alternative learning environment. Search for better-suited educational options ranging from modified homeschooling to college programs.

If your child has no serious academic liabilities, there's a good chance that treatment woke him up and he now realizes he can achieve more. Better yet, he might even want to. Such internal motivation is best, but if your child is not on fire for school then you can create external expectations—rewards and consequences—to keep him moving in a positive direction.

Issue: Education.

Vision: We see our kids growing up with a love of learning, and attaining an education that will afford them a fulfilling lifestyle.

Value: We value education and the way it opens up the world to the person who is learning.

Expectation: Our kids will maintain a "B" average or higher because they're capable of it. We will help them research colleges and prepare for their higher learning in the summer between their junior and senior years. And we'll do our best to help them pay for college, according to what we can afford.

Rule: We expect you to earn a "B" average or higher. We also expect that you will try your hardest in school and be respectful to your teachers and other school staff. School is your job, so, to the best of our ability, we will pay for your education through college.

In getting an education, abilities and learning styles can vary greatly among siblings. This is an area where your vision and values are the same for all your children, yet your expectations and rules might vary.

Technology: Friend or Foe?

Technology is a pervasive element of modern life that really can't be avoided. Laptops, tablets, smartphones, social media, and games galore—the vast entirety of the Internet—are all literally at your child's fingertips. This generation has a lot to teach us about this worldwide, culture-shifting phenomenon, and we have much to teach them about the wisdom of limiting it.

The difficult thing about technology is that it is ever evolving. Just when you think you know what's "in" and "up" with your kid, there's something new out there—a new device or a new way for him to get in trouble. Since technology is here to stay, it's not about banning electronic systems from your child's life, but rather about allowing them in moderation.

I encourage you to develop a cautious approach to technology. Social pressure regarding it is severe. Not only are your kids' peers involved in this equation; so are other parents. I say never mind what others are doing in this case. It's your home, your roof . . . and it's okay to limit technology to your comfort level and to keep it only as available as you choose. Maintain access to your child's technology (through full disclosure of passwords, if necessary) so you can monitor potential threats such as drug deals, online strangers, pornography, or too many hours lost in the world of online video gaming.

The way parents achieve success in "fighting the technology battle" is with transparent and loving communication, and by creating strong awareness in their children. If your child still abuses the privilege of the technology supplied and paid for by you, then dole out a consequence, such as denying use of the technology for an amount of time that gets the point across (think weeks, not days).

Young adults will most likely use technology regularly, and you won't easily be able to manage it. The exception is that you can control what you pay for. Limit what you purchase, especially if you think your young adult will misuse or overuse the gift.

Some kids are in treatment *because* of technology. When determining rules about usage for such a child, take his specific situation into account. It is best if the Rules of the Road for technology can be sorted out with your child and his treatment therapist long before he comes home.

One final suggestion, and I know that, for some of you, taking this precaution won't come naturally or feel right. But, when it comes to technology, don't hesitate to snoop. The bottom line is your kid's health and future. If checking up on him through his technology can keep him on the road to recovery, go there.

Cell Phones

Phones seem to be the form of technology that causes the most contention in families. Most parents these days believe cell phones are necessities. I'd like to offer an alternative point of view: having a cell phone is a privilege—not a birthright—for our cyborg generation!

We can live without cell phones. Most parents fight me on this one, as they see all the "safety" benefits of the phone more than the dangers. Cell phones can be used for unethical behavior and as a manipulation tool. Your child can manipulate you if you're really convinced she needs to have a cell phone. Yes, a phone, if she has it turned on, allows you to connect to her and know her whereabouts. It can provide safety in case of danger, and the list of benefits goes on. But if you really want to get the best use out of a cell phone, make it an earned privilege.

In treatment, technology is so limited that, when your child gets home, she'll most likely argue for the latest and greatest smartphone. Because she wants it so much, her manipulative impulses might be triggered. You have many options regarding how you respond. Some parents let the child work for and buy her own phone. Some purchase a basic phone—with no bells and whistles and limited minutes and texting. This is wise, as texting (especially with a camera feature) opens the door for sexting. Many parents choose to allow texting, but block it during school hours and after curfew. Be creative with your boundaries and stay within your comfort zone, not your child's desired zone.

> Be creative with your boundaries and stay within your comfort zone, not your child's desired zone.

You might wonder, *How out of hand can it really get?* When I was working in wilderness, I had a client who sent 17,000 text messages in one month to a girl with whom he had a codependent relationship. He eventually broke up with her, and the phone bill became more manageable. I'm letting you know this to get you thinking. What is an appropriate amount of texting minutes, talking minutes, aps, gadgets, and bells and whistles? The variations are seemingly limitless. Why not discuss this topic with other parents to find out what has worked for them, and then make cell phone rules that work for you and your kid? Perhaps you will develop a rule such as this:

> **Issue:** Ethical use of the cell phone.
>
> **Vision:** We see our child using the cell phone for necessary communication and not abusing the privilege by using it for inappropriate activities such as sexting, which has been done in the past.
>
> **Value:** Technology is a tool to be used, not abused, especially when Mom and Dad are paying for it. :)
>
> **Expectation:** We expect you to use your cell phone in a responsible and ethical fashion.
>
> **Rule:** Mom and Dad will pay for a basic cell phone with a limited texting package. We request that you use it responsibly and stay within the package usage limitations.

At the heart of the cell phone issue is the idea that, at least initially, you will want to keep a close eye on your child and his relationship with technology. If you allow certain latitudes on the phone, consider having your child pay for the phone and/or the extras, and most assuredly use the withdrawal of phone privileges as a consequence if he breaks major rules.

Computers

Most families see computers, like phones, as necessities, so the issue is again about access and limitation. Computers offer a means to do homework for school or college, access to the world through the Internet, a way to engage in social media and be connected via email, and, for some, pornography.

Most problems start when a child is allowed too much computer time alone in his bedroom. Not only can your kid be spending the time breaking rules with the aid of the computer, but this also interferes with sleep. Moreover, isolation might set in, which can lead to depression.

Many parents come to regret having allowed computers or phones in the bedroom late at night, and they start collecting technology nightly until responsibility is evident. You might be able to put in controls for inappropriate programs on TV, but this is much harder to do on laptops in the bedroom. Again, how much control is needed depends on your child's specific circumstances. A court-ordered treatment for sexual misconduct dictates strong parameters around computer use, whereas a child who has awakened academically might need a lot of computer and Internet time. Still, none of it needs to be accomplished by your child late at night, alone in the bedroom.

And that leads me to the other relevant topic mentioned: pornography. It is easily accessible over the Internet, and often too much of a temptation to your child for you to ignore. Probably you face more apparent problems with your child, and feel pornography is not as pressing an issue. That might be the case, but be forewarned. It is quite easy, through pornography, for a child to move from curiosity to aberrant sexual behavior. The leap can be one more click away. Monitor and supervise.

Unless you are absolutely certain that pornography is not a part of your child's life, I strongly encourage you to write down your expectations and consequent rules for the issue. It can be a one-liner, but please do address pornography in your Home Agreement if it is in any way relevant. Again, beliefs about pornography fall on a spectrum from absolutely none allowed to moderate "curiosity" use being tolerated. I caution parents not to be overly permissive or end up on the other side of the spectrum by burying their heads in the sand. Again, this is an area where taking the occasional snoop might be warranted.

Social Media

Facebook, Twitter, and other social media are here to stay. This way of connecting is a new cultural phenomenon, and we still have a lot to learn about the ramifications and consequences. Many predators gain access to children through technology—more specifically, social media. Also, much illegal activity, such as drug dealing, happens online. It's a good idea to monitor what your child is doing with social media until you feel comfortable and trust her behavior regarding its use.

Some parents feel it's an invasion of privacy to be their child's friend on Facebook, while others demand it. How you handle it will depend on your family culture, and yet I see better outcomes when there is a fair amount of supervision—especially when there's been a history of technology abuse. The treatment program your child just left watched social media closely, or perhaps didn't allow it all. Consider an immediate baton pass on this issue.

Proceed with caution in allowing your son or daughter unsupervised time with social media. Too much, too quickly, might lead to regression. Once you see healthy behavior, you can let her have more privacy. If your child is legally an adult, you might still want to ask for access to her computer and phone. I have more than once seen parents monitor a 22-year-old while the young adult still lives under their roof.

In conclusion, social media are neither good nor bad. They provide a tool—one that I myself use. Some get addicted to using it and neglect their responsibilities; others use it to connect with the outside world in a healthy, supportive way. It really comes down to intention and moderation on the part of the user. As a parent, you can help guide intention with your expectations.

Video Gaming

Gaming either was or wasn't an issue for your child prior to going into treatment. If it was, you might have already responded to the problem by jettisoning all gaming devices or removing technology from the bedroom and allowing very limited use in clear view of the family. The bottom line, however, is this: If gaming was a problem pre-treatment, it might very well continue as a problem after treatment.

Males tend to struggle with gaming much more than females do. Teen boys and young men, even into their late twenties, can spend ten hours a day gaming. So I no longer have a problem saying that gaming can be addictive. For many, it can be a fun, positive experience, but I'll let someone else write a book about the many merits of video gaming.

For my clients who are trying to jump-start life outside of treatment, these games are especially alluring, as boys home from treatment have most likely spent months or years deprived of something they sorely missed. When treatment is over and gaming is back on the menu, it can lead to a quick downward spiral. Gaming might replace the real life young people need in order to mature in the world outside of treatment.

While your child was away, his habitual use of gaming was replaced with healthier activities. Most programs limit gaming to once per week for less than a few hours, and in wilderness it is obviously not used at all. Your child learned to live without it, and became active in healthier ways without the use of this technology. Why not maintain that momentum?

I've noticed, within my clientele, that kids allowed to game have a harder time getting a full night of sleep, waking up on time, keeping up grades, and finding work. Gaming seems to erode healthy sleep habits, and can create more laziness, isolation, and belligerence. Some games seem to have highly addictive psychological processes built into them, so their effects appear to be much like those produced by drugs.

I'm not denouncing all video gaming, as it can serve as a form of entertainment and also as a social connection in virtual reality. I do, however, urge caution in this area. If gaming was your child's issue, don't make access easy for him. If gaming wasn't your child's problem, I still recommend that you be conservative and pro-moderation. An excellent reference for learning more about gaming addiction is *Video*

Games and Your Kids: How Parents Stay in Control, written by Hilarie Cash and Kim McDaniel.

The Keys to the Car

Driving has always been a significant rite of passage for teenagers in our American society. It is a definitive marker on the way to adulthood. My recent observation, though, is that close to half the teens I work with are actually hesitant to take on all that's required to drive a car. More and more kids are waiting until they're 18 to obtain a license, let alone a vehicle. Surprisingly, and contrary to what you might have known growing up, more girls than boys consistently follow through on their goals to earn a driver's license and obtain a car. Young men tend to delay this by years, and they often expect their parents to continue the taxi service.

The topics of safe driving and car ownership by teens and young adults often create dissension in a household. Worries might come up about expenses, kids driving under the influence, and their freedom to go anywhere. These worries, which can cause tension and friction in the family, can be alleviated by clear expectations and boundaries for driving.

> **Issue:** Driving and car ownership
>
> **Vision:** We see our children driving safely and responsibly in a family vehicle or a vehicle they have helped pay for and also maintain.

Value: Driving is a privilege and a responsibility. We believe that having a driver's license and a car is a major step toward adulthood, one that will allow you to get from home to your workplace and school.

Expectation: We expect our kids to take driver's education and to have a valid license and insurance. Our kids will pay for half of their vehicle and all their own gas.

Rule: Because driving is an important life skill that should be approached responsibly, we ask that upon your return home you take a professional driver's education class, and then take the driver's license test within six months of your return. We will help you practice driving. We will pay for half of a safe vehicle, for insurance, and for maintenance. You will pay for the other half of the car and for gas.

Alternative Rule for a Working Young Adult: Upon return from treatment, you will get your car back. You will be expected to pay for gas, maintenance (oil changes, tire rotations) and insurance. We will pick up repair bills for the next year. If you have any speeding or parking tickets you will need to pay for them. On a funny or maybe not so funny note: your lead foot will increase your insurance premiums!

To come up with the appropriate rules for your family, don't feel you have to follow the above examples. Draw upon your experience as a teen and what your parents did for you. Look around at other parents and figure out which rules out there are working and align with your own beliefs. Don't be afraid to put more of the responsibility for safe driving and car ownership onto your child. You might find that your child doesn't want to drive and wants you to shuttle him around. Also, many urban centers have mass transit systems available, and bicycles work perfectly on most college campuses.

Lastly, you might want to include within your rules, consequences for irresponsible behavior. Sometimes teens and young adults do very dangerous things with cars, and I suggest adding a clause in your rules to cover this. Something like: "If any damage caused by you happens to the car, you will be responsible for the deductible and increase in premiums. If any irresponsible behavior happens when you are using the car, your privileges can be suspended."

And this ushers us to the topic of the next chapter, consequences.

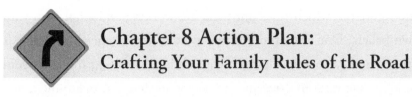

Chapter 8 Action Plan:
Crafting Your Family Rules of the Road

(To download blank worksheets, visit www.TheRoadHomeBook.com/downloads.)

#1. Rules of the Road

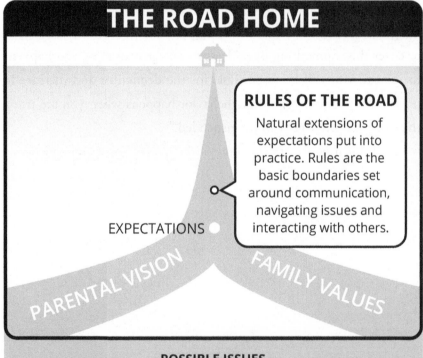

THE ROAD HOME

RULES OF THE ROAD
Natural extensions of expectations put into practice. Rules are the basic boundaries set around communication, navigating issues and interacting with others.

EXPECTATIONS

PARENTAL VISION

FAMILY VALUES

POSSIBLE ISSUES
Communication & Attitude   Dishonesty   Laziness & Lack of Motivation
Hygiene, Exercise, Diet & Sleep   Piercing & Tattoos   Smoking, Drinking or Drug Use
Cutting   Eating Disorders   Peers   Dating, Love & Sex   Curfew   Money
Counseling, Therapy & Medication   Spirituality & Faith   Chores & Work Ethic
Education & Academics   Technology   Pornography   Video Gaming   Cars & Driving

This chapter laid out the issues that often warrant Rules of the Road to ensure your child's successful journey home and to becoming a healthy mature, adult.

The idea is, again, to have rules grow from your vision and your values. Here is an example of the process using "work ethic" as the issue:

Issue: A work ethic.

Vision: Our child will be a hard worker like his grandparents and like us.

Value: We believe a work ethic leads to a more fulfilling job and life. We want that for our son.

Expectation: We see our son willing to work hard like his grandfather and like us. We expect our child to learn to value a strong work ethic, and to pay his own way in the world.

Possible Rule #1: Mom and Dad value hard work and want every family member to have a work ethic. We will pay for your college education and your room and board, but a car, gas, a cell phone, and entertainment money are up to you.

Possible Rule #2: In the culture of our family, it's very important to work and earn your own keep. However, we don't want work to interfere with your schooling. During the summer, working 20 hours a week will result in self-pride and allow you to afford the extras that a teen wants.

> **Possible Rule #3:** It's important that we all work hard and contribute to the household. Mowing the lawn, clipping the hedges, and taking out the weekly garbage are ways of being a contributing member of this family, which is greatly appreciated by us all.
>
> **Possible Rule #4:** We work hard in this family for what we have. Also we value the money we earn. We expect our children to start working as soon as possible, in a way that doesn't interfere with school. By age 16, they will need to have a job and pay for entertainment such as dates, movies, eating out and so on.

Now it's your turn to try doing this, using one of the following issues that are most likely on your family's radar: drugs, sex, or technology.

Issue: _____

Vision:

_____

_____

_____

_____

_____

_____

_____

_____

Value:

_____

_____

_____

_____

_____

_____

_____

Expectation:

_____

_____

_____

_____

_____

_____

_____

Rule:

_____

_____

_____

_____

_____

_____

_____

#2. Action Step

In past Action Plan steps, you have chosen issues that are relevant to your own situation with your child returning from treatment. You have looked at your vision, values, and some expectations. Now is the time to create the Rules of the Road that will be the foundation of your Home Agreement. Use the chart that follows (also available for download at www.TheRoadHomeBook.com/downloads) to draft some rules. Don't worry about filling in all the blanks if it seems like too much busy work. But do make sure the rules you create are rooted in your vision for your child and your values. An example has been provided for guidance:

Issue	Vision	Value	Expectation	Rule
Gaming	Our child will use technology to enhance, not hinder, his life.	We value how technology helps and entertains us, but we do not abuse technology.	We expect you to use technology in a healthy way.	You may game for three hours on the weekend for your first three months at home. If you use this time responsibly, we'll discuss additional time down the road. No gaming in the bedroom.

Issue	Vision	Value	Expectation	Rule

Adding Truth and Consequences

You've heard the old saying "Rules are made for breaking." What do you do, as the leader of your family, when your well-thought-out rules are trod upon? The most important thing is to stand by your values and defend your family culture. The best way to do this is to have an open conversation, loaded with transparent and loving communication (TLC), about what went wrong, and to follow up with a consequence.

We've looked at how kids need boundaries or guardrails to keep them on the road to health and help them succeed in the world outside of treatment. When your child comes home, direct him in such a way that he learns to respect your rules as you learn to hold him accountable. Transparent and loving communication is one of your best tools to accomplish this, and so are reasonable and appropriate

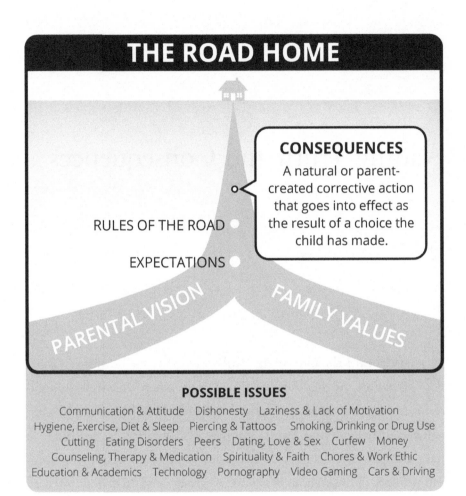

THE ROAD HOME

CONSEQUENCES
A natural or parent-created corrective action that goes into effect as the result of a choice the child has made.

RULES OF THE ROAD

EXPECTATIONS

PARENTAL VISION

FAMILY VALUES

POSSIBLE ISSUES

Communication & Attitude   Dishonesty   Laziness & Lack of Motivation
Hygiene, Exercise, Diet & Sleep   Piercing & Tattoos   Smoking, Drinking or Drug Use
Cutting   Eating Disorders   Peers   Dating, Love & Sex   Curfew   Money
Counseling, Therapy & Medication   Spirituality & Faith   Chores & Work Ethic
Education & Academics   Technology   Pornography   Video Gaming   Cars & Driving

consequences. Remind your child that consequences are put in place to guide, not to punish. Creating consequences is not about punishment, but correction. Neither you nor I desire to see kids suffer. The desire is to see them learn and grow.

In treatment, kids are often taught that consequences happen directly from their choices. If you do "A," then "B" happens—cause and effect. This is an objective reality. It just happens, so there is no need to preach, teach, or defend when a consequence is given. It's not a punishment, but the result of a choice. This approach respects a child's, teen's, or young adult's volition to decide his or her fate. This learning from choices made promotes maturity and growth as responsible people. It's good to remember that a support or reward is just as much a consequence as a deprivation is. Receiving a good grade or an earned privilege is as much of a consequence as losing a privilege, such as cell phone usage.

Consequences can come from two places. They can come from parents when a Home Agreement rule or other value is breached. They can also come from the outside world. This is called a natural consequence. When I punched my truck as a hotheaded teenager, I had to watch a doctor put a pin in my broken hand. I made a choice and paid the price. Believe me, I haven't punched a truck since.

Parental consequences are really about getting a child's attention. It's letting her know you mean what you say and that you're not messing around. Your rule is like a stop sign for your kid. Have you ever been cited for a rolling stop or, worse yet, failing to stop altogether? The expensive consequences, a

> Parental consequences are really about getting a child's attention.

fine and traffic school (or even a collision), probably stayed with you. You most likely don't roll through stop signs any more. Consequences given to a young person have to be bold and memorable because the goal, as with that ticket, is to effect change. If the consequence really stings, it will put up that guardrail boundary. Your kid will avoid hitting that rail again.

It's good for your child to know what kind of fines she might incur, so make consequences simple, easy to remember, and quick and deliberate in execution. It's easier on the child and the parents when the expected consequences number two or three rather than ten. For example the loss of technology can be a universal consequence appropriate for many broken rules.

Keep consequences appropriate and proportionate to the offense. If your son broke the agreed-upon rules regarding gaming, take away his gaming time or computer for a week. If your daughter with a history of cutting says she hasn't been doing it, yet the evidence is irrefutable when she is confronted to roll up her sleeves, you might ground her for lying and ask that she visit her therapist more often. You may also decide to inspect her body regularly for cuts. In all these cases, a by-product consequence should be an increase in transparent and loving communication.

Freedom Is the Holy Grail Consequence

Kids value freedom most: freedom to hang with friends, connect with friends, cruise the mall, drive around, do their own thing, hole up in their rooms, surf the net or the ocean, and so forth. Limiting or taking away what gives them freedom, such as the phone, laptop, or car keys, is an effective consequence. You know what matters most to your child, so use that as leverage.

If you dialogue with your child, you might be surprised when he comes up with an even more suitable and freedom limiting consequence than you. The dialogue may go something like this for a dad who feels he needs to ground his son for at least a week:

Child-Chosen Consequence

Dad: Okay, son, we need to chat about you deciding to break so many of the rules. You broke curfew twice this week and refused to do your chores. And you're gaming way beyond what we agreed upon. I told you the consequence would be restricting your freedom with friends.

Son: Dad!

Dad: I know. But I have let you slide this last week and I don't like where this is all going. I need to follow through on my word. This is hard on me, too.

Son: No, it's not.

Dad: Hey. Let's get to the bottom of this. We need to discuss how long you will be losing your freedom to hang with your friends, because the last time I gave you that consequence it did not get your attention. Apparently three days wasn't long enough.

Son: It was more than enough.

Dad: *(reflecting what he heard)* So you thought it was long enough?

Son: Yes!

Dad: Look, I don't want to punish you. I want you to learn.

Son: *(exasperated and sarcastic)* So what are you going to do? Ground me for a month?

Dad: Okay, I get it. You're frustrated and you're getting sarcastic. Let's try to understand each other.

Son: *(sighs)*

Dad: So how do I get your attention? I'm still going to limit your freedom. What are your thoughts? I need you to come up with something that works.

Son: Okay, ground me for two weeks, not a month. I'll make sure this doesn't happen again.

Dad: That sounds good. I like your idea.

Son: *(a bit shocked his dad just went with his idea)* Okay . . .

Dad: So, no going out with friends for the next two weeks. In that time I want you to earn back your freedom by following curfew, doing your chores, and gaming within our agreed parameters.

Son: I got it, but it sucks.

> **Dad:** *(reflecting)* It does. Please learn from this. This is hard on
> all of us, and I'm committed to you following through. You
> can do it.

This dad totally scored! He was going to disallow his child's time
with friends for one week, but his son, fearful that it could be even
longer, chose two weeks. In a weird way it's a win-win for all involved.
Take your child's suggested consequence and run with it, as he is empowered by this and then has to live with a consequence that was his
own idea. Also, taking away the phone for a day or two seldom has the
necessary bite. I like it when parents go a little longer on their consequence than their first impulse. The theme that runs through a solid
consequence is time—time for your child to contemplate and reevalu-
ate. If you're thinking of taking the phone away for the evening, go for
a week. If you do it big, often you only have to do it once. If you go
small, you might have to do it over and over and over again, and that
wears everyone down and builds resentment. Take the car for a week.
No allowance until *all* chores are done. No gaming for a month.

Timing and Style

When delivering consequences refer first and foremost to the Home
Agreement. If a specific consequence isn't written for the infringement,
agree as parents on an appropriate consequence and hand it out quickly
and decisively.

Consequences have a shelf life. They are best given out immediately after a boundary has been crossed, especially for lesser infractions

to the Home Agreement, such as going over cell phone minutes or not cleaning her room. For more serious infractions having to do with safety, health, relapse, or integrity, however, feel free to not decide immediately. It might take a day or two to contemplate options or discuss them with your partner or a professional.

It's always best to deliver a consequence matter-of-factly. In treatment programs, consequences are delivered with little fanfare. This takes away shaming but still gets the person's attention. And that's what parental consequences are all about: getting her attention and letting her know that you're evaluating and have the courage and resolve to stand behind whatever expectations you put forth. When parents don't get punitive or overly energized, and dispassionately deliver their justice without fanfare, the child accepts the consequence a bit more readily.

If you deliver a judicious consequence that isn't personal, it will come off better. Something like, "You took the car without permission and stayed out an hour past curfew. As a consequence, no car for a week." After the consequence is delivered, don't walk away. Let your child vent a bit.

If you put too much emotion into a consequence, your child might see this as ambivalence and seize an opportunity to manipulate or get your goat. All too often I watch this scenario play out in my work with families. A child pushes one rule for the first time and sees wishy-washy parents, too intimidated to follow through on what they said they would do. This is especially true if things are going really well. Parents justify not following through because they think a consequence for one violation will send the whole process south. This is rarely true.

If you don't follow through, you have just told your child that she can manipulate the system again, like she did before treatment. Follow-through confirms to her that you stand behind your values. When she knows you're sticking to your guns, she'll fume with frustration but "have to" go along with your justice. When she feels the firmness and fairness of your family culture, it's more likely that she'll quit giving her energy to futile results and move forward with her healing.

Support As a Consequence

Some infractions need to be handled with consequences that are supportive as well as those that can be seen as restrictive. For example, drunk driving will most likely need to be dealt with through a combination of consequences. If drug and/or alcohol abuse are of concern for your returning child, then add several expectations in your Home Agreement about these issues. Include rules and consequences to encourage respectful behavior, discourage irresponsible behavior, and set up fail safes for relapses and slips. If drunk driving occurs, you might limit contact with certain friends (restrictive), cut off access to the car for a month (restrictive), and insist that your child attend AA meetings three times a week for a good period of time (supportive).

Proactive consequences that provide support, such as going to 12-step meetings or more frequent therapy sessions, are ways of attending to lingering mental health concerns. If signs of depression and anxiety, such as panic attacks or serious mood swings, are occurring routinely and contributing to rule breaking, then more support (consequences) is warranted, whether it be an increase in sessions with a caring therapist, psychotropic medication, or alternative modalities of healing.

POSSIBLE CONSEQUENCES

RESTRICTIVE the phone, the computer, gaming, the TV, the Internet, the car, seeing friends

SUPPORTIVE additional support (therapy, yoga, AA), earned freedom (no curfew, extra car privileges), earned praise, earned college tuition, earned and appropriate affordable material rewards (such as a laptop for the diligent student), an earned allowance if age-appropriate, special-recognition dinners or family outings

The Consequence-Resistant Kid

When consequences, including those that act as rewards for good behavior, don't seem to work with your child, it might be indicative of an underlying problem. Before I expound on this, though, let me be clear. For the majority of kids, consequences work if they're the right consequences.

If, after a few months, your child is not responding to your consequences with positive change, your first recourse is to try different consequences. How do you know which will work? Those that impinge on what your child most values will get him motivated. Again, teens and young adults value freedom. So if you increase privileges (supportive consequences), such as more car use for being responsible, or decrease privileges (restrictive consequences), such as no car for two weeks for staying out all night, then you'll most likely get your child's attention

For the young adult at college or trying to launch a career, two of the more effective consequences are giving or taking away financial support or use of a vehicle.

If your consequences aren't motivating your child to "do the right thing" no matter how creative you get, then there's a possibility that your child might be dealing with an underlying mental health issue. What gets in the way of a teen's or young adult's healthy motivation and functioning are anxiety, depression, psychosis, anti-social personality traits, addiction, eating disorders, and the like.

If your son or daughter is consequence-resistant, the first order of action is a TLC discussion or two, maybe with a professional, to get to the heart of the matter. When someone struggles with motivation around consequences, often he is confused. He needs compassion to allow him to explore his ambivalence and whatever internal or external barriers are in the way of his success. You might discover that your son is not attending work, despite your cutting him off financially, because he's having panic attacks on the bus. Consequences in a case such as this might need to be therapeutic in nature. If your daughter is stealing your jewelry, despite being grounded from all activity but school, the drug addiction might be back and thus she might need to receive more professional help.

If an underlying mental health issue is the reason your child isn't functioning well, it's time to be honest with yourself and him. Your child, though trying hard to succeed, might be letting his process be foiled because he knows deep down that he needs more help and is waiting for you to suggest added support. Be proactive, and explore the myriad of supportive actions available. Get him the help he needs, but don't be afraid to follow through on the other consequences. If he's using drugs and stealing, let drug counseling be one consequence, but also insist that he pay back the debt he's incurred by stealing from you.

Ineffective Consequences

False threats will get you and your kid nowhere fast. When you dole out a consequence, speak the truth and do exactly what you say you're going to do. False threats will only encourage manipulation. Lack of follow-through will undermine your authority. One thing your child learned very well in treatment is that when an adult says they're going to do something, it gets done. Staff members and counselors know that their unwavering word means everything. At home, just like in treatment, there has to be consistent behavior to back up any spoken words. This creates emotional stability within your child. It stops manipulation quickly. If your child can't trust what you say, then trust is fundamentally broken. Trust is the heart of relationship, the very thing you want your child to have with you.

Physical punishment is not an appropriate consequence. Resorting to it will create aggression or fear and might place the parent in front of the law. There are better consequences and tools, lots of them. If this is a situation within your family, I urge you to seek professional help.

Using cash as a parental bartering tool is mostly ineffective. Many children who have been in treatment are not motivated by money. "He can live off fumes," I hear parents say. Money often doesn't get the child's attention or have lasting impact as a consequence. Offering a financial reward for six months of sobriety will not serve as sufficient motivation for success. Expecting sobriety because it's attached to a family value and offering support in the form of love and counseling is a much more honest and effective consequence.

If you provide your younger or college-attending child with an allowance, determine what chores or behavior earn that money; don't shell out just for expected healthy behavior. If money is attached to valuable work and the work is completed to your satisfaction, pay the allowance. Alternatively, withholding the allowance for poor or incomplete work might be effective, but only if you aren't still slipping him a twenty when he says he needs it.

Consequences in the Home Agreement

Writing a specific consequence for every rule isn't advisable. Your Home Agreement will be too long in pages and heavy in content if you try to cover every possible scenario that could happen. If rules and consequences are too detailed, they'll feel like prison for you and your child. Thus the goal is to strike a balance. Write up rules based on issues that have been prevalent in the past. Focus on the crucial issues and a consequence as an extension to the rule. Here is an example of adding a consequence to a rule if a child's gaming has been an issue:

> **Issue:** Gaming.
>
> **Vision:** We see our kids enjoying technology and using it as an effective tool to assist them in their life endeavors.
>
> **Value:** We value our mental and physical health and want to enjoy all things in moderation.
>
> **Expectation:** We expect you to use technology in a healthy way.
>
> **Rule:** Moderate, ethical use of the computer/TV/phone is okay, but no gaming of any kind is allowed.
>
> **Consequence:** If gaming begins, then your use of technology will be suspended for at least a month.

Rewards and the Home Agreement

To move your child toward healthy, mature goals and expectations, I encourage you to include some earned rewards (supportive consequences) into your daily life and even into the Home Agreement. Your child will appreciate earned rewards and those given for diligence in the areas where she struggles. A simple and yet magical reward is honest praise—not always accompanied by constructive feedback.

Rewards and praise are most effective when they're proportionate to the positive act. Your daughter will be suspicious if the reward is too much or the praise not justified. Wait until she has 100 percent earned what was stated in your agreement, or completes what was expected.

This gives her a sense of confidence and self-esteem, and teaches her to finish what she starts to get the reward. Give an "A" for results, not just effort. It's just fine if she misses the mark and doesn't earn the reward. There should be no shame. Remind her to strive to achieve the reward next time. Be patient. It might take a year for her to earn that car, but accepting delayed gratification is a sign of maturity.

The message here is to reward what is above and beyond satisfactory. Don't reward normal. So many times I've heard in living rooms, post-treatment, "Mom, Dad, why are you giving me something for being normal and just doing what I should be doing?" She won't want to get special treatment for accomplishing the basic stuff of life. For instance, a modest allowance is a plenty good reward for chores, because she knows chores are expected.

> The message here is to reward what is above and beyond satisfactory. Don't reward normal.

Sobriety, on the other hand, is hard work and can be rewarded with more fanfare. If your son remains sober for an extended period of time, say several months, roll out a reward that seems appropriate, such as taking him golfing at his favorite course. But don't break the bank or go overboard. Your child *should* be sober if he has substance issues. If his sobriety continues for a full year and proves a hard earned, life-changing commitment, then maybe his dream of taking a National Outdoor Leadership School course is appropriate.

Academics and study habits are pretty easy to regulate with rewards. If your kid comes home with a 3.8 GPA and your expectation was a 3.0, then go nuts and have fun for the day, but don't buy her a car. Give her a privilege, preferable to material rewards. It's better for her to experience the benefits of maturity (curfew an hour later on Saturday night) than an extra fifty bucks.

If you include a reward or two in the Home Agreement, make them count. Make sure each is something your child really wants. For example, if you want him to be driving within the next few months, and he concurs, you can offer an incentive: "Once you take the driver's safety course and earn your license, we'll chip in for half the cost of a car." If you want your daughter to consider higher education, then write into the agreement that you will pay for a trip to tour campuses once she finishes the semester successfully.

A very sweet reward for kids is access to their friends. How often do you hear something along these lines? "Dad, can I ask Hannah to join us on our vacation to the lake this year?" It might be very worthwhile to write in the Home Agreement that if your daughter stays sober and pulls a 3.0 in her fall semester, Hannah can come along. Follow through if your daughter earns the reward, but definitely don't allow Hannah to come if she doesn't.

One final thought on praise and rewards. Positive reinforcement that is sincere and honest works. It's given daily in treatment, and it also plays out effectively in human relationships at work, church, and home—as long as it's genuine. But if you're trying to bribe your child and control her, she'll resent you. She'll look down on you for trying to buy her efforts. Yet delivering praise and rewards in the form of gratitude can be very effective. For example: "I've noticed that you've been

"Honey, I am so proud that you have maintained a 3.0 and kept your job for an entire semester. You deserve a reward!"

surfing twice a week for the last four months, and I know this is really hard for you; you'd rather chill and channel surf instead. It makes me feel good to see you doing something healthy for yourself. How about some fish tacos—my treat?"

Reward your child in a range from genuine gratitude to full-on praise, but only when it's earned. Try out lines like: "I'm really proud of you for walking Grandma to the car." "Thanks for helping me get through that tough conversation. I was angry and you really helped me de-escalate." "It was great that you remembered to call me when you said you would. That meant a lot to me." Add a hug to these and life doesn't get much better.

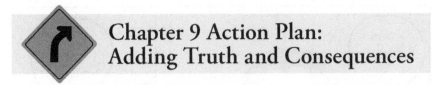

Chapter 9 Action Plan: Adding Truth and Consequences

(To download blank worksheets, visit www.TheRoadHomeBook.com/downloads.)

#1. Restrictive Consequences

Take a minute to think about what matters to your child. What freedoms, pleasures, and privileges lost would make the best restrictive consequences? For example:

If you choose to go out with red light friends then you will lose your cell phone for a month.

_____

_____

_____

_____

_____

_____

_____

_____

_____

_____

_____

_____

_____

_____

#2. Supportive Consequences

Now think about consequences could be supportive such as:

If you stop taking your medications we will have a TLC discussion and ask you to go to your psychiatrist to discuss the side effects and adjust medication.

#3. Issues, Rules and Consequences

Refer back to the chart you filled out at the end of Chapter 8. Which issues or rules do you feel will be best reinforced with a consequence, either restrictive or supportive, written into the Home Agreement?

#4. Reinforcing the Home Agreement

Fill in a consequence on the next page for each issue or rule you identified. Remember to include supportive consequences. Here is an example using the issue of substance abuse and sobriety:

Issue	Rule	Consequence
Substance abuse and sobriety	We expect sobriety for at least one full year after you come home.	If you slip you will be drug-tested regularly, and will need to go to NA and see your drug counselor weekly until you're back on course.

#5. Rewards

Think of healthy goals you want your child to attain. When she does accomplish the goal or exceeds it, how can you reward her? An example would be:

If you maintain good hygiene and exercise regularly for six months, Dad will take you on that weekend motorcycle trip to the desert.

Issue	Rule	Consequence

10

Addressing Mental Health and Addiction

We're human, and part of being human can be getting ill—be it a bothersome flu or a short-term, treatable depression. Other illnesses, such as agoraphobia, opiate addiction, and eating disorders, are more destructive to individuals and their families. Some psychotic conditions, such as schizophrenia, can so internally tear apart the individual that they interfere with the natural development into adulthood.

In the past, you've watched your child become seriously dysfunctional, which manifested in concrete ways: lying, stealing, plummeting grades, fluctuating moods, and antisocial, argumentative, or aggressive behavior. Such pathology displayed by a child triggers action by a parent, often resulting in some form of treatment.

The goal of treatment is to heal your child so that his journey home and back into the world will be full of forward movement. Occasionally, though, pathology creeps back in to a child's life. What to do?

Try stepping back and viewing mental health issues as separate from the individual. Much of our culture wants to integrate the body and mind, which I very often support. Yet I would say that the Western medical model helps us look at mental illness more objectively.

Too many youngsters have over-identified with their illness and made it part of who they are. For example, they might use past depression or panic disorder as the reason they can't function today: *I'm depressed; I can't get off the couch. I can't go to school. I might have a panic attack. I'm too nervous to apply for a job.* Simple life experiences become debilitating, or rationalized as undoable, because the young person has been continually treated with kid gloves due to his mental state. An unused mind, like muscles that atrophy, will become less strong.

The Western model, in viewing mental health problems as illness, allows a child to separate from the illness. It can be viewed as transitional, and therefore must be endured only until treatment is successful. True, some illnesses last a lifetime, but these too can be treated as separate from the person.

I find this model more hopeful, in that it doesn't allow the mental illness to become a lifelong identity. Depression, anxiety disorders, substance abuse, eating disorders, and oppositional personality traits can disappear with good treatment and the client's choice to take responsibility for his mental health.

Individuals with mental health conditions that are lifelong, such as narcissistic personality disorder, schizophrenia, chronic addiction, bipolar disorder, and borderline personality disorder, can manage them and be functional and successful in the world. It's beyond the scope of this book to go into the how, but I would like to make it clear that the appropriate medical, psychological, and spiritual professionals should be involved. The heart of the matter is for a child to realize she is not the disease which might be genetic in nature. As with any physical illness such as lupus or diabetes, she must learn to manage the challenge life has given her if she is to get the most out of her wonderful life.

Nature vs. Nurture

As I have gained experience in my field, it has become painfully clear how great a part nature plays in the debate of nature vs. nurture. Much has been written in the prestigious medical journals of our time about the major role of genetics in mental health.

During treatment, your child might be asked to look into her family history. It would be prudent for you to assist. Knowledge is power in this case. Identify the common challenges and weaknesses woven into your family lineage, and prepare appropriate contingency actions to take regarding your child. If addiction, depression, or panic attacks were known in your family forty years ago, then a genetic predisposition may exist. Such genetic loading should be addressed in treatment, and the issues honored at home. This doesn't mean your child's path is predetermined, or that family history should become a crutch for your child to use to rationalize dysfunctional behavior. If there is adequate planning and support, much of life's potential chaos can be contained and focused with environmental structures and follow-through; i.e., Rules of the Road and consequences.

On the bright side, take some time to recognize that physical and character strengths, from resiliency to adaptability, are genetic, too. Maybe you come from a long line of brilliant thinkers, violinists, or exceptional athletes. Look for the lightness that will balance the darkness.

> Nature is a birthright, and your Home Agreement is the nurture part.

Nature is a birthright, and your Home Agreement is the nurture part. It can be the final word and have lasting effects, so assess your family history carefully and take seriously any potential issues.

Mental Health and Manipulation

Sometimes your child might use his or her mental health issue or addiction to manipulate you. For example, "Mom, if I don't hang out with Johnny (red light friend), I will get depressed." Honestly, when I see such blatant manipulation, a questioning "are you for real" look of my eyes says it all, and my client is almost embarrassed for trying such a ploy. That being said there might be some truth in the manipulation. Use TLC and see if you can explore what is going on. This can lead to a solution to an honest issue or problem. In the above example, maybe a discussion would lead to the importance of having more friends who are healthy and could help keep depression at bay. Also, perhaps that red light Johnny could earn the family's trust and become a green light friend someday. If you see such manipulation of using one's illness as an excuse to ramrod your Home Agreement, call it out and potentially explore if there is a legitimate concern.

Putting Order into Disorders and Addiction

To date, your son or daughter might or might not have been diagnosed as having a mental illness. If he or she has been, educate yourself thoroughly on the specific pathology. I'll briefly identify the mental health concerns that seem to visit my clients most often. This list is not by any means comprehensive, but a quick recap of what I see in my practice.

- Mood disorders

- Anxiety disorders

- Oppositional defiant disorder (ODD)

- Personality disorders

- Reactive attachment disorder (RAD)

- Eating disorders

- Psychotic disorders (psychosis and thought disorders)

- Cutting

- Post-traumatic stress disorder (PTSD) and other trauma issues

- Attention deficit hyperactivity disorder (ADHD)

- Addiction

Mood disorders are common among teens and young adults who find themselves in treatment. Debilitating depression, dysthymia (a low-grade depression that lingers), and bipolar disorder are some of the more common conditions of which you might have heard.

The illness of clinical or unipolar depression is not the same as the blues we all feel from time to time. It is a mortal enemy that saps the life out of someone, a devastating melancholia that is potentially life-threatening. Symptoms might include appetite and sleep problems, weight gain or loss, a low sex drive, lack of interest in life, not feeling part of life, hopelessness, and suicidal thoughts and acts.

Dysthymia is more malaise and the "blahs," akin to a low-grade fever of depression. I call it the Eeyore illness.

Bipolar disorder, formerly known as manic depression, includes mood swings and degrees of mood swings. The up mood, called a mania, can range from irritability to psychotic symptoms such as hallucinations, delusional beliefs, and disorder in the stream of thought. An individual diagnosed with bipolar disorder often needs medication, and med compliance often becomes an issue, especially with young adults.

After your child comes home, his debilitating mood disorder might also return. This is definitely something to discuss with the professional managing your child's disorder, and to address in the Home Agreement. Have contingency plans to support him if his mood becomes a struggle.

He learned a multitude of coping skills in treatment, and therapy and medication are often appropriate, but clinical problems don't always need clinical solutions. Often real-life opportunities, such as taking on a new job or interacting with friends and family members in positive situations, can really help.

A natural, healthy response to anxiety is to exert some control into one's life. This lessens nervousness. When someone has pathological anxiety, his response to the stress of life might turn into illness—an anxiety disorder. Common anxiety disorders are panic attacks, obsessive-compulsive disorder (OCD), specific phobias such as agoraphobia and social phobia, and general anxiety disorder (GAD).

After working in wilderness, my conclusion is that the majority of teens and young adults entering treatment do so with a combination of mood (depressive) issues and some form of excessive anxiety as well. Upon your child's return, if anxiety disorders are a concern, watch for avoidant behavior such as not applying for jobs, refusing to go out with friends, or holing up in the bedroom. Also keep an eye out for excessive controlling behavior such as rigid routines. Sometimes anxious kids can fall into addiction with marijuana, benzodiazepines, or opiates, as these drugs provide temporary relief when an individual is overly stressed.

Although anxiety disorders are worrisome, the bright side of this story is that there are very effective treatment options such as cognitive and behavioral therapy. A great resource for learning more about these and other alternative holistic approaches is Edmund Bourne's *The Anxiety and Phobia Workbook*.

Anxiety, similarly to depression, is best addressed from multiple angles: diet, nature, massage, exercise, meditation, medication, relaxation, psychotherapy, spirituality, vitamin supplements, improved relationships, EMDR therapy, and exposure and desensitization therapy are some of the options. Each person is so unique in his or her pathology that there is no one-size-fits-all solution. An individual has to figure this out for himself under the guidance of a professional and go with what works.

Personality disorders are not diagnosed until someone is in his late teens. The idea behind these disorders is that they can be integrated into the person's character and prove to be lifelong. If you've been exposed for a while now to treatment jargon, you might have heard terms related to personality disorders such as: borderline, dependent, narcissistic, antisocial, and histrionic, to name a few. Personality disorders create problems in relationships, whether personal or professional, and this has deleterious effects on the person when it comes to functioning in society.

ODD, oppositional defiant disorder, is a common diagnosis given to those entering treatment, and for the most part it is remedied in treatment. ODD behaviors include negativity, hostility, anger, being argumentative, short temper, defying adults, annoying and blaming others, and spite and vindictiveness. ODD may cause impairment in social, academic, and potentially occupational endeavors. Your child would not be coming home if she still had this problem. If untreated, ODD could lead to serious antisocial behavior and personality traits in adulthood. If you notice a strong antiauthority attitude or disregard for society's rules, such as breaking laws or getting arrested, ODD is creeping back into your child's life. Being oppositional at home is not ODD. Oppositional tendencies must be more generalized outside the home to truly be of concern.

Attachment theory is back in vogue for good reason. Researchers are discovering solid evidence that the way in which we attach to our caregivers in childhood influences how we relate to others throughout life. When someone has significant trust issues with those who raised her, a diagnosis of reactive attachment disorder (RAD) can be made. RAD is at its core an attachment issue, meaning that a relationship in a subject's early development caused a core problem around trust and emotional safety that affects that person into adulthood. Children affected by RAD have insecure attachments to their caregivers and overall don't trust life. When stressed, they feel sure they are about to be abandoned, emotionally and perhaps physically. Many programs and treatment protocols are focused on healing that core issue of trust and relationship within the individual's psyche.

If you suspect your child is insecure and doesn't trust, you and the world must become very predictable to this child. She needs to know that you have her back and that you can be counted on. Affection matters, but consistent, grounded parenting is the real key to helping her feel stable enough in life to trust.

Eating disorders affecting both women and men are prevalent in our culture. They can last for years, and sometimes a lifetime. Some of the more common types are anorexia nervosa, bulimia nervosa, and binge eating disorder. These disorders can have severe physical ramifications, including death. Yet treatment can be highly effective if the patient is matched to the right program. An important factor in eating disorders is that significant depression is part of this diagnosis, and depression is a serious risk factor in and of itself. If an eating disorder has affected your child, watch for depression and treat it, but do not neglect to look at the entirety of the issue.

Psychotic disorders (psychosis), often complex and more difficult to diagnose, usually develop in the teen and young-adult years and basically mean the patient is having a temporary or permanent break with reality. A person can have bizarre, illogical beliefs, disorganized thoughts that don't add up, and hallucinations involving any of the five senses. For example, someone might see and hear aliens in the room telling him that the FBI is after him. He might also be speaking nonsensically and incoherently. Alcohol, or drugs such as crystal meth, can also induce psychosis.

It's not out of the ordinary for those with psychotic disorders to hear demons—auditory hallucinations—telling them to do harmful things. Some psychotic disorders develop without explanation. For example, schizophrenia, a rare disorder, appears in the late teens and early twenties, seemingly from nowhere.

Medication and cognitive therapy are both effective in treating psychotic disorders. These disorders are not something a parent can handle alone. Outside help is nearly always imperative.

Cutting is a form of self-mutilation that can be done with scissors, knives, razor blades, rocks, sticks, paper clips—you name it. When under intense duress, some people make cuts into their skin.

They report that, as a coping habit, it creates emotional relief, albeit harmful. Cutting is not a suicide attempt. It is self-injury for psychological reasons.

While cutting can be an ongoing issue well into adulthood, I find that my clients stop the practice once honest-to-goodness therapy has taken root. When emotional relief can occur in a healthy way, cutting usually stops. If your child has a history of cutting, watch her closely when she's distressed. People can resume this habit after treatment, and if they do, they'll hide the places where they cut themselves, commonly on the belly, underarms, and inner thighs.

An experience of trauma, whether from sexual violence or aggressive acts such as being physically attacked or witnessing a murder, can stop the natural psychological development of a child. Often referred to as PTSD, post-traumatic stress disorder can be treated, but the symptoms might be lifelong and the afflicted one has to learn how to cope.

Trauma is a serious mental health issue, and traumatized people exhibit symptoms and behavior that clearly interrupt their life progress. Mood, sleep, trust, relationship, emotional stability, and daily functionality can all be affected. If a trauma has occurred to your child, compassion is the name of the game here. If equine therapy worked in treatment, try to integrate it at home. If other therapeutic processes worked, create a bridge to similar supports at home. There is no quick fix for trauma. It can be a lifetime companion.

One common and often over diagnosed condition that stands alone is ADHD or attention deficit hyperactive disorder, formerly known as ADD. There are three types of ADHD: predominantly inattentive, predominantly hyperactive-impulsive, and combined hyperactive-impulsive and inattentive. Many of the parents I work with do not believe that ADHD is an illness, and I tend to agree. Many kids given the diagnosis are gifted in ways that are exceptionally positive. They simply have a hard time fitting into our culture's sit-on-your-fanny-all-day method of education. You can decide whether you think this is a clinical issue for your child or not, and as he matures he'll decide for himself. Medication might help, but finding a lifestyle, alternative form of education, and work life that complements this type of person helps significantly.

You and your child should know with which mental health issue you are dealing. Most such issues are remedied, if not healed, by treatment, and that is why your child is ready to return to your home. Discuss the ramifications and important factors of your child's diagnosis with his treatment therapist, and incorporate the clinical and psychological needs of your child into the Home Agreement. Watch him closely to determine whether anything significant is developing, as some pathology becomes more apparent and can be more clearly diagnosed as a child matures in years.

On Addiction

Addiction and the fear it sends through a person's mind and body have people buying a lot of books and going through a lot of programs. We're fortunate to live in a time when so much knowledge and help is available, and yet this is little solace for the parent who is dealing with a child addicted to heroin, alcohol, prescription drugs, food, sex, or gaming. No question, this is a heavy burden on parents, and yet I invite you to take a deep breath and work on approaching this seeming catastrophe with a more hopeful or even clinical perspective.

Addictions can be categorized as clinical or cultural. Clinical addictions can be found in the *DSM-V* or *Diagnostic and Statistical Manual of Mental Disorders, Fifth Edition*, published by the American Psychiatric Association. The *DSM-V* mostly refers to substance addictions ranging from coffee to cocaine and also gambling.

Cultural addictions are also hot topics today. These include sex, pornography, love (which occurs when a person will not or cannot give up a toxic romantic relationship), food, shopping, the Internet, and electronic gaming. It's noteworthy that sex addiction, gaming and the Internet are all being further researched to perhaps be included in the DSM's clinical addictions.

Substance Addictions

Addictions to drugs and alcohol are ravaging our culture. Prescription drug abuse is on the rise, and hard drugs like cocaine and heroin are easily available to kids at younger and younger ages, and at low cost. Many of the drugs out there today are not the drugs you knew as a teen or college student. Most of us experimented with substances in our young adult years; experimentation seems to be natural for teens. But for those with a predisposition to addiction, it is in this young, experimental phase that the switch for a lifelong struggle is flipped. Unfortunately, the adventurous and exploratory type who starts a journey of curiosity with substances might find a monkey on his back that will be difficult to shed for a good portion of his life.

Substance addiction is probably the number one reason teens and young adults enter treatment. It is also the type of addiction that most of my young clients are dealing with. When a teen or young adult moves beyond experimentation and begins to build a lifestyle around substance use, parents and professionals attempt to determine whether this particular individual is just going through a phase. Not all who go to treatment develop chronic addiction issues, and yet for some it's the beginning of a struggle that can debilitate the child, inhibit her functional development, and become a lifetime illness.

Some of the more prevalent dependencies I work with are addictions to alcohol, marijuana, and such prescription drugs as benzos or benzodiazepines (diazepam, alprazolam, clonazepam, and lorazepam) and opiates (oxycodone and hydrocodone). Prescription drug deaths due to overdose have tripled in the last ten years.[1] From my observations, heroin is making a comeback as a dangerously affordable drug. Cocaine is in full swing in young urban areas. Crystal meth is hitting rural areas due to its ease of manufacture and fairly low cost. Many students in high-pressure academic settings appear to be abusing amphetamines as their study buddies.

My most recent work in Southern California has unveiled a rise in the use of K2 and Spice among high school teens. These are synthetic drugs with effects similar to marijuana, and they might not be detected

---

[1] CDC Policy Impact: Prescription Painkiller Overdoses, http://www.cdc.gov/homeandrecreationalsafety/rxbrief/

in home drug tests. Bath salts, which cause reactions similar to those of cocaine and amphetamines, are being used by teens as well. The issue with K2, Spice, and bath salts is that your teen can walk into any local smoke shop and purchase drugs that are very serious in nature. If you see small packets of "incense" or "bath salts" in your child's possession, research what those packets really contain.

If your child identifies as having a substance addiction, it's a good idea for you to understand the language in which he and the treatment world speak. Try not to let terminology confuse you. A person's substance addiction can be considered either *substance abuse* or the more grave *substance dependency*. Abuse means basically that the use is to such a degree that the user's life is disrupted: health, legal, employment, interpersonal, and other key life issues come to the forefront as matters reach a crisis. Dependency reflects an increase in these psychosocial stressors, along with pronounced physiological problems such as tolerance and withdrawal issues. Whether abuse or dependency, when substance use gets to this pathological level, the patient (and I use that word intentionally) needs professional support.

Load your Home Agreement with accountability and include counseling, support groups, and random drug and alcohol screening. Rely on your child's Relapse Prevention Plan (RPP) for material on which to base such consequences and attach it to the Home Agreement. As you observe your child over the next year, be looking for signs of substance use, from paraphernalia to missing money and suspicious behavior. The surefire way of knowing is to drug test. A dirty drug test resolves the suspicion immediately.

The Relapse Prevention Plan

A Relapse Prevention Plan (RPP) is usually a hefty, stand-alone document created by your child and her treatment team or counselor. Include it in your Home Agreement as an addendum. This document lays out a very personal strategy, with goals and objectives specific to one individual's addiction. It delineates how that person is going to address environmental stressors and triggers for relapse, as well as red light people to avoid. It also specifies healthful practices to maintain sobriety, recovery, and the continued healing of core issues. An example of an RPP will be included at the end of this chapter, so that you might become more familiar with this important and informative document.

Within the Relapse Prevention Plan, structured supports will have been written out: such actions as keeping the home free of drugs and alcohol, addiction counseling, outpatient meetings, 12-step programs, spiritual practices, random drug testing, and identifying certain places and people that could trigger use. There will also be a plan for consequences in the event of a relapse. Use this important information to inform the Home Agreement, in which you can create Rules of the Road that will help you catch derailment early.

How Randomly Do You Randomly Drug Test?

Parents ask me on occasion to clarify what "random drug testing" comes down to. How random? How often? What drugs? First, random drug testing is necessary, as your child will not be able to plan ahead and fake or alter the test if he is using. I recommend that you schedule on your personal calendar the dates on which to test your child. Don't forget to pick some Mondays, after those tempting party weekends, but don't just choose Mondays—remember the random idea. That the tests stay random is a must, but if something looks suspicious, you should test him then also.

Drug testing, whether random or as the result of a red flag, lets your child know you care and are keeping your side of the bargain. It doesn't matter if he gets angry about it; inside, he sees that you mean business and have his back. Not too long ago, a client told me that they had been hesitating to drug test their child. They had let it go for two months, and finally they garnered the courage to test him. He complained. He got angry, but he did it. Within minutes—*minutes*, mind you—after he did the test, this young man was walking around the house whistling. Why? Because he knew his parents cared. He knew they were going to help him stay sober. (By the way, the test was clean.)

Drug testing is an external structure that supports your child's sobriety and gives you real measurable information on how he is doing. I do recommend testing for all drugs possible (a 10-panel drug test). Drug addiction is a moving target, and people change their drug of choice, especially if they think they will only be tested for one drug. Also, there are newer synthetic drugs that will not be picked up on standard tests purchased at a pharmacy. For more entrenched addiction, go for professional services that have fewer false positives and test for the new designer drugs. Contact your local treatment centers or hospitals for professional drug testing available in your town or near your child's college. A search engine perusal will also provide you with testing sites.

If alcohol is an issue, or if perhaps you suspect it might be the new "drug" of choice, randomly drug test on a Monday morning and screen for alcohol. Or, out of the blue, breathalyse your child. You can order a Breathalyser over the Internet and can also find them in pharmacies. It is up to you, depending on your family culture, to decide if this is what you want to do, especially if your child is of legal drinking age.

If you suspect your son or daughter is drinking or using again, don't ignore your gut feelings. Investigate your suspicion. This is no time to be naive.

Slips vs. Relapse

The clinical world uses two words consistently when it comes to addiction recovery: slip and relapse. The words slip and relapse mean exactly what they imply. When someone slips, she uses for a very brief time and quickly gets back to sobriety and her recovery work. She is highly motivated to do so, recognizing that she took a brief turn for the worse. For example, if she identifies as an alcoholic and after two months of being home drinks a few beers or gets drunk one night, but returns immediately to her 12-step meetings and stays sober, that would be called a slip.

> The words slip and relapse mean exactly what they imply.

Many addiction specialists state that a slip is part of the normal pathway to sobriety and recovery. While not all addicts in recovery will have a slip, it's a common mistake from which the addict can learn. If your child slips once or twice, quickly instill consequences, including additional supports, to underline the urgency of the situation. A slip can move into relapse if not addressed right away. The key is to catch the slip, enforce consequences, and hope the supports and pressure from you are significant enough to get his attention. If motivated, he will self-correct. Your child's motivation to change is key. It's the reason people stop addictive behaviors. If he doesn't care enough to do this for himself, then a relapse might be imminent and help outside of the home would be a next step.

Slip . . . or relapse?

Relapse is a significant regression back to the substance of choice; the addiction has returned. It means your child has come back fully to a habitual, addictive behavior such as drinking, drug use, gambling, video gaming, self-mutilation, or an eating disorder. Relapse is a time for concern, but not frenzy. Quickly employ the consequential supports stated in the Home Agreement, and ramp them up if the relapse continues. If the relapse is full-blown and your consequences aren't working, engage your backup plan, which is usually treatment. The earlier a slip or relapse is caught, the better, so your child can get back on the wagon.

To Be or Not to Be Dry

Many parents ask this question: "How do we manage our home and personal life when it comes to substances when our kid has serious substance issues?"

If your child has struggled with a substance addiction, it's an issue the entire family needs to address from a few different perspectives. First, take an honest look at your own substance use; is it out of control? Some parents do smoke a lot of pot, drink too much, or abuse prescription medication. This is the time to be clear with yourself if you have a problem, as your child will be coming home with greater awareness. He will want to see what you're doing to heal, and what you're doing or not doing will either give him incentive to work harder or justification not to. If you have a substance use issue, please seek help and stop the maladaptive use before your child comes home. Then continue getting help after he returns; if not for yourself, then for your child.

If you are a moderate partaker of substances, you should also consider how and if you will use them in front of your child. It's not what you say but how you live that speaks to your child the most. The modeling of healthy behavior when it comes to substance use is extremely important to a child trying to stay sober. If you do enjoy the occasional beer with the ballgame or a glass of champagne on the holiday, you might still have angst about this with your child. Consult with his treatment counselor and create a dialogue with your child on this issue. I've worked with many parents who, as an act of solidarity with their child, chose to go sober. This might or might not work for you. There's no rule of thumb here; it's unique to your family culture.

It's also worth deciding how readily available substances will be in your home. I can direct you down the safest route, gleaned from my years of working with families, and that is to have no substances, including alcohol, in your home and to lock up any necessary prescription medications. This prevents impulsive substance slips from occurring easily under your roof. But not all parents agree with this approach. They don't want to send their child the message that he has drastically changed their lifestyle. You might choose to drink a beer during the football game or keep your nightly ritual of a glass of wine. If this is your choice, monitor the amount of alcohol in your home. Check levels on bottles and count beers. It takes some extra effort, but don't let a few cans of beer jeopardize all that money spent on treatment.

Creating Sobriety Boundaries

Because addiction causes so much devastation, here is an example of how you might create rules around a dependency (in this example, alcohol addiction), informed by the Relapse Prevention Plan:

Issue: Alcohol addiction.

Vision: We see our daughter as a healthy, functioning, and honest individual. We see her unencumbered by dependency on drugs, alcohol, or tobacco.

Value: We believe that our minds, bodies, and lives are not to be wasted.

Expectation: We expect our daughter to live a rewarding life without dependency on drugs or alcohol.

Rule: Because we love you and want you to get the most out of your bright and positive future, we do not want you to drink. No alcohol is allowed in our house. We will randomly breathalyse you and request that you attend AA twice a week. You will do this for three months upon your return, and then we will reassess. Red-light friends include Jessica, Billy, and Jon, and Lookout Point is off-limits.

Consequence: If you relapse, we will discuss this as a family and determine the core issue or what the triggers were. We'll decide then if you should resume addiction counseling. We'll

| also determine at the time if any other consequences
| are needed.

If addiction is affecting your family, the approach to take is one of proactivity. Engage this process by educating yourself and learning how to cope with addiction. You'll then be better equipped to support your child and other family members. Families who don't learn about the disease or seek outside help might find themselves in vicious and tormenting cycles that can tear the family apart.

Putting in some research hours will pay off greatly. A resource I often refer clients to is *www.addictiondoctor.com*, where books and DVDs based on the work of Dr. Kevin McCauley are available. Dr. McCauley does an excellent job of explaining the whys of addiction. Accepting the fact that addiction is a medical illness, like cancer or diabetes, might give you greater understanding with which to address this issue. Attend Al-Anon or Nar-Anon meetings. Discuss the situation with your therapist.

> Do what you can as a loving and loyal parent, but please be cognizant that the person with the addiction is ultimately responsible for his or her own health.

Two books I recommend to parents are *Terry: My Daughter's Life-and-Death Struggle with Alcoholism* by George McGovern and *Lost, Found, and Forgiven: How One Mother Prevailed Against Teenage Rage and Brought Her Daughter Home Again* by Lisa Marie Jackson. Through the eyes of these parents you can grow to further understand the reality of having a child with addiction. Also *Codependent No More: How to Stop Controlling Others and Start Caring for Yourself* and *Beyond Codependency: And Getting Better All the Time*, both by Melody Beattie, are helpful for people close to someone with an addiction.

Lastly, and I know I sound like a broken record, always hold your child who struggles with addiction accountable to his Relapse Prevention Plan and the Home Agreement. Fight hard for your child, as addiction can render him unable to fight hard for himself. And at the same time, do not become codependent and instill more pain and suffering into your life. Do what you can as a loving and loyal parent, but please be cognizant that the person with the addiction is ultimately responsible for his or her own health.

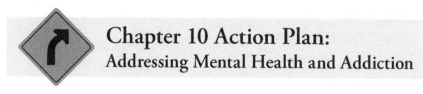

Chapter 10 Action Plan:
Addressing Mental Health and Addiction

(To download blank worksheets, visit www.TheRoadHomeBook.com/downloads.)

#1. Identifying Issues

What mental health or addiction issues pertain to your child? What led to treatment? For example:

Cutting, bipolar, borderline personality disorder, and bulimia..

#2. Visions, Values and Expectations

If you haven't already, fill in the following for the issues you've listed above. I've provided an example.

Issue	Vision	Value	Expectation
Bulimia	We see our child healthy and not hurting herself.	We believe in taking care of and not hurting ourselves.	We expect you to come home and to manage your bulimia. We are here to help you. We want you to openly communicate with us and make sure you have the support in place that you need.

Issue	Vision	Value	Expectation

#3. Relapse Prevention Plan (RPP)

If addiction is your child's issue, schedule a time to talk to your child's treatment therapist. Ask for advice on what supports your son will need when he returns. Ask to see your son's Relapse Prevention Plan (RPP). In the unlikely event that one has not been made, ask the therapist to assist your child in creating one. For those unfamiliar with a Relapse Prevention Plan, here is a sample of the type I most often come across.

Josh's Relapse Prevention Plan

Date: June 6, 2014

Commitment: One Year of Sobriety

Why I Used and Why I Stopped
I used drugs and alcohol because I was very stressed with school. My motto was "I work hard, therefore I play hard." This got old as my substance abuse worsened. I got tired of partying, but couldn't stop. I was out of control until wilderness therapy stopped the chaos. Down deep I don't want to slip or relapse and am very worried that I will.

Road to Relapse
For me it's all about who I hang out with. If I'm around my friends that party, it's just a matter of time. I have learned that I'm not stronger than my environment. I have to be careful of people, places, and events that trigger my urge to use. Concerts and school parties were my downfall every time, and I need to avoid these for now. If I try to start telling myself or others that I can attend these events or hang out with my old party friends, I am on the road to destruction. I will need help from my healthy peers and my parents to keep me honest. I promise to be open to their input.

Josh's Relapse Prevention Plan   *1*

Warning Signs

If I start to avoid my healthy friends or family, this is a serious red flag that I am starting to consider using. Also, if I get easily defensive this means I'm stressed. If I start getting dishonest, I'll know that I am too overwhelmed and am looking for excuses to relapse. If school starts to be more than I can handle, I need to make sure I'm not taking on too much, and need to remember that a 3.0 is better if it means I'm sober, instead of a 4.0 and I relapse. I could be really screwed if I don't see that I'm stressed!

To Prevent Relapse

I am committed to meeting my goals in life, and this means maintaining my motivation to not self-destruct by abusing alcohol and drugs. I will not make any of my goals if I am addicted to anything. I need to maintain balance and moderation to truly enjoy my life and those I love. In order to do this, I need to maintain my body, spirit, and relationships. This means surfing three times a week, eating mostly organic, and lifting weights for fun. I will also be attending weekly mass with my parents and journaling my soul work and dreams daily. I will only hang out with friends that have my back. I will also need to protect myself from addiction by attending the appropriate supports. This means seeing my therapist weekly and attending two 12-step meetings a week for the next 12 months. If necessary, I'll increase both therapy and 12- steps if I'm especially stressed. I will also volunteer once per month at school tutoring, as I need to give back to others.

The New Me

I have worked incredibly hard at my recovery, and my parents have sacrificed a lot to save my life. I owe the world and myself my best giving of my time and talents. This is my life and I need to make the most of it. Life is to enjoy and I need to do the inner soul work and live from that place. I need to stay grounded in life and connected to Mother Earth, God, my loved ones, and most importantly myself. I am resolved to make this plan work!

Plan B

If the struggle to stay sober is too strong for me, I will be honest with my loved ones and myself. I always feel better when I'm honest

Josh's Relapse Prevention Plan   2

with myself and my parents, because it takes a weight off my mind. I'm human, and it's okay to not be perfect. If I fall off the wagon, I will receive whatever help I need, including going back to wilderness. I'm also open to going to a long-term program that supports me finishing high school and starting college in a sober environment. It's okay to need a plan B and use it, though I have faith that I won't need it.

Josh Doe

Signed: Josh Doe

Josh's Relapse Prevention Plan   3

#4. Backup Plans

Once you have a better understanding of your child's clinical issues and RPP, if applicable, determine what your backup plans might be and add them on the following pages. An example of this is provided here.

Issue	Rule	Consequence	Backup Plan
Bulimia	You will continue to see your therapist and we will all use TLC to keep this issue out in the open.	If you relapse, we will discuss alternative support with your therapist. We will use TLC to get to the why.	If you continue to relapse, we will look into additional in-patient therapy.

Issue	Rule	Consequence	Backup Plan

Issue	Rule	Consequence	Backup Plan

Writing the Home Agreement

D rum roll, please! This is what you've been working so hard toward—the culmination of reviving visions and dreams; searching for and clarifying family values; discussions with your partner, your child, and the treatment team about expectations and more; and all that therapy. You've learned how to write rules and consequences. You've looked at issues of concern to your family including mental health and addiction. Now it's time to put everything together. This is where you actually get to create your Home Agreement, the impetus for this book, and the map that will help guide your child back home and into an eventual life as a mature young adult.

Treatment programs have different templates and names for the Home Agreement, such as home contract, behavior contract, and transitional contract, to name a few. The goal of all is the same: to create

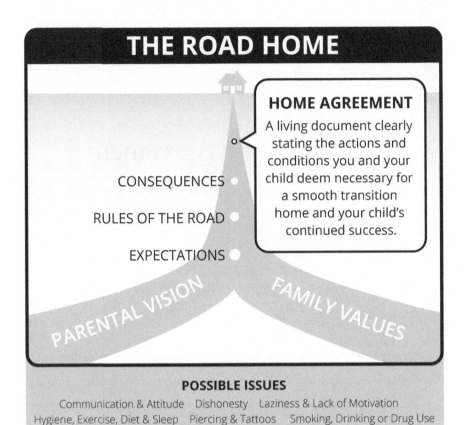

a living document that states clearly the actions and conditions you and your child deem necessary for a smooth transition home and your child's continued success.

This document is a baton pass from the treatment-program team to the parents, with the collaboration of the child. It is the result of open dialogue between the treatment team, you, and your child, and it defines the structure of the therapeutic goals to be maintained at home. If the program your child is in does not pass the baton, then it is up to you to start the race. Use this book to create a Home Agreement with your child's input, and present it and put it in use ASAP when your child returns. The Home Agreement outlines the practical expectations regarding everyday life, from chores to boundaries. It also implies choice, and explicitly puts the responsibility of maturation onto your child's shoulders and into his heart.

I believe the Home Agreement can be a comprehensive family-driven document that honors the spirit of your family as well as your child's endeavors. It can let all involved know who your child is, but also who you are, as people and as parents. The Home Agreement can be the place for previously unsaid words that establish your family culture, stating them boldly and concisely for all to understand and honor. It delineates what is hoped for and expected of you and your child, so the entire family can continue to grow from the therapeutic process.

When I began to work with kids returning from treatment, I clearly saw parents' frustration and confusion. My role quickly included being the reminder and clarifier of parental visions and values. When parents search their souls and have the courage to stand firm for what they find there, the child has the best chance of success. True, there's no guarantee that your child will succeed with any home

> When parents search their souls and have the courage to stand firm for what they find there, the child has the best chance of success.

contract in place, but the concise and thorough process outlined here for creating the Home Agreement will give him his best shot.

The Home Agreement is not just a contract. It represents hours and hours of sweat and tears, because it takes lots of taxing work to create something so simple, valuable, and effective. Once complete, this soul-searching process offers relief and peace. The Home Agreement represents one more effort of the countless efforts you've already invested, to express love for your child.

By answering such questions in this book as "What do I value and what do I hope for?" you've already completed much of the work needed to create an effective Home Agreement. You might have realized, while reading these pages and working through the chapter Action Steps, that there are some dreams and goals your family has achieved and others you have not. This can be sobering and sometimes saddening. With awareness and consciousness, though, comes hope and renewed strength to strive on and achieve your dreams.

There's something magical about committing dreams and goals to paper. It seems to create a momentum to help us finish what we've started. Holding the Agreement in your hands somehow gives your effort validity. Granted, the first draft of your Home Agreement won't be perfect, and maybe not even the final draft will be. Perfect doesn't exist. Just follow your heart and your beliefs, and be informed by your child and her treatment team, and you'll have a workable tool you can all live with. It's not in stone; it's on paper. The Home Agreement can be modified as your child settles into life and you see what is and isn't working.

Teamwork

It's likely that, while you're working on the Home Agreement, your child and her treatment therapist will be working on their version of a home contract. It's up to you to voice your interest in being part of the process to your child's therapist. Longer-term programs are accustomed to taking the lead and doing the bulk of the origination.

So that the resulting document will be useable and practical for you and your child, drive the creation of this document as much as necessary for you to have some owner-ship in the result. If you're not invested in the Home Agreement, don't expect your child to be. That being said, co-ordination and collaboration with your child and his treatment counselor is essential. Your child needs to be part of the process to own his part. If he takes responsibility for giving feedback and offering solutions to inevitable dilemmas, he will be more apt to follow the agreement upon his return home. Yes, I recommend that you be the foundation and author of the Home Agreement, but your child needs to contribute to the shaping of it. He will have an opinion! Consequences and rules will rub him wrong in places and you can listen to his suggestions and work things out. Don't back down from non-negotiable issues such as core values of sobriety or honesty, but be open to modifying less important rules and consequences. If you take his input, he will feel heard. Besides, this

> If you're not invested in the Home Agreement, don't expect your child to be.

creates more of an opportunity to know what your child's real buttons are and what issues are less important. It might surprise you to know that he is fine with drug testing but hates the curfew. Listen and work with your child. If he has no input and feels lorded over, the Home Agreement will probably be ineffective.

Be persistent. To sort through the range of issues in the Home Agreement, several telephone conference calls should be scheduled. Emailing drafts back and forth can also be helpful. Your child's thoughts and considerations should be heard as well as his counselor's, and if there's a Relapse Prevention Plan attach it to the Home Agreement. Just make sure that you drive the heart and soul of the process and "own" what is put on paper.

The Family Part of the Home Agreement

Creating the Home Agreement is such an exhausting labor of love that parents often wish to share the "gospel" with all their children and at times to have the same rules apply to all the children in the family. But this document is solely for the sake of the continued health of your child who needed treatment. The Agreement is a private document to be worked out and shared with the child returning from treatment, his counselor, and you, the parents. Other siblings privy to the new rules and expectations of the entire document might find the Home Agreement dumbfounding and could feel resentful, even resistant. They'll balk at the idea of having the same tight rules as their post-treatment sibling. And they're right. They don't need the same support structure as your prodigal child. Share your values and expectations with your other children. Share enough that they too can be supportive of their returning sibling and of what you are doing. Some transparency is healthy for the family, but some of what is in the Home Agreement could embarrass your returning child if it is freely known, so be judicious about what you share.

Consider holding a family meeting before your child comes home. Explain what a Home Agreement is, and why you're putting it in place for the returning brother or sister. Listen to your family's thoughts concerning the sibling coming home, but don't veer away from your core beliefs. Your newly minted Home Agreement is based on your values, and these can be openly shared with all your kids. You might even want to roll out a second, more general, Home Agreement for the entire family. In essence, get the other kids on board so they can understand how to support their returning sib.

The Mechanics

As you've probably noticed, writing out expectations, rules, and consequences for issues pertinent to your child can use a lot of ink, so brevity is wise in a Home Agreement. If your child's eyes glaze over when she's reading your Agreement because there's too much content, you'll lose her. The objective is to hand your kid a two-to-four-page document with plenty of white space. It should be simple and concise, so your child understands exactly what's expected of her and buys into it, and so it's easy for you to implement.

To make the Home Agreement user-friendly, the elements—vision, values, expectations, issues, rules, and consequences—should be condensed into Integrated Statements. Integrated statements join family beliefs and rules into sequential, logical declarations that embody expectations, consequences, and the "why" in one fell swoop.

Constructed of three or four sentences, each Integrated Statement sounds as though the parent is talking to the child. However, some issues need to be very thoroughly spelled out, so do not stop short of saying what you need to say. The tone is direct, unflinching, to the point, and yet loving. No diatribes wanted. The strongest Integrated Statements stay away from the "Thou shalt not" format and are positive and affirming of the child's progress.

An effective Integrated Statement has all the above-listed characteristics and also has impact and teeth, as this is your truth made transparent. Instead of stern, antiseptic lists of rules in the manner of the usual behavioral contracts, kids more readily accept Integrated Statements that are nonthreatening, conversational, and backed by values.

Crafting an Integrated Statement

I recommend combining the vision and value in the first sentence or clause, the expectation and respective Rules of the Road in the second, and a consequence, if one is desired, to conclude. The fewer consequences the better, and this brevity can be accomplished by giving similar issues the same summarizing consequence. This keeps it simple, takes less ink, and minimizes the punitive nature that a "contract" can convey.

Here's an example of an Integrated Statement distilled down from the work done on the issue of honesty.

Issue: Honesty.

Vision: We see our children as honest individuals, living a life of integrity.

Value: Honesty in all aspects of life is something we value greatly, as individuals and as a family.

Expectation: In our family, honesty and integrity are very important, so lying, cheating, stealing, or illegal activities are not what we do.

Rule: Lying and stealing have happened in the past. We're clear that these are not acceptable or tolerated in our household.

Consequence: If you lie, cheat, steal, or engage in dishonest or illegal actions, you'll lose a commensurate privilege like use of the phone, computer, or car.

Integrated Statement for inclusion in the Home Agreement: We are honest people who embrace integrity in all that we do. Lying, stealing, and any other form of dishonesty or illegal activity is a grave violation of our family code. If any form of deception occurs, we'll have a family meeting using "I feel" statements and you will lose all car, phone, and Internet privileges for at least one week.

An Integrated Statement for Education might be written like this: *We believe education beyond high school ensures a fulfilling life that opens*

doors to this wonderful world, so we will help you with the college application process and support you financially in college to the extent we can
afford to do so. Besides good conduct at school, we know you're capable of
a "B" average or better, so if you drop below a "B" average we will not pay
for cell phone or the Internet until your next academic review shows a "B"
average or better.

For the Driving and Car Ownership of a 16-year-old, you might
choose to write this Integrated Statement: *Becoming a responsible, safe
driver who shares in the financial cost of driving is part of becoming an
adult. You will need to take a safety class prior to your permit, drive for six
months with us before earning your license, and share in half of all costs of
the car, including the car itself, gas, and insurance. If you abuse the driving
privilege, as evidenced by poor maintenance or irresponsible use of the car
such as speeding, you'll lose the driving privilege for at least one month.*

In the following Integrated Statement concerning chores, notice
that the family chose not to include a consequence. It works, because it
assumes that chores are "just what we do in this family."

Household Upkeep and Chores: *You are expected to keep your room
and clothing clean. These actions are what is expected of you in life. Clean
means all clothes put away, sheets clean, bed made, vacuuming and dust-
ing complete, and the bathroom sink, toilet, floor, and shower clean. You
and your sister will divide the following chores equally to keep the house
running: taking out trash, loading and unloading the dishwasher, and
cooking dinner one night a week each.*

Integrated Statements are powerful. They put the onus squarely on your child's shoulders. The expectations are there in black and white—no wiggle room.

It takes time to cut and edit important information, but crafting good Integrated Statements is well worth it. If this book hadn't been edited, you'd fall asleep fast, and the same is true of your Home Agreement. If you edit and really hone in on what you want to say and the guidelines that you want to lay down, your child will read your Home Agreement with interest (even if that isn't openly expressed). I'm not saying she'll agree to it all on the first pass, but she'll know that things have changed back at home. So mine those worksheets, keep the gold, and toss whatever muddies the water.

When you have Integrated Statements for the issues key to your child and family, set them aside for a day or two and then look at them again. Pay attention to the tone of the communication. Do you come across with love and understanding? Do you sound preachy? Do you seem a bit too much like a dictator? Words are powerful, especially those that carry values and expectations. Take the time to hone your tone.

For example, you could write a preachy and judgmental Integrated Statement like this: *You must take care of both your mind and body to be happy. In the past your eating disorder has caused you to jeopardize your life, and we won't let that happen again. If we find you slipping into the eat-and-purge cycle you had before, we will immediately put you back in treatment.*

Or it could sound like this, which will most likely be met with little resistance: *We value health, both in mind and body, and believe it is one avenue to a fulfilling life. We wish for you to live a life full of possibility, so we want to help you stay healthy. Please talk to us regularly about your feelings around food, and if you slip, we'll be here to back you up with additional support.*

See the difference? The two statements are saying the same thing, but in two different tones. Which one would you react to better? The same is true for your kid. Don't be afraid to add a few more sentences if those added words soften the blow, are inspirational, and make the message more acceptable to your child.

The Home Agreement Format

Although I'm going to provide a basic Home Agreement template, be clear that it is only that: a template, a guideline, and an example. It's a starting place for you; feel free to adapt it to what feels natural. Use the examples of Home Agreements and a College Agreement at the end of this chapter to help you determine how you want your own Home Agreement to look and communicate.

The Home Agreement that seems to work best for my clients is divided into the following parts:

- **The Family Mission Statement** - This could also be called your goal or "what we are about." This is where you clearly state for your child your family culture and basic belief system.

- **The Communication Style** - Here is where you lay out what you consider to be respectful communication in your family. Transparent and Loving Communication (TLC) is the goal and a topic worthy of some considerable spelling out in your Home Agreement. What habits need to be bypassed? What new communication techniques are to be used?

- **Expectations** - You can also use the term Rules or Guidelines. Within this section lies the meat, the stuff your child is going to be looking for. Here is where you clearly state what day-to-day-life is going to be like and, if expectations (rules) are not met, what consequences will come into play. This is where you put your Integrated Statements dedicated to specific issues. As you'll see in the provided examples of Home Agreements, some families choose to put more than one Integrated Statement into an issue category. It all depends on what works for you. Remember, brevity, clarity and honesty are your best friends when writing the Home Agreement.

- **Parent Commitment** - This is often the section your child likes to see, where you let him or her know what you're willing to do to ensure that the Home Agreement works. This might include continuing therapy, using new communication techniques, and what additional support you intend to provide. The idea is to let your child know how invested you are in this process.

- **The "If Things Don't Work Out" Clause** - This section provides a space for parents to clearly state what can be expected if the child can't live up to the Home Agreement and regression occurs. It's the place to articulate your backup plan. It should include a progression of Action Steps to be taken, such as additional and tougher consequences, outpatient programs, and additional therapy and counseling.

Before your daughter or son comes home, please have a serious dialogue with the treatment therapist or educational consultant about a backup plan if things don't go well. Know where you can reach out for fresh opinions and whom you can lean on and trust in the tribe or village you've created. Which friends, family members, and professionals will you use as a sounding board? Have backup plans, and backup professionals to call, when a scenario you could not have imagined pops up.

- **Attach the Relapse Prevention Plan** - If your child has struggled with addiction, she will very likely have created in treatment a Relapse Prevention Plan. Reference the information in the RPP to help you write the Home Agreement, but attach this document, which can be quite hefty, to the back of the Agreement and have it stand alone.

- **Title, Date, and Signatures** - Finally, for clarity, title your Home Agreement, date it, and provide a place for signatures. This is your family document, so you can give it any title that works for you. Possibilities include: Home Understanding, Rules and Expectations, Home Creed, Family Pledge, Christopher's Contract, or any mixture of the above. Again, the title and tone should reflect who you are as a family. The following example will give you a clearer idea of what the Home Agreement and all its parts might look like.

The Johnson Home Agreement

Date: July 20, 2014

Family Mission: Our family is a support system, built on love, respect, and trust, in which we can all grow to our full potential. The purpose of this agreement is to help you continue your positive growth into a fulfilled and sober young adult and a contributing member of our family.

Communication: We wish to have transparent, loving, respectful communication in our house, built on honesty, so we all feel safe. We should respect one another's viewpoints and emotions, and use the communication skills we have all learned to allow for de-escalation, transparency, and recognition. Dialogue over issues is welcome, but Mom and Dad are the ultimate decision makers for what occurs in the household. Because communication is important, we want to have family meals together in the evening as often as possible. If this doesn't give sufficient time to talk about what is going on in life, we'll set up a regular weekly meeting time.

Expectations: The purpose for expectations is to ensure that your transition home is successful. We truly see the change in you, and our trust has gone up dramatically. At the same time, coming home can be a triggering event in itself, so we will be putting expectations and limits in place to help all of us with this transition.

Sobriety and Overall Health: We value good health, so we want you to stay sober and not use tobacco. We expect you to choose friends who are sober and not triggers, to follow your RPP (to be attached), and to set up a support system for home and for college.

The Johnson Home Agreement   *1*

As a starting point, we suggest that while you are home you meet with your therapist weekly and attend AA weekly, and we will randomly drug test you. We are open to adjusting this as time moves on and you feel you need less or more support.

We know you've done a lot of work around cutting. Your RPP clearly lays out stressors and triggers. Your therapist will help you here greatly, but know that we are also here to support you 100 percent. We have no reason to think you will be cutting again, but if red flags come up—long sleeves and no shorts, disengaging from the family, long hours in the bedroom, etc., we reserve the right to invade your privacy to ensure that you're not cutting.

You have expressed that yoga "saved" you. This is awesome. We want you to continue practicing your yoga three days a week, and we will pay for the class.

Curfew: 10 P.M. initially. Once we have all settled in, and you turn 18, this might be adjusted to a later time. As a courtesy to us, we would like to know when you're leaving the house and when you expect to return. Also, please inform us if your plans change. If this is an area that becomes problematic, we will discuss it fully but a consequence will be put in place.

Friends: We hope you choose healthy friends whom you respect and who respect you. Let us know when you're going out, and please know that dates and friends are always welcome at our house when we are home. At no time should you be alone in the house with a member of the opposite sex. Bedrooms are off-limits. Boys have been a big issue in the past. We truly hope you will choose boyfriends who respect you and value who you are. If you violate any of these guidelines, you'll be grounded for at least two weeks.

Technology: We like technology, but it can be detrimental to physical and spiritual health when it's abused or used for unethical purposes. We hope that you will make balanced use of technology and maintain healthy habits, e.g., shut off computers well before bedtime. The same rules apply to TV, streaming, and downloading.

Computer: The computer is a tool that we all use extensively in our household. With regard to computer usage, we will not pay for gaming, unapproved purchases, etc. We should be friended on your social media sites. No X-rated material or unhealthy sites, chats, etc., are allowed. If this privilege is abused, you'll lose the computer for one month.

Phone: Phones are not to be brought to the table during meals and need to be shut off at bedtime. We will pay for your phone as long as the rules are followed and you don't go over limits. Eventually you'll be responsible for paying for your own phone and service.

Work: We believe that developing a work ethic and earning money is important for all people if they are to develop into responsible adults. Working during the summer is expected, and working part-time during the school year will also be necessary if you want additional spending money. We will cover your food, haircuts, toiletries, basic clothing, and health club dues, but you are responsible for "fun" money to use for entertainment, outings with friends, movies, CDs, iTunes, concerts, etc. We will pay for basic clothing (as determined by us) and sports gear and clothing. You will pay for extra items such as jewelry, cosmetics, and special clothing.

Household upkeep and chores: Because you're 17, chores are expected of you as a member of the family. They include keeping your room and clothing clean, vacuuming the upstairs each Saturday, washing the dishes every other night, and helping Mom maintain the garden.

Car: When it comes to driving, we are most interested in your being safe and taking responsibility for others when you get behind the wheel. You must take a certified Driver's Ed course and a driver's practical course (we will pay for these) and pay for your license. If you want use of one of our cars, you must get permission. If you wish to have a car of your own, you will be responsible for paying for half of it. (We must approve for safety any car purchased.) You will pay for gas.

As long as you are a safe driver and get the good student insurance rate, we will pay for your vehicle's insurance and maintenance. Driving under the influence will result in the loss of your driving privilege.

Education: Because education is important to our family, we expect you to put your full effort into schoolwork and studying for the SAT or ACT in preparation for college. You have shown you can maintain a 3.5 GPA or above. If you do, we will support you wholeheartedly and invest in your college education, as well as travel with you to see college campuses.

Parent Commitment: Our commitment to you is to continue working on our communication skills and our relationship. Mom will stop yelling, and Dad will be more present. We will also keep a dry house, free of alcohol, to support you in your sobriety.

If Things Don't Work Out: As long as you are honest, respectful, hardworking, and open with us, we will support you 100 percent. If honesty, respect, and transparency are abandoned, then consequences will be put into effect. These will include restrictive consequences such as loss of the car and supportive consequences too. If sobriety and/or cutting become issues, we will watch for triggers, slips, and relapse. We will support you emotionally and financially to recover. We want you to have resources to fall back on. We will request even more professional help outside of the home, if it becomes too difficult for us to manage together, which may include residential treatment.

In signing this document, all parties agree to uphold their part of the bargain, even if parts of the agreement have been negotiated and compromises have been made.

Agreed Upon

_____ Date_____
_____ Date_____
_____ Date_____

The Johnson Home Agreement   4

Presentation

Once you've drafted your first version of the Home Agreement, it's again time to collaborate with your child's therapist. Present your work. You might find the treatment therapist pleasantly surprised by your proactivity and eager to weigh in on many points. Listen and adapt. This person knows intimate details of what makes your child tick, and some nuances that might be new to you, so please take her suggestions to heart. Ask your therapist to hold off on presenting your first draft of the Home Agreement to your child. Go back to your desk, and when you have a second draft that takes into account feedback from the therapist, it's time to formally present the Home Agreement to your child.

Initially, this collaborative experience might be unsettling to your child because it means you've been doing your work alongside him. He might feel suspicious and put on the spot, because his therapeutic process has just become about the family and not just about him.

> When your child first reads the Home Agreement you've created he might feel scared beyond belief, because he now realizes he's going to be held accountable at *home*.

When your child first reads the Home Agreement you've created he might feel scared beyond belief, because he now realizes he's going to be held accountable *at home*. This fear might come out in the form of anger. Expect him to fight you on some issues. Expect him to be angry, grumpy, and snotty. These first-response emotions will dissipate as he feels more settled and safe and realizes that, although the onus is on him to tow the line, you are now in charge and have his well-being held firmly in hand.

It might take a few letters, emails, or phone conversations before you can get down to the nitty-gritty and enter into a full dialogue about the Home Agreement. This is a time when the family gets to be practical about what life is truly going to be like. This will lower your anxiety as well as your child's. It will be time to roll up your sleeves, use TLC, and collaboratively get the job done.

Your child will usually struggle with, and want to discuss, one or two issues and often some specific consequences. This is good, as it means he's read the Agreement and has his own thoughts. If your child raises no objections to the Home Agreement, this might be a red flag that either he hasn't read the document thoroughly or he's not taking it seriously. Most kids just want out of treatment, and signing a "contract" is the last hoop they need to jump through to land back in their own home. So you actually want to have some tension about what is written in the Home Agreement, as this means your kid is digesting the future.

When your child brings up these issues, it will be a perfect time to practice TLC. Having your child's therapist in on a call can help you and your son or daughter use healthy communication skills. Approach this dialogue with a willingness to negotiate, as long as the result doesn't go against your vision or values. For example if you hear: "Mom and Dad, I think I should be able to have an extra hour of gaming on

Saturdays." You could respond to this with a "Fine." However, the response to "Mom and Dad, I still want to smoke a little weed" might be "No way."

There may be a few heated discussions about consequences, but this is mainly due to the fact that your "hard line" comes as a surprise to your child. He might have been hoping you were not going to be so attentive. Kids don't want to believe that you're going to be on the ball when they return. You can't blame them, really, as they've been in the spotlight for their whole time in treatment.

> Approach this dialogue with a willingness to negotiate, as long as the result doesn't go against your vision or values.

When you're negotiating, it might help you to see that, in the grand scheme of things, the conversation is not really about gaming or pot smoking or any other issue of debate. The conversation is about your child using his voice, exercising some power, and desiring the impending freedom outside of treatment.

Once you have had enough TLC to agree on the content and spirit of the Home Agreement, you and your child should sign and date the final draft. This "ceremony" often takes place on the day your child graduates or is released from his program.

The Home Agreement Used to Get Home

Your child might say yes to many of the rules in the Home Agreement only to struggle with them when he gets home. He said yes just to exit the treatment facility and get back into his own comfortable bed. Months or just weeks later, this can make the road bumpy as your child challenges your boundaries and admits he only agreed to rules and consequences to get home. In my experience, this happens 50 percent of the time if not more. The issues that your child gave in on, in order to appease you, will become the power-struggle issues. What you can do is hold firm on the bumpy ride. Let him push and pull. Let him run into the boundaries.

A benefit of the Home Agreement as outlined in this book is that a teen or young adult will find it hard to challenge core issues embedded within the family culture. Kids sense this resolve, this integrity. They feel the strength of the firm boundaries that result from belief.

Once your child is home, have weekly or monthly check-ins to ensure that boundaries are holding firm and your authority is being respected, as it is quite natural for adolescents and young adults to challenge you. Pull out the Home Agreement and assess progress. In other words, open up the can of worms. Sometimes, out of fear of sacrificing warm feelings and creating a potential for regression, parents don't adhere to what is written. Also, parents who are still ambivalent about the process and unsure of its value will stall when the effort to enforce the Agreement becomes more than they can handle. If you can't stand behind your Home Agreement, why should your child follow it? So bring it out of the drawer, sit down as a family, and see

> If you can't stand behind your Home Agreement why should your child follow it?

how you're doing. The more you keep the Home Agreement alive, the more you protect the work you and your child have done since the very beginning of treatment.

Some families post the Agreement on the fridge or on a bulletin board in the child's room. Its placement doesn't really matter. What matters is how well you keep it alive in minds, hearts, and daily accountability.

A quick side note here. I have noticed that parents often treat the Home Agreement as the fall guy. They say something like, "The contract says," or "The Agreement states that . . . " This is not always a bad thing, as it does reinforce the work and importance of your well-thought-out living document. However, the child can start targeting the Agreement as something to resent or despise. I recommend that you state that it's *you* deliberating, evaluating, and doling out the consequence, and not the piece of paper in your hands. The Agreement is a symbol of your soul work around parenting your child. You are the parent, and that's where the buck stops. So instead of deferring to The Home Agreement, refer to yourself. For example, "We told you we were not going to allow that behavior." "I'm not okay with this action as I stated in the Agreement." "We are all about healthy bodies, which means no more loafing around and video gaming all day long."

Take the hit—be the heavy, and your child will respect you more. If the Home Agreement gets too removed from you by being referred to as something other than you, then it actually loses its power. The Home Agreement should be who you are, not something that has to be reviewed daily or worried about. If it truly is an extension of you, this will be easy to enforce. So please put the soul searching and painstakingly developed consequences in the Agreement now, so you don't have to make it up on the fly when your child messes up. Save yourself the panic of *What to do? What to do?* As long as you follow through, life at home can be peaceful and enjoyable once again.

> The Home Agreement is created as much for the parents as it is for the child.

Here's a secret I share with my parent clients about a month after their child returns home: The Home Agreement is created as much for the parents as it is for the child. Parents need to know—just as much, if not more—what the game plan is. The Home Agreement creates boundaries for you so you can remain sane and effective and maybe even get a little sleep at night.

Adaptation

As your child returns and you settle into your new life together, you both might see what issues should have been put in the Agreement or what consequences were inadequate or overbearing. Don't hesitate to modify the Agreement if something isn't working, but do not back down on what you know is right as a result of pressure from your child. This is a delicate dance, listening and adapting to the "new," more mature child before you and doing what you feel you need to do as a confident parent. Transparent and loving communication is what you use to find the compromise, if one is indeed necessary.

If you hold her accountable, she will most likely settle into a healthy pattern. After about six months, give the Home Agreement a formal review. If your daughter has continued to make her journey home and out into the world a healthy one, you might indeed want to reward her with more freedoms and privileges.

If, on the contrary, she has had trouble towing the line, enlist the actions you put in the "If Things Don't Work Out" clause of the Home Agreement. You might learn that your child needs more structure, and choose to offer professional help. Even when you're doing all you can to support your child's success, it's still ultimately up to her. There are no guarantees, whether your child went to treatment or not, that it will all work out. But know this: you have read hundreds of pages, sorted your priorities, and edited your many heartfelt thoughts into a succinct plan for your child, and in fact your entire family. You've done a lot! You're a good parent.

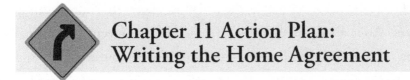

Chapter 11 Action Plan: Writing the Home Agreement

(To download blank worksheets, visit www.TheRoadHomeBook.com/downloads.)

#1. Integrated Statements

Refer to the issues you've been addressing in Chapters Seven through Ten. Write Integrated Statements for those issues most important to include in your Home Agreement. Keep in mind your child as of today, but let the past inform you. For guidance, refer to your child's Relapse Prevention Plan or her version of a contract if there are any. Be sure to address triggers (more on these in Chapter 12).

Here is an example of an Integrated Statement written for the issues of sex and love:

Love and sex can make life either ugly or beautiful. Since you are now a young adult, you have freedoms, and yet we hope you will respect yourself and the person you love. Your boyfriend is always welcome in our home, but having sex is not allowed under our roof. If you break this rule, we will regretfully ask you to move out of the house.

Issue #1: _____

Integrated Statement:

_____

_____

Issue #2:_____

Integrated Statement:

_____

_____

_____

_____

_____

_____

Issue #3:_____

Integrated Statement:

_____

_____

_____

_____

_____

Issue #4:_____

Integrated Statement:

_____

_____

_____

_____

_____

_____

Issue #5: _____

Integrated Statement:

_____

_____

_____

_____

_____

_____

Issue #6: _____

Integrated Statement:

_____

_____

_____

_____

_____

_____

Issue #7: _____

Integrated Statement:

_____

_____

_____

_____

_____

_____

Issue #8:_____

Integrated Statement:

_____

_____

_____

_____

_____

_____

Issue #9:_____

Integrated Statement:

_____

_____

_____

_____

_____

Issue #10:_____

Integrated Statement:

_____

_____

_____

_____

_____

#2. Example Home Agreements

Here are two examples of Home Agreements, and one College Agreement. Please read through them so you can get a feel for what your Home Agreement will be like and what its overall tone might be.

Example 1:

The Garcia Family Understanding

Date: September 1, 2014

Family Statement

It's our hope that our family will always be close emotionally and that you'll live a fulfilling and meaningful life. We value being authentic individuals who have integrity, a strong work ethic, and a balanced life with times for travel, recreation, good friendships, and an effort to give back to our world and leave a lasting legacy. We hope you use and enjoy your sharp analytical mind and let it be a tool that serves you well. Now that you've succeeded in addressing your mental health concerns, we hope you stay healthy.

Communication

We have been so fortunate to have learned excellent communication skills in the last two years. During your residential treatment, we learned that active and reflective communication works wonderfully, and we are now so practiced at it that it is second nature. We will integrate healthy communication daily, and more particularly when tense moments arise, as we know we can solve most issues this way.

Guidelines

The rules explained here are based on our values and the spirit of our family. We hope they will give you the basic structure to succeed in life. The choice is yours every day to live within these parameters. There are privileges and freedoms gained for doing so, and consequences for not respecting the rules.

The Garcia Family Understanding 1

Health

You have worked hard at getting in shape while in treatment, and we have, too. We believe life is better when we're exercising regularly, eating a healthy diet 80 percent of the time, and staying sober. We expect you to go to the gym or play basketball three times a week, minimum. We also have gotten rid of junk food in the house, and expect it to stay that way.

We do not approve or agree with your rationale for using tobacco. You will need to smoke your cigarettes 100 yards away from the house, and pay for your smoking habit out of your own money.

Sobriety and Bipolarity

As you know, we're in support of you maintaining a healthy mind, as that is the key to an enjoyable life. A stable mood is a priority, and we will support your ongoing work with the psychiatrist in maintaining the best medication regimen. For addiction you will be seeing your therapist at least once per week and attending two 12-step meetings per week, and random drug screens will be required. We expect you to follow your Relapse Prevention Plan, which we support wholeheartedly.

The backup plan, if you start to really struggle with either sobriety or mood swings, is that we will do whatever it takes to keep you safe. We will follow through with professional support such as the ER and Inpatient, Outpatient, or Residential treatment until you are stable and able to function. We will rehire your therapeutic educational consultant to find the best support possible and ask that you work with her and us on this together. If you refuse treatment, we will ask you to leave our home until you're willing to receive help. If any drug dealing occurs, we will report you to the police, which will be a painful but necessary action.

Curfew

Until you are on your own in college, you have a curfew. Since you will be home for only another five months, we expect you to be able to pull this off. Sunday through Monday, we expect you to be home by 11 P.M., and Friday and Saturday at midnight. If you have a problem here, we will take the car for two weeks. We will also sit down with you and discuss why this rule is being broken.

Friends

As we have discussed, the friends you choose should support your sobriety and mental health. You have identified certain friends who are not to be trusted any more, and you have committed to not bringing dysfunctional people into your life. If we see any issue here, we will have a family dialogue and figure out what is going on and how to resolve the matter. Dating is encouraged.

Technology and Phone

We believe the computer and phone to be wonderful tools when used responsibly and with moderation, and they are a reality of today. As long as we don't find you staying up past midnight on technology or using it irresponsibly (no drug dealing, porn, etc.), we will not interfere. You are responsible for the costs of your new phone and the monthly charges. If we see any abuse of technology, we will sit down and discuss an appropriate, fair consequence, most likely limiting or denying use. If any drug-related activity occurs with technology, we will indefinitely rescind the privilege to use it.

Work, Money, and Chores

We value a strong work ethic, and this has been an issue in the past. We expect you to find a job in the first two months upon returning home. No smoke shop jobs allowed. You will be responsible for paying for your phone, gas, and activities with friends.

We also value responsible use of money by saving and budgeting. You will be expected to save two thousand dollars for college between now and this fall and to not spend all of the $3000 you currently have in your account. We expect you to keep your room and bathroom clean, and to help out with random chores when asked. If cleanliness becomes an issue, you will lose the car until a correction occurs.

Car

We believe the role of an adult is to handle a car responsibly and enjoy this privilege. You get the Mustang back, and will be able to have this car indefinitely as long as you maintain it. If you have any incident involving drugs or alcohol, you will lose the car. If you complete college, we will buy you a new car valued at twenty thousand dollars upon your graduation.

Education

Our family believes in college, and we are happy you plan on going. We know you are capable of going far, and support your goal of becoming a music teacher. We will pay for your tuition and give you a moderate allowance. You will need to apply for schools as soon as you return home. If you want help with this, please ask. We will develop a college agreement this summer to spell out the specifics, much like this agreement.

Parent Commitment

This treatment journey has shed light on issues within our entire family. Our commitment is to be the best parents we can be for you. We will remain firm and follow through. Mom will continue to go to weekly AA meetings and remain sober. Dad will go to Al-Anon weekly as well. We will always be here to talk out issues, fears, and successes.

If Things Don't Work Out

If you are not succeeding at home, it will most likely be due to struggles with sobriety or your mood issues. We will help you fight the good fight and get the right help. If we see red flags, we will hold a family meeting and up the support. If you refuse help, we will ask you to leave the house until you're willing to receive support. If any illegal activity occurs, we'll report it to the police and we will not pay for an attorney. This is our backup plan, but our sincere hope is that things will work out and we will not have to employ it.

Love you.

Rudy Garcia
Rudy Garcia

Adriana Garcia
Mom

Dad
Dad

The Garcia Family Understanding   4

Example 2:

The Kim Family Covenant

July 20, 2014

Family Spiritual Mission

Our family believes in being strong Christians. The purpose of our lives is to find our calling and gifts and give them back to the world in service to one another and for the greater glory of God. This agreement is to further Tommy's effort in finding his life's purpose and continuing the great gains he has made in wilderness and therapeutic boarding school.

Communication

Mom and Dad set the tone for the house and will model honest, healthy, nonviolent, respectful communication as we have learned in your programs. There needs to be respect for the hierarchy of the family, and the parents will guide emotional safety and discussion around serious and tense issues. We know it is okay to agree to disagree. We have proved that we can work through anything. We are a close family, and love wins the day.

Rules

We have worked hard as your parents to envision our hopes for you and we have looked hard at our heartfelt values. We expect you to live by our rules, and there will be rewards of freedom and more privileges if you do. If you choose by your own free will to disobey our wishes, we will with love and care deliver judicious consequences, as this is right and fair.

Spirituality

We hold faith and spiritual development above all. Thus we expect you to attend weekly church service with the family. We also expect you to rejoin the youth group band as you desired, and to attend summer Bible camp. If we see you falling away as you did in the past, we will sit down and have a family meeting to decide if it is appropriate for you to stay home or move on to a Christian boarding school.

The Kim Family Covenant   *1*

Health

We believe your body is sacred and that part of life is honoring the temple God gave you. We expect you to play your usual sports this year (baseball and basketball) and limit sodas to two per day. If this privilege is abused, we will have no more soft drinks in the house.

Curfew

This is the same as always. Everyone is to be home by 9 P.M. on school nights (Sunday through Thursday) and 11 P.M. on weekend nights (Friday and Saturday). If there are violations, the consequence will be no cell phone for two weeks and an earlier curfew of 8 P.M. for the next seven days, no questions.

Friends and Dating

We're excited that you're reconnecting with your old friends who are supportive and have good values. As you have agreed, your old gaming friends are on the red-light list, and we expect you to hang out only with green-light friends. If and when you bring new friends into your life, we expect you will have them over for dinner so we can meet them. All friend activities need to be approved by us.

Dating is allowed, and we will need to meet this young woman. We hope you find someone who supports you. You are expected to be a gentleman with her, and premarital sex is not permitted. When she visits us, you are allowed to be alone with her only in the family living spaces, meaning no bedroom or private areas.

Technology

Now that you have healed from your gaming addiction, we hope you will use technology responsibly. Since this has been a major reason why you went to treatment, we decided to empty our home of all video games, as gaming is not allowed. You may use the laptop and Internet for school, and will be expected to hand in the laptop at night, as computers aren't allowed in the bedroom. If your gaming addiction returns and is too much for our family to deal with, we will look for outside support.

Phone

If you choose, you may purchase a basic phone with a texting function (no smart phones due to your gaming addiction) with your own

The Kim Family Covenant   2

money, and pay the monthly fees. This phone needs to be turned in to us every night and no inappropriate phone use (sexting) is allowed. If this becomes an issue, we will prohibit the phone indefinitely.

Work

We're proud that you have a strong work ethic, as this is very important to us. You can return to your pizza delivery job, but we expect you to not work over 20 hours per week due to school being a priority. From your earnings, we expect you to tithe 10 percent to the church or ministry of your choice and save 40 percent for college. The remaining 50 percent is your spending money, to be used for gas, dates, and fun with friends.

Chores and Work Ethic

We need your participation in doing chores and helping with meals, as you are an important part of the running of our home. We expect you to help cook Thursday's dinner and do dishes every night with your brother. Your chores are the same: lawn mowing, snow shoveling, and cleaning the upstairs bathroom on Saturday. You are also expected to help Dad with special projects like landscaping or painting the house. We will pay you extra for this. We so appreciate your efforts. If we see you getting slack on your chores, we will limit your time with friends and have a family meeting to remedy the situation.

Car

We know you worked hard for your car, and we're happy to give it back to you. You will pay for gas from your job earnings, and your car insurance will be earned by completing household chores. As you know, you pay for any parking tickets or traffic fines. We are not too worried here because you have been responsible in the past. If any serious infractions occur, such as reckless driving, we will take away your car for the rest of the year and you can ride your bike to school. Remember, you need your car for your pizza delivery job.

Education

We believe college or tech school is a good way to ensure a solid future. We wholeheartedly support your maintaining a 3.0 GPA minimum. If you drop below this at report card time you will need to stop working and give up your car. We will pay for your college or tech school as long as you are maintaining a healthy, ethical life and a 3.0 GPA.

Parent Commitment

We are loving Christian parents. We will always be here for you, to help you and guide you, especially if you're trying to do the right thing. We are both going to open our hearts and listen with all our being. We want you to know we hear you and that what you think is important to us.

If Things Don't Work Out

We can handle mistakes and lessons, but will not tolerate major regression into old ways. If you regress to gaming addiction or significant belligerence, we will sit down and discuss with you the options we support, such as additional treatment. If you refuse professional support and cannot return to a healthy way of life, then we will look into other therapeutic programs or boarding schools. This being said, we really don't think any serious regression will happen. You have changed, and we see that.

This is an agreement. Sign it if you mean it. Love you.

Tommy Kim
Tommy

Karen Kim
Mom

Tom Kim
Dad

The Kim Family Covenant 4

Example 3:

Sarah's College Agreement

Family Statement: It is our hope that you will take this wonderful opportunity to open your mind and find a passion that matches your gifts and talents. We hope you develop yourself by rigorous study and find great opportunities to further your life in pursuit of your goals.

Communication: This year in treatment has been a life-changing event for all of our family, and we have learned how to communicate with you effectively. We are committed to keeping the lines of transparent dialogue open so we can tell each other what we're truly experiencing. We will employ the skills we learned in your program to solve any issue that comes up. Emotional safety is our top priority.

Expectations: As we've discussed before, we have some basic rules to support your college journey. In this document we are laying out what we expect of you so you can receive our financial assistance for college. College is a privilege that will need to be earned each semester.

Health: We believe your physical and mental well-being is the first priority, before anything. You can only fully share your gifts with the world if you are alive and well.

We totally support your joining any sports or taking on any physical activity. For example, if you want to join an intramural sport or a yoga class, or try skiing or river running, we will be more than happy to pay the extra costs.

Your struggle with schizophrenia has been hard, and the therapy and medication have really helped per your own report. This summer, before you start school, we will assist you in locating a good therapist and psychiatrist, as we expect you to stay in therapy and remain on your medication. We know you enjoy group therapy and will support that option. If you start to struggle with your mental health, we request that you bring this up as soon as possible, and we will bring in the appropriate additional support systems (more therapy visits, review of meds, hospitalization, etc.). If you refuse to take medication,

---

this is very serious, as your symptoms will quickly return. If this happens we might need to consider more treatment options, such as an adult living program that has a college component.

Academics: Our family values the pursuit of academic excellence, and we know that you're capable of good grades. We don't expect perfection, but we do expect a 2.75 GPA. If you drop below this goal, we will withdraw financial support and you can continue college by taking out your own student loans. You've stated that your goal is a 3.5, and we know you can do this. If you choose to pursue grad school, we will most likely be able to financially support this effort. We can discuss this option when you're closer to graduation.

Room and Board: For the first year you'll be living on campus as agreed, which is a wonderful opportunity to connect with fellow students who might end up being your lifelong friends. We believe a successful college experience is balanced with social opportunities, including joining clubs, student government, and the like, which we will support.

We will pay for your housing, food, and incidental costs as long as you follow the basic expectations in this agreement (open communication, managing your mental health, good grades, responsible use of the car, etc.). For your second year, we will pay for a room off campus with friends and give you a food allowance, but you'll be responsible for the financial costs of having fun.

Money, Job, and Car: Because we want your studies to be your number one job, we will give you an allowance of $250 a month. We do believe that a job is important for self-reliance, and we know you'll need a car to get to that job and do other fun things. The first semester will be the test. If you do well academically and manage your health, we will give you the car at Christmas time and ask you to look for a part-time job starting in the second semester. We ask you to keep school your priority and not work more than 15 hours per week. Once you have a paycheck, we will ask you to pay for your own gas and entertainment such as movies, concerts, etc., and your discretionary allowance will be dropped to $175 a month.

Breaks/Summer: Time together is very important in order for our family to stay close. We want to see you over the winter break, and will fly you home for two weeks. Spring break is probably important for building friendships in college, so we will consent to your going on a vacation with friends who will support your healthy choices. We hope you take advantage of your college's study-abroad trips this summer, and will support that if you so choose. If not, we will ask you to return home and work full-time.

Parent Commitment: We want you to have every opportunity to live a fulfilling life. We will support you emotionally and financially and at the same time help you develop the goals necessary to be a well-functioning adult in this demanding world.

If Things Don't Work Out: We have full faith in your desire and motivation to succeed at college and in your subsequent career. If you should struggle to the point where your mental health is seriously compromised, we will work with you to find the right place and situation to allow you to succeed in life. We will need your help and collaboration, so please work with us, and with your therapeutic educational consultant, in finding the right fit for you. If you should learn that college is not your path, we will look into other options like technical degrees or working for Dad's contracting company. Our main hope is that you will develop independence and have a satisfying career.

Date: August 20, 2014

Sarah Kramer
Sarah

June Kramer
Mom

John Kramer
Dad

#3. Your Home Agreement

Here is a template to help guide you in creating your Home Agreement. Write a draft and then reflect on it. You might want to finish this book before you send the Agreement to your child, as more information on triggers, regression, etc., will be coming up in these pages. When you're pleased with your Agreement, have incorporated feedback from the treatment therapist and feel certain that it's an extension of you that you can stand behind, share it with your child. And then, congratulations! That's a huge achievement.

Title for Your Home Agreement:_____

Date:_____

Family Mission Statement:

_____

_____

_____

_____

_____

_____

_____

_____

_____

_____

Family Communication Style:

_____
_____
_____
_____
_____
_____
_____
_____
_____
_____

Expectations:

_____
_____
_____
_____
_____
_____
_____
_____
_____
_____
_____
_____

Issue #1: _____

_____

_____

_____

_____

_____

_____

_____

Issue #2: _____

_____

_____

_____

_____

_____

_____

_____

Issue #3: _____

_____

_____

_____

_____

_____

_____

_____

Issue #4: _____

_____

_____

_____

_____

_____

_____

_____

Issue #5: _____

_____

_____

_____

_____

_____

_____

_____

Issue #6: _____

_____

_____

_____

_____

_____

_____

_____

Issue #7: _____

_____
_____
_____
_____
_____
_____
_____

Issue #8: _____

_____
_____
_____
_____
_____
_____
_____

Issue #9: _____

_____
_____
_____
_____
_____
_____
_____

Issue #10: _____

_____

_____

_____

_____

_____

_____

_____

Parent Commitment:

_____

_____

_____

_____

_____

_____

_____

_____

_____

_____

_____

_____

_____

_____

_____

_____

_____

If Things Don't Work Out:

_____
_____
_____
_____
_____
_____
_____
_____
_____
_____
_____
_____
_____
_____
_____
_____
_____
_____
_____

We pledge to honor this agreement completely, with honesty and integrity.

_____ Date _____
_____ Date _____
_____ Date _____

12

Rolling Out the Welcome Mat

At last the day has come that your child and you have worked so long and so hard for: homecoming, in a different sense of the word. You have both dug into your "stuff," gotten honest, and put your hearts on the line so she can start a new life, rising out of the one previously derailed by dysfunction. With treatment under her belt, your child is more authentically herself, and she now possesses coping skills to guide her along the road of life.

You and your family have discovered much about your child's situation, have soul-searched, and have learned how to communicate effectively with this precious child. Her crisis and her truth—her gifts to you—have helped the family heal. Hopefully, your child's treatment program included you in your child's recovery and you have delved into your own work along with other members of the family. Great stuff. Good work. You'll need your tools, because the truth is that the consistent day-in-day-out work begins now, when your child returns. What the treatment staff managed (holding your child accountable 24/7, managing the treatment environment, offering care and compassion) now falls back to you. Yes, you and your child have traveled through shadowy valleys and made the exhausting climb to this exhilarating mountaintop, so it's time for a loving reunion at home. Just beware that you have a little more climbing to do before you reach the summit.

You are excited and nervous at the prospect of your child's return. This is a new adventure, and your anxiety is to be expected. Parents usually have a swarm of questions buzzing in their minds: *Will he immediately regress? Will we be able to carry forward the gains she's made? Do we have the right skills, and know what to do if the going gets tough? Will she respect our values and us? What will we do if this doesn't work out?*

Your questions might be numerous, but don't let yourself become overwhelmed. After everything your family has been through with this child, anxiety, fear, and even some dread are natural feelings. Allow them to remind you that your child and you will undoubtedly make mistakes.

Confident parenting, TLC, and the Home Agreement will now be your constant companions. If there are setbacks, and there will be a few, rely on the Home Agreement. Get behind your words, as they are real symbols of who you are as a parent. When you make a mistake, own it and get right back on track.

See the New Child Before You

Often a well-meaning parent filled with joy and good intentions will say to his child, "I'm so glad treatment gave me back the old you." And the parent will be so sincere and so happy that he misses the nonverbal cues the child gives in response, such as grimacing, clenching her jaw, or rolling her eyes. She's afraid to say what she's really thinking, but she does tell me, and it goes something like this, "Even when I was messing up, I was still a good person. I just made a few mistakes and did some bad stuff." She wants her parents to know that her past experiences, both the dark and the light, have made her who she is today. She's proud of what she has accomplished, and proud to now be free to be exactly who she is.

A way to honor this whole child is to see her in the present and not project old images, or even future ones, upon her. Be totally interested in who your child is today, right now in her life, not who she used to be or is going to become. Treatment had an effect. Your child is different now, and she knows it. As a result, she'll want you to trust her 100 percent. Give her the benefit of the doubt, because she has worked incredibly hard and has changed, but keep up your radar. Your child needs to be trusted . . . to a certain degree. By having faith in her, you actually increase the odds of her doing well.

> Be totally interested in who your child is today, right now in her life, not who she used to be or is going to become.

Observe her, affirm positive behavior, and correct her when she veers off course. Without micromanaging, subtly redirect her energies in the direction of making good choices. As long as she abides by the rules of the Home Agreement, let her explore life. She might have said in treatment that she was going to play soccer and study art. Perhaps now she'll find something else more in tune with her true self. As long as she keeps moving in a positive direction, allow her the space to change her mind. This requires, from you, the ability to be flexible with your child.

Communicate Changes

Sometimes, with all that parents have to do when a child is in treatment, there can be an omission in clearly communicating shifts that have taken place on the home front. If your family system has changed significantly while your child was in treatment, please address this directly. Have you moved? Has a separation or divorce taken place? Has a parent come out of the closet? Has Dad become sober or has a loved one passed away?

Don't overlook the sharing of changes such as these, or fail to communicate them because you think your child is already facing so many issues. When he comes home, he'll be looking for familiarity—for things at home to be the way he's always seen them. He might resent or struggle with having to adapt to a new family system, structure, or environment. He might not like the "new you," because parents who do their work do change. He may struggle with the loss of the family retriever who grew old and died. He could even have trouble with the fact that you painted the dining room Umbrian Red.

Sometimes a parent will feel sympathy for the child and be guilt-ridden about a sad situation their child has to face when he returns home. This can lead to overindulging. Instead, be empathetic. Let your child know she can talk to you about her grief or feelings of loss at any time. Try to understand and reflect back to her what she's going through, but don't parent from feeling sorry for your child. This can be an opening for manipulation on her part. You can't prevent your child from feeling loss or abandonment, but you can walk with her through the valley.

Establish a Home Based on Middle-of-the-Road Parenting

The preceding chapters' Action Steps have helped clarify and shore up what your family is about. You, as the executive branch, now have firm ground beneath your feet for leading your child, in fact the entire household, with intention and strength. Lead with a sense of vision, values, and assurance. This confidence will create a home environment where everyone can flourish, including a child returning from treatment.

On the following page, again, is the model for middle-of-the-road parenting first presented in Chapter 5. In treatment, the middle-of-the-road approach to parenting is what your child became used to. Here's the key to making this balanced approach work at home. Use firmness to stay true to the values and boundaries held in the Home Agreement.

PARENTING STYLES

| AUTHORITARIAN DOGMATIC | ↔ MIDDLE-OF-THE-ROAD ↔ | FLAT HIERARCHY DEMOCRATIC |

Do not negotiate: "Drugs are off the table, period! Aggression toward your mother will never be tolerated again, period!" Notice that these strong statements (that have a hint of authoritarianism) can initiate awe or healthy respect—earned, because you're confident in your values and your capabilities. Balance this firmness with TLC that leans to the democratic, more open, side of the spectrum.

As a coach, I strongly believe in and aim to model the middle-of-the-road approach. When I become flustered and err in my coaching practice, I quickly take stock and notice that I've left the center and swung to one or the other side of the spectrum. Then I get grounded, recalibrate, and once again guide my teen or young adult client from the middle.

It isn't always easy, because it's a balancing act. Some boundaries pushed by a child require us to use great strength and resolve to hold fast to our rules. Yet it's important to allow your child to make choices so she can continue to find *her* way. If you don't parent from the middle of the road, I respectfully ask that you consider trying it.

To help you understand even better the difference in parenting styles and the results, let's imagine a scenario. Alyssa, 17, has been home from treatment for four months. In the last month she has broken her curfew for a third time, despite her parents' twice following through on the consequences. In response to this third infraction, what would the different parenting styles look like?

Authoritarian/Dogmatic Parenting Style

Alyssa: It's not my fault! My phone battery died, and—

Dad: I don't want to hear it! I've had enough. Go to your room and think about the fact that you're grounded for a month!

Alyssa: But . . .

Dad: No buts, you know better than this. Why do you keep doing this to your mother and me?

Alyssa: Will you just listen to me?

Dad: No. I've given you enough chances. This is the third time, and I'm sick of it. Now get to your room.

Alyssa: You never listen. I hate you. I hate your stupid rules.

Dad: And leave your phone with me.

(Alyssa throws her phone on the sofa, runs upstairs to her room, and slams the door. She has shut down.)

Flat Hierarchy/Democratic Parenting Style

Alyssa: Hey, Dad. Sorry I'm late. My phone died.

> **Dad:** Well, what matters is that you're safe at home now. But try not to do that again. Call from someone else's phone, okay?
>
> **Alyssa:** Sure.
>
> **Dad:** So, did you have a good time?
>
> **Alyssa:** Yeah, it was fun. I'm kind of tired, though. I'm going to go to bed. 'Night.
>
> **Dad:** 'Night, Alyssa. Sleep tight.
>
> *(P.S. Alyssa broke curfew again two nights later.)*

Middle-of-the-Road Parenting Style

> **Dad:** Hey, we talked about this. You've crossed the line three times now, so you're going to get a stiffer consequence.
>
> **Alyssa:** But, Dad, that's not fair. My phone died.
>
> **Dad:** I hear that you think it's not fair, but it shouldn't be unexpected. This time no phone for a month, and for two weeks you only go out to school, work, church, and family functions. No friends.
>
> **Alyssa:** That totally sucks!
>
> **Dad:** I suppose it does. So what's really going on?
>
> **Alyssa:** Nothing's going on.

Dad: No, really. I'd like to understand why you're staying out so late. Something about the curfew makes it hard for you to follow. Midnight isn't horrible, and the rule isn't going to change. Please tell me what it is you are struggling with.

Alyssa: I'm struggling because everyone else gets to stay out all night, practically. It just seems so unfair that I can't be like everyone else, just because I was in treatment.

Dad: Yeah, I guess that does seem unfair. And maybe in a way it is, but I also know it's unfair for you to stay out past our agreed-upon time and not call. We love you; you know that. Your mother and I really worry when we don't know where you are and if you're okay.

Alyssa: *(pauses)* Yeah, I suppose that does suck. I guess I'll try to do better.

Dad: I hope so, honey. In the meantime, I'll take the phone, okay?

Alyssa: Okay.

The middle-of-the-road method got the desired result. That's because the parent guided the process and created a safe environment where mutual respect existed. Dad was firm, but he listened and kept the dialogue going. As a result Alyssa felt validated and ultimately accepted the boundary.

What to Do with Siblings

Parenting a child who is home from treatment right along with children who have remained home creates anxiety for some parents. Do you parent these kids in the same way? Do they receive different consequences? Are they granted different privileges? The basic answer here is this: A family culture is the same for the entire family. Values don't vary from one child to another. Your values are your values to pass down to each of your children; they don't fluctuate. But the differing ways in which your children accept and respond to those values might require a little finesse and variation in your parenting.

Rules very often need to be age-and-maturity-specific. A 16-year-old might be expected to hold a summer job, but not younger siblings. Siblings who stayed home have earned privileges that your child in treatment has not. For example, one of your young adult children might be able to drink alcohol while the one returning from treatment might not, due to addiction. Or perhaps there are limitations on the friends your child returning from treatment can hang out with, while the other kids have no such restrictions, having chosen their friends well all along.

Most kids, not just those from treatment, will balk at any difference. "Why does she get to spend the night at a friend's house?" "Why do I have to take the garbage out?" "Why can't I see an R-rated movie?" Some of this moaning is typical, age-appropriate kid stuff. Some of it is the beginning of manipulation. Stick hard and fast to non-negotiables. For less important complaints such as what day her room has to be clean, get into listening mode and then compromise only if you feel right about the compromise.

Siblings might also have a negative response to changes in the family due to the growth of the parent while one child was in treatment. When you define your family values, you raise expectations and create rules. You'll begin holding all kids accountable and chances are there will be some grumbling. If so, smile and use TLC to create a safe space for all to speak openly and honestly.

At times, in order to balance the dysfunction created by the child who went to treatment, some siblings assume the role of the "perfect child." If this has been true in your family, you might find that those siblings left at home aren't acting so perfect any more. Good!—because now these kids can be authentic and test their world. They can explore their full personalities and learn how to live within the safe context of your home.

Also, a sibling at home might have mixed emotions, including anger, toward the sibling in treatment. You'll see this on home visits, and in particular in the first few months following the prodigal child's return. In my practice, I have not seen this dynamic become destructive, so my suggestion is to not interfere. Let the siblings sort it out. Things that weren't said in treatment need to be expressed, and often they need to be said outside of the parent's purview.

If your family is truly healthy from the treatment process, one of the rewards for the parents is to see their children deal with tension and become closer because of it. This tension is natural, and the child returning now knows how to communicate and lead. If resentment and other consequent emotions run high for too long, then step in to call a family meeting with TLC.

Another factor to take into consideration: The child returning from treatment will have a big war chest of wisdom, a skill set way beyond the years of many of his peers and siblings. This differential might intimidate other members of the household, including you. I especially witness many siblings feeling insecure, resentful, and intimidated, as well as—paradoxically—relieved. In his new authority, the returning child often drops into a leadership role, and siblings might feel angst until the new pecking order has been determined.

Again, step back and let the natural reshuffling of the deck happen. This is not the time to referee; instead, let each family member experience this event. Let the kids jockey and vie. Call it pack behavior. Just make sure all siblings are being respectful and following the spirit of your household. If someone gets snotty, correct the dysfunctional behavior, as you still are and always will be the leader of the pack.

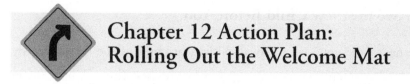

Chapter 12 Action Plan: Rolling Out the Welcome Mat

(To download blank worksheets, visit www.TheRoadHomeBook.com/downloads.)

#1. Communicate Changes

Have there been changes in your family structure or your personal life that you have not communicated to your child when she was in treatment? Has there been a death of a family pet? Have you been diagnosed with a disease? Has Uncle Joseph been jailed after his third DUI? Make a list of things you may have not wanted to communicate while your child was healing in treatment. Circle those that matter and, using TLC, communicate these to your child.

_____

_____

_____

_____

_____

_____

_____

_____

_____

_____

_____

#2. See the New Child Before You

The next time you visit or speak with your child (if she hasn't already returned), pretend you're meeting her for the first time. What do you like about her? What impresses you? Also talk to your child's therapist. What virtues does he see in your child? The purpose of this is for you to see the "new" person before you and not get mired down in the "old" troubled kid who left home. Start out on the right foot. Give your child the credit she deserves for her hard work and her journey thus far. What have you discovered?

_____

_____

_____

_____

_____

_____

_____

_____

_____

_____

_____

_____

_____

_____

#3. Siblings

If there are siblings in the house, sit down with them and have a TLC discussion about their feelings concerning their sibling in treatment. Openly discuss fears, irritants, and feelings of love. Let your other child or children open up; make the space safe for them to do so. After you have this conversation, take a moment to write what happened. What insights did you gain?

_____

_____

_____

_____

_____

_____

_____

_____

_____

_____

_____

_____

_____

_____

_____

_____

_____

_____

13

Navigating the Reunion

I call the period of a few weeks to a few months after a child's return the honeymoon / shell shock phase. Like a coin, this period of time has two sides. It's both a euphoric state for your child to be back home and also a shock. On the honeymoon side, you'll see joy and a reveling in the love of family and familiar surroundings; "I'm home, and it's all good." On the flip side, there's shell shock. You might notice anxiety, even sheer terror. Your child will most likely try to hide this side from you, and yet it's important to realize that he has not yet settled into an ordinary routine.

There are many reasons why your child returns disoriented and not quite himself. Imagine not living in your "real" home for months or even years. Not hanging with friends you've known since kindergarten, eating Aunt Millie's chocolate chip cookies warm from the oven, laughing at Grandpa snoring after Thanksgiving dinner, or arguing with Mom over dirty socks tossed behind the sofa. It's just plain weird to lose out on the comforts of this everyday life.

Reacquainting to the way it was is both exciting for kids and hard on them. My young clients have reported feeling "out of it" and in a daze. Often they don't want to tell their parents because they're afraid their parents might think something is off and send them away again.

When your child returns, I hope your communication skills will afford discussion and validation of these feelings. If your child pretends he's fine, allow him to fake you out. Take a back seat, but watch. Time is needed. Your child might have thought he'd be off and running when he returned, but just the opposite might prove true. He might find himself not going out much, because just hanging out at home is his way of adjusting and taking in the sensory overload of being back.

Returning to one's old school or starting at a new one is stressful to kids who have been in treatment, and might emotionally exhaust yours. This can show up as his being edgy or irritable. Give him some space, and validate his experience once you're clear as to what it is: "Yeah, it is tough starting at a new school."

During the honeymoon phase, the Home Agreement might be mildly tested. Your child might drag his feet regarding school and work expectations. For example, if procuring and holding a job was laid out in the Agreement, he might wait a week or even a month before pursuing employment, or even question whether you really meant what you said. Reaffirm to him that, yes, you meant every word. It's okay to give him a few weeks to settle in, as long as he clearly knows the consequence for not working and when it will kick in.

These hiccups will occur, but please know that your youngster is truly excited to be home. It's just that he couldn't completely know what it would be like. And now he's home and it's . . . not exactly what he expected. He'll be excited, and yet nervous and bewildered. He'll be psyched to eat Dad's spaghetti again, and yet might be enjoying it in a state of semi-shock.

If your child . . . and you . . . have changed for real, the honeymoon might last for a very long time. If she has become more grown-up and self-motivated, you might find her incredibly agreeable and compliant in this initial stage. You might have never had the "mature" daughter in your home. Enjoy this wonderful experience. Savor it, and intentionally use this golden time to build rapport, closeness, and mutual respect, all of which you can call upon if ever the going gets rough.

When the Honeymoon Is Over

When the honeymoon is ending, it can be disconcerting and downright scary. It can look and feel like all is lost. You may think that "treatment didn't work" and experience moods ranging from feeling dispirited to anger and depression. Even when the transition home is going well, there will be times when you doubt how much your child has really changed. You will most likely experience days when she is surly, irritable, disrespectful, and even downright rude. Rules will be shunned and tested.

Take faith, for the end of the honeymoon is when the work at home begins in earnest. It is now time to manage the chaos and the push/pull of boundary challenges. I like it when the honeymoon ends. It's an exciting and revelatory time. It's after the honeymoon that your child's authentic self can show up and be present for a true relationship with you and others.

Ah yes...the honeymoon has ended at last.

The honeymoon is over when you see signs of your child returning to her true nature; now the whole person, both light and dark, is present. Usually between two weeks to two months after her return home this total person will become more apparent. She'll start to be bored, or things will start to feel ordinary to her. She might start pushing certain boundaries she considers "stupid."

Don't be surprised if you hear your child say something like, "I only signed that agreement to get out of treatment. I didn't even read the whole thing." It's unrealistic to think your child won't challenge a rule or two at some point after she comes home. This is normal, and even arguably healthy. It means she's realizing that she is her own person and can disagree with you. The truth of whether or not she's going to follow the Rules of the Road isn't revealed until after she has pushed against the boundaries and learns that you mean business.

> The truth of whether or not she's going to follow the Rules of the Road isn't revealed until after she has pushed against the boundaries and learns that you mean business.

Imagine what your child is going through. She honestly feels like she's being controlled, and wants to feel like she has her own power. Her push against a certain rule might be more about exercising free agency. She may also be expressing anger toward you for having so much structure in place. Don't let her get your goat. If she sees your frustration she'll sit back and gloat, thinking, *Good, now you know what it feels like to be me, frustrated by your stupid rules!*

Your aim is to use TLC and hold the line. Let her know she will not get her needs met by being defiant. She will eventually, at some point (after weeks, not months), drop into a more agreeable mode. Here is an example of the use of TLC in such a situation:

Transparent and Loving Communication (TLC) & Defiance

Mom: Maddie, we keep arguing about pot. What's going on here? Why is this an ongoing issue?

Daughter: I'm going on 19 and pot is almost legal, but you keep treating me like I'm a kid. I can't do *anything*.

Mom: *(reflecting)* Okay, you're frustrated that you can't smoke, so that's why you're arguing with me. And then you get even more frustrated because you feel you're being treated like a kid. Is that it?

Daughter: Yeah, it really pisses me off.

Mom: *(reflecting)* I don't blame you for being frustrated, but the rule is not going to change and I'm not going to get into arguing with you about this every single day.

Daughter: But all my friends smoke weed and they don't get hassled.

Mom: It's your choice. I can't stop you from testing the rules, but the consequences are the consequences. If you want our support in all the ways we support you, then don't smoke pot. Hold true to our Home Agreement.

Daughter: *(rolls her eyes)* I hate that agreement.

Mom: That may be, but it has a purpose.

Daughter: Yeah, to make my life miserable.

Mom: *(smiles)* Is it really all that bad?

Daughter: *(cracks a smile, too)* Sometimes . . .

Notice how Mom guided this conversation? She listened, but she didn't cave in. She also didn't feed into her daughter's defiance and argue back. In treatment, staff members do not argue with their clients, simply because it doesn't work to anyone's advantage. Mom, in this example, knows that it is the Home Agreement and what it stands for that will help her daughter stay on the straight and narrow. After this conversation, Maddie undoubtedly understands where she can turn for support and what's being requested of her.

When your son or daughter is clear on your expectations and support, then eventually your curiosity will be satisfied. When the honeymoon is over, you'll see what work is complete and what work she still needs to accomplish to reach full maturation.

Most likely she will struggle with the issue she mentioned on that last tense phone call before leaving treatment. A discussion may reveal that her grumbling and small infractions reflect a larger issue. For example, her refusal to see a therapist and attend 12-step meetings is actually about her belief that she is "done" with therapy and ready to get on with life. Delaying getting her driver's license might be indicative of a fear about college and adulthood. When the Home Agreement is challenged, take it as an opportunity to have a rich dialogue to find out who is now living with you, and as a chance for developing a more authentic relationship.

It's About Both of You

This time of reunion is very much a journey toward health and authenticity. Your child spent months or years becoming genuine and discovering her true self. She has learned to be transparent in communication, and has the coping skills to continue healthy patterns. If she has been honest and forthright in her change, this self-knowledge and awareness feels good to her. If you can now be as authentic as possible about who you are, your child will notice this modeling and a very positive cycle of healing will begin in your family.

When arguments and other relationship-based tensions arise between you and your child, it is vital to be self-reflective. Such conflicts trigger you as well as your child, and your reactions might create a downward-spiral effect. To help prevent this, check in with yourself during and after conflicts. Take time to reflect on how you felt physically and emotionally. Don't be afraid to share what's happening inside you with your child. Extend this sharing to everyday life. Show your child who you are every now and then. Open up, but make sure, of course, that the topics are appropriate. For instance it might be helpful for your child to know about how you were bullied in high school, but maybe not so much your drug history.

I still appreciate it when my parents talk about where they are in life in an honest way. I remember my grandmother doing it. When I was a teen, I would ask my grandmother how she was, and often her answer startled me with its genuineness. "Oh, today was the pits!" she might say, or, "Sometimes I'm tired of life." Or, "Swell! Fit as a fiddle!"

Grandma's authentic responses modeled to me that it was all right to be whoever I was in the moment. This same basic awareness is taught to your child in treatment, and you can keep this tradition alive. When we stop being authentic with others, and with ourselves, we begin to walk toward dysfunction. Awareness and a commitment to being genuine lead us toward health.

> When we stop being authentic with others, and with ourselves, we begin to walk toward dysfunction. Awareness and a commitment to being genuine lead us toward health.

How to De-escalate

You'll know all too well that the honeymoon is over when your child has a big meltdown or initiates a doozy of an argument. Your job is to not melt down yourself or argue back.

If, in the discussion, your kid keeps arguing, it's because you're doing something to perpetuate the argument. Take responsibility for this and change tactics. You don't have to rule with an iron fist. As a matter of fact, I advise against it. Reflect back and validate your child's feelings and her journey. Get in the habit of using TLC regularly and develop a dispassionate approach. The end of the honeymoon is not a personal affront to you. It is a natural and to-be-expected response from your child.

The ultimate technique I use to deal with argumentative and defiant teens and young adults is based on the precepts outlined in the book, *Motivational Interviewing: Preparing for Change* by William Miller and John Rollnick. I know the concepts presented in this book inside-out and backwards. I trained my wilderness guides with these concepts, because they do not fail. The basic idea that parents could benefit from is this: Learn to reflect your children's ideas back to them. Reflect like a mirror—without personal opinion expressed.

> Learn to reflect your children's ideas back to them. Reflect like a mirror—without personal opinion expressed.

How do you do this? Remember that most communication is nonverbal. Watch your child. See what he is saying with his body as well as his words. When I have a TLC moment and need my clients to lower their defenses, I raise a mirror to them. I reflect back what I'm hearing and seeing. I see the rapidly shaking leg and the lack of eye contact. I see the tears. I hear the monotone voice, and I let my client know exactly what I believe I'm seeing and discerning. This, without fail, lowers defenses and allows us to have a more genuine encounter. Note that I do not necessarily agree with what my client is saying. Rather, I listen and hear with all my senses and offer back those ideas to him. If I'm correct, he will affirm my reflection, and this gives me the information I need as I see him, in that moment, for who he is. If I'm wrong in my perceptions, he can clarify, and then I still get the information I need. Either way, I win and so does he.

Process vs. Content

When a defiant, perturbed client is venting at his parent about the car being taken away or some such issue, I look for a lull in the emotions and then come in directing the experience by first pointing out the process, not the issue at hand. The process is the frustration and defiance. The issue of the car is secondary. Reflect on the process, not content. I most often say something like, "Wow, you are so mad right now." Or, "I can see this is a serious issue for you and you are torqued at your dad, and I notice you're really venting at him right now." I usually reflect and engage in the ensuing dialogue at least three times before my client lowers his defenses. At that point, I go into open-ended questions such as, "Well, what do you mean by that?" "Tell me more." "Explain to me how important the car is."

After my client responds, I reflect back *either* the content/issue or the process: "So you need the car for dates and work." "It looks like your dad is holding firm to the rule and consequence." "Frustrating, isn't it?" By this time, the teen or young adult has de-escalated and is reacting in a more reasonable manner. This does not mean we have resolved the conflict, but most of the time each person feels heard, accepts the reality of the situation, and starts moving through the issue instead of getting stuck and aggressive.

Just to let you know, it has taken me more than ten years to perfect this skill. There is a science to Motivational Interviewing, and it took a full semester of rigorous group critique from graduate school associates to truly learn the art. But a little of this science, even if it isn't smooth or is downright bumbling, can help immensely. The essence of the technique is to focus on reflecting or mirroring back what you see in the moment with your child in a genuine and nonjudgmental way. This allows your kid to see who he is, and it will take a charged atmosphere back to a TLC atmosphere. If meltdowns and arguments are not handled with TLC and maintenance of boundaries, they can trigger regression. Don't teach, preach, or lecture; hold up a mirror dispassionately. A mirror doesn't lie.

> Don't teach, preach, or lecture; hold up a mirror dispassionately.

Sometimes, when a child loses it, it can be very alarming for a parent. Don't avoid conflict. Move into it with the intention of learning, and manage it carefully. In treatment and in my coaching practice, we are diligent about letting conflict become an opportunity for productivity. When handled correctly, the natural tension that accompanies arguments can lead to more closeness, forward movement, and a better understanding of your child. Don't underestimate your child's abilities. She knows how to de-escalate and make conflict productive. She did it a hundred times in treatment. She has the skill set, but if she's hell-bent on raising Cain, relax into the tension and realize that nothing will be accomplished until you allow the rage to run its course.

I have spoken to many moms in my practice who sometimes feel quite frightened when their six-foot man/boy loses it. It's scary when someone seems out of control, but these situations can be de-escalated. Here is a sample dialogue where a mother is able to calm down a situation and also stand by her beliefs. She is able to listen to her child, understand where he is coming from, reflect back, and talk transparently about her own feelings. The mom does this from a distance, and yet her son, in this scenario knows that he is loved.

Deescalating a Potential Meltdown

> **Son:** *(raised voice, but tears in his eyes)* I am so sick of this crap. I hate this contract. You only did this because you read that book. It's BS. I'm fine and don't need another contract telling me what to do. I hate this family and don't want to be here anymore.
>
> **Mother:** *(gently)* Hey, sit down on the couch. Tell me what's going on?
>
> **Son:** *(plops down onto the couch)* I'm tired of your rules and tired of *you*. You don't want to be embarrassed by me, so you just want me to stay home where it's totally boring. I don't have a life. I can't go out with my friends. I can't do anything. *(punches sofa pillow)*

Mother: *(reflecting)* You really are tired of all this.

Son: Yes! It sucks. You would hate it too, if you were me.

Mother: I am sure I would. It does suck. And I am tired of this, too.

Son: Then why are you doing this to me?

Mother: *(chooses to pause and let the question hang in the air)*

Son: I know you're worried about me, but don't.

Mother: Yes, I do sometimes worry.

Son: Mom, I promise, I'm doing okay.

Mother: Actually, I think you are doing great overall. I mean, I'm struggling with your tone right now and it feels a bit disrespectful, but I do think you've been doing great since you got back home, and I'm proud of you.

Son: *(raises voice again)* Then why all the rules?!

Mother: You're very upset with me and raising your voice. I know you aren't happy with the Home Agreement and it's stupid in your eyes, but it stands for ideals that are important to me.

Son: *(lets out a sigh that could be frustration or acceptance.)*

Mother: *(reflecting)* I see you're frustrated, but once I see that you're continuing to do well we can change the more restrictive rules. And, by the way, I'm not okay with the way this conversation went. It could have been done with more care for my feelings.

Son: I know. What rules are you going to change? I hate my curfew.

Mother: *(reflecting)* Yeah, I get it. You hate the curfew. Let's discuss that in a few weeks. I think we can modify the curfew if you continue to show me that you're mature. But remember, some rules may change, but my values won't. This is who I am.

Son: You're not going to change your mind, are you? *(tosses the sofa pillow into the corner of the sofa)*

Mother: No. I'm not going to change my mind, but I do get how frustrating this is for you.

Yes, this young man didn't hug his mom and say he was sorry for all the mistakes he'd made, but he heard his mother and accepted her rules. Just as important, the mother heard her son, reflected back and de-escalated the situation. That's an accomplishment.

Disrespect Hurts

The heart of good family relations is mutual respect. Thus, if your child drops into blatant disrespect, address the issue immediately. If an old pattern of insolence is reinstated and goes unchecked, your child will think it's allowed, despite knowing from treatment that rude, belligerent, or aggressive behavior is not tolerated. Follow through with what you stated in the Home Agreement and have a TLC discussion about it. Don't give it more energy than is warranted.

On occasion when a kid comes home she will most likely go through a completely self-absorbed and seemingly selfish period that can feel very disrespectful. This behavior can be understood when one realizes that this child has been away from home and wants to reclaim her entire life now. It's not "all about the family." She needs to reconnect to her environment; her other loved ones, her "people, places, and things."

It might hurt your feelings to see her decide she would rather do many things without the family, especially if you saw a more compassionate personality come out while your child was in treatment. This "selfish" phase is particularly true for older teens and young adults. That's because it is important and age-appropriate for them to establish a life outside the family as well as in it. If this phenomenon occurs in your home, define what events are paramount and congruent with your vision and values and what are less important, and be clear about your expectations. Going to temple together might be a high priority and something you put your foot down on, while the July 4th picnic in the park is something she can do with friends.

TLC and the "Selfish Phase"

Daughter: Dad, I don't want to go to out with the family tonight for dinner.

Dad: Why not?

Daughter: I want to go hang with Carla and see that new vampire movie.

Dad: *(feeling frustrated because this is the third time this month his daughter has bailed on a family event)* I'm pretty sad that you don't want to hang out with us.

Daughter: I know. I feel bad, but I get tired of being with you guys all the time.

Dad: *(reflects back and validates)* You think you're spending too much time with us.

Daughter: Kind of. Yeah.

Dad: Okay. Well, I wish you would join us tonight, but I do understand that your friends matter a lot, too. This is hard for me because we haven't seen you much in the last few years. Look, I am going to ask you to be at major family events like birthdays and holidays for the next few years, but I guess I

| need to let you go more. So, tonight, go be with your friend
| and try to understand where I'm coming from.
|
| **Daughter:** Okay. See ya!

Notice how this dialogue does not show a lot of empathy by way of the daughter. As she matures she will develop more empathy for her parents, but in the interim this can be tough on them. Please take some solace in understanding that getting a full life and developing strong social ties is part of maturation. This venturing process can likely be the beginning of the "leaving the nest" inevitability. As difficult as it may be, encourage this maturation, though always within the scope of the Home Agreement.

The Coffee Shop Technique

For those times when you are just plain worn down, when you are feeling less than enamored with your son or daughter, times are tense, or you feel like the fifth wheel, I can offer a simple technique that might help. I've noticed that the minute I become emotionally overwhelmed when working with a young client, whether it be with sadness, anger, or disappointment, my attitude and language toward him will become condescending and paternalistic. And guess what? My client will then become defensive and shut down. This prevents me from doing my job, which is to keep the person before me moving in the direction of maturity and health. It's the same job you have as a parent.

I've taught myself to step back at such times, assess the situation, and get grounded. I then approach the client with fresh eyes, a new heart, and less of an agenda. It's true that I'm a clinician, a professional who drops in and out of a family's life. I'm not the parent who has a 24/7 commitment. I do believe, however, that parents can achieve this clarifying distance as well, by playing pretend.

Make believe your child is a stranger that you just met in line at a coffee shop. How would you strike up and maintain a conversation? You wouldn't harp, would you? You wouldn't criticize. You wouldn't lecture, or feel compelled to give advice. There'd be no talking down, and probably that new acquaintance would like you and maybe even think you're cool.

So, just pretend—that's my secret for achieving appropriate nonattachment when emotional flooding looms. Or maybe think of it this way: Meet your child for the first time. Blank out the history and look at her with fresh eyes. Look at her as someone new and interesting . . . someone you want to learn about.

> Meet your child for the first time. Blank out the history and look at her with fresh eyes. Look at her as someone new and interesting . . . someone you want to learn about.

Ending the Honeymoon with a Bang

Occasionally, if a young person was being insincere about his change in treatment, he might end the honeymoon period in a very significant way. For example, let's say that after a month of being a model citizen, the boom falls. Your son stays out for two days with people you don't know, and then tests positive for pot and Ecstasy.

Most likely the thought of this scenario unnerves you. If something like this should happen to you, please realize that your child is testing you all at once in one day. It doesn't mean that treatment didn't work, though you might wonder if you just wasted a lot of money and energy. All honeymoons end—and some with more volatility than others.

A dramatic ending of the honeymoon is an all-out attempt to move toward regression, and a challenge to your entire road map home. If your child ends the honeymoon with a big bang, then meet that with a strong tour de force of TLC (transparent loving communication). Use TLC to get to the root of the child's misbehavior.

Please realize that your Home Agreement was violated—your values and beliefs. So immediately dole out a consequence, a medicine that won't be swallowed easily no matter how much sugar you offer. Then follow through on your consequence without flinching. A big blowout doesn't deserve negotiating over curfew or the car. Negotiations can occur once trust has been regained over several weeks or months.

If your child repeats the offense and continues to regress significantly, despite follow-through with consequences and TLC, this will certainly suggest that he was brought home too early or was insincere with his commitment during treatment. Your child might need more guidance than you or the treatment staff knew.

How can this be, you ask? How can treatment professionals not "know?"

Clients who have been in treatment have shared with me that, in essence, they played a good poker hand or chess game with all the adults in their life, including the treatment pros. It does happen. If your child happens to be this person, he will most likely come clean and confide this reality to you in a moment of anger or to a confidential source such as a therapist or transition coach. If this is the case, it is tough news to receive, and yet you finally know with whom you are dealing. He may need more professional help, or if you hold true to your Home Agreement he may self-correct. I have seen Home Agreements steer even the most masterful manipulating clients onto healthy ground. Not all is lost if your child fooled the treatment team and you, but don't get fooled again. He has shown a great lack of trustworthiness, and needs solid accountability to make that Home Agreement work.

Keep an Eye on the Triggers

There is another concept that's worth understanding so that you can maintain a healthy home environment: triggers.

For your child, triggers are the sights, smells, people, places, and other sensory and environmental elements that could cause a relapse into his or her challenge. Triggers can cause someone to get depressed, have panic attacks, or fall back into addiction, eating disorders, or defiant and illegal behavior. Triggers are omnipresent.

It's often hard for parents to accept that their child can't be sheltered forever and needs to come back to life, which means interacting with life, which means encountering triggers. Some triggers can be avoided, and your child knows to do this. If he's serious about staying healthy, he'll work to avoid triggers and work through those that can't be avoided. It's challenging, but it can be done, and many do it.

Greater difficulty arises when someone thinks he can be around his serious triggers and function just fine. Rarely is this true. We are not always stronger than our environment. Your child needs to avoid the triggers that led to his misery and dysfunction. He might not be able to avoid the smell of weed when walking downtown to grab a burger, but he *can* avoid the park where he started and continued his heroin addiction. The task for your child is to stay out of harm's way and use his learned coping skills to counteract triggers. The task for you is to know what your child's triggers are and address them in the Home Agreement.

Triggers differ for each individual. Listening to that old party music can trigger an alcoholic's desire to drink. Mom turning out the lights can prompt the promiscuous young woman to want to sneak out. A conversation with an old boyfriend and a paperclip on the desk can trigger a cutting relapse. It can be just that simple. Furthermore, if a family doesn't change with the child in treatment, their dysfunction can trigger old patterns. A parent's behavior might be triggering. For example, if a parent remains verbally aggressive or alcohol-dependent, it's quite possible that these behaviors will counteract a child's gains once she gets back home.

> If a family doesn't change with the child in treatment, their dysfunction can trigger old patterns.

Although triggers are specific to each individual, for youths I find some shared villains. The classic for those with a marijuana dependency is a whiff of marijuana smoke. It sometimes happens, when I walk a beach or a trail with a client, that we encounter the smell of someone smoking pot. I use these moments to assess how my client is doing. It doesn't make sense to run away. The smell is there, the weed is there, the trigger is there, and so is my client.

This is an opportunity for me—and for you, if you encounter such an instance with your child—to talk openly about the experience and learn from it. The responses I hear from kids when I ask them what the smell of weed does to them range from "This is hard; it makes me crave pot" to "It doesn't bother me. I don't even want it any more."

Other triggers common to kids are: unwholesome friends from pre-treatment life; the sight or smell of drugs or alcohol; the smell of and access to cigarettes; places your child hung out when he was dysfunctional; weekend party time; technology, such as warring games, that allowed him to become unhealthy; the phone with the drug dealer's info and social media sites; his bedroom, if he isolated himself there and became reclusive; arguments in the family, if family strife was the issue; and the school that holds so many bad memories. There are more, many more; the list can be infinite, but these are the predominant types of triggers I hear about—the types of places and things that you want to make sure have been addressed in the Home Agreement.

Parental Triggers

Some parents are surprised to learn that they have triggers, too. All humans do. Parental triggers, though, are different from those of their children. They're all about falling into old patterns of communication and enabling the child. Once home, your child will test the water with manipulation and rule breaking to see if you still react the way you used to. These challenges will be your triggers. They'll come at you like fast pitches, not lobs, so be ready. Parental triggers coming from your child might appear harmless, but they're not. In fact, they can be perilous in the sense that their effects can stall your child's continued maturation into adulthood.

> This simple rule of thumb might help you resist falling for your own triggers:
> If your child can do something for himself, let him.
> Don't do it for him.

A classic communication trigger is when she comes home and works you to let her have the wrong friends around. If you wavered in the past, she's not only trying to get her way, but also testing to see if you've changed. It's up to you to demonstrate change and stick to what's written in the Home Agreement. Firmly insist that no red-light friends are allowed. Don't be triggered and give in.

Here's another example. If you were accustomed to rescuing your child instead of letting him work through difficulties (and so were inadvertently denying him valuable lessons), when he acts helpless again you might very well feel the urge to save him. Let's say you used to advocate for him at school when his grades suffered, but in treatment he has learned to be a good student. When he returns home, he might slip into old, lazy study habits and expect you to sympathize and talk to the teachers on his behalf.

Don't take the bait. Don't let his manipulation be your trigger. Realize that your child, in this example, is capable and has full potential. He's choosing not to do all that he can do. A supportive consequence, such as a tutor or a different school, might be appropriate if the child needs additional help. But if the child is choosing to remain lazy with consequences both supportive and restrictive in place, back off. Let the struggle become the teacher's. Harvard may be lost, but City College is still a possibility.

This simple rule of thumb might help you resist falling for your own triggers: If your child can do something for himself, let him. Don't do it for him.

Managing Triggers

The key to managing triggers is consciousness. You can halt regression if you're vigilantly mindful of the pitfalls that can lead to a decline. Identify the triggers that contributed to parenting that didn't work. Identify the ones that prompted your child into regression, or led you and your child into mutual backsliding. Talk to your child about them openly and honestly before she returns.

Your daughter might now be adept at managing her triggers, and able to teach you what she needs for support. She probably included them in her Relapse Prevention Plan, and you should address them in the Home Agreement. Do all this in preparation, and know that managing triggers will be a normal, everyday part of life. Your child is experienced in this. You might be less so. It takes practice so don't expect perfection. Accept stumbles, talk about them, and learn from them. Mistakes are normal, but if you identify and neutralize the triggers, fewer mistakes will be made. Identifying and managing your own triggers is excellent modeling for your children.

You Can Honor and Reevaluate Values

To maintain a home where everyone feels safe, staying true to what you have worked so hard to create in your Home Agreement is of utmost importance. Honor the work you've done, and stand firmly behind the words created for this symbolic yet very practical document. You know who you are more clearly than ever. Don't be cowed into abandoning what matters most to you. This was not an exercise in futility, but in freedom for you and your family.

What's more, you've created something user-friendly that isn't laden with a hundred hard-to-track rules and consequences that could squelch your child's spirit. Quite the opposite—you've created an easy-to-use road map based on what you hold dear as parents. It is based on your spirit and your love.

If your child consistently challenges a boundary, it is most likely situational, meaning she dislikes a specific rule, such as the 10 P.M. curfew or the monthly drug testing when she's had a year of clean tests under her belt. If the rule continues to be challenged even after TLC and follow-through with consequences, take the time to reassess where you stand. You might discover that you actually agree with your child that the rule is unrealistic or unreasonable.

Smoking is a behavior that I often see parents negotiate with their child after he returns from treatment. Most parents write in their Agreement that no cigarettes are allowed. You might discover, months after his return, that your 19-year-old secretly still smokes. The good part of this is that he's doing it behind your back because he knows where you stand on the issue.

If you repeatedly catch him smoking, and he continues to defy you despite the consequences, engage in TLC. Perhaps you'll learn that your young adult has a different value from yours in this regard and is going to keep smoking. After deliberation, you might decide to keep peace in the family, and your son at home, by changing your rule concerning cigarettes.

Your expectation and The Home Agreement might then be amended to: "We don't agree with you smoking, but you're 19 and we recognize that you can choose how to treat your body. As long as you live under our roof, you need to smoke away from our home and yard, and you'll use your own money to buy your cigarettes."

As your child transitions to home life and some rule breaking occurs, the question will arise: *On which issues should I consider being flexible?* I can't tell you; no one can, because it depends on your values. Between your well-thought-out expectations and the clinical information from your program, you know what is crucial to your child's success. Don't flex on issues close to your heart, or on those that are in place to keep your teen or young adult safe. If an issue is minor to your child's well-being and not a strongly held belief of yours, there might be some wiggle room. For example, you might agree to spending more on a car than the contract says because the car in question is safer, very reliable and a sensible choice by your child. If you do adjust, don't do it in such a way that you give your child an opportunity to start maneuvering. She might mistake your willingness to be open-minded as a return to the kind of parenting that can once again be manipulated.

When I taught high school, I learned that on the first day I had to be firm and set the stage for high expectations. But, as the semester progressed, I could be more flexible and reasonable as the atmosphere of the class allowed. Once my students knew I was a man of my word, they didn't test the waters. So start out tough, and after a few months show more mercy, understanding, and flexibility. Once respect has been established, TLC can be as well, and with that any situation can be managed.

> You are not here to control your child, but to manage your child's opportunities.

The idea of being flexible might be a bit worrisome for you, as your child could try to manipulate you. In this case, sort out if your child just wants to get rid of rules or if he has genuinely earned more privileges. You can discover this with TLC. If you're being manipulated, then don't change the rule. If there is a legitimate reason to change the rule and you agree it's a good idea, then go for it. Remember, you are in charge of this whole process. You are not here to control your child, but to manage your child's opportunities.

Using TLC to Enforce the Home Agreement and Change a Rule

(Mom and Dad talk with their daughter after they have privately discussed and agreed on their approach.)

Dad: We want to talk about how you're not holding up your part of the bargain. You're refusing to see your therapist. Mom worked hard to find that therapist, and you even said you liked meeting with her. And you agreed to meet with her twice a month. It's been over three weeks and you keep putting this off.

Daughter: I didn't know you guys were watching me so closely. Geez. I didn't think it mattered that much. I mean, I'm doing so well.

Mom: So why not tell me what's going on with you?

Dad: Yeah, let us know what you're thinking.

Daughter: I don't know . . . it's nothing.

Dad: Look, this issue is important and we want to get to the bottom of this so we can figure out how to support you. Please be honest with us.

Daughter: Honestly? I'm sick of therapy. I just spent a whole year of my life doing it, and I'm just not into it.

Dad: *(reflecting)* You're tired of it and don't want to go anymore.

Daughter: Exactly.

Dad: Okay. Well, I agree you're doing really well; you seem happy and I feel I can trust you. Your mother and I would be open to changing the rule on therapy.

Daughter: All right . . .

Mom: I agree with your dad, but let us ask you a few more questions. Do you like this therapist? Can you trust her with your ideas and emotions?

Daughter: *(thinks and then lets out a sigh)* Yeah, she's pretty cool. I like her. I can tell her all kinds of stuff, and I do.

Dad: That's good to hear. Thanks for being honest.

Mom: Yeah, it means a lot that you shared that with us.

Dad: So here's what I think could happen. You go see her one more time in the next two weeks and let her know you're stopping for now. However, I want you to keep that door open if you ever need her.

Mom: I agree. Please communicate to her that you want to be able to reach out to her if you ever need her support. Also, I think if you should begin struggling with your mood for a few weeks or so, then we will ask you to go back to therapy.

Dad: That's a good idea. Does that work for you, Natalie? Do you feel like we've heard what you were telling us?

Daughter: Yeah . . . thanks, guys. I didn't know you would be willing to hear me and change.

Dad: We're always willing to hear you out. Mom and I both want you to continue to manage your own life as much as possible, and yet it's important that you follow the rules while you live under our roof. Is that understood?

Daughter: Yeah, I got it!

Now, if you negotiate too much and too often, then you may experience another dynamic that is of concern: the issue of "If you give an inch, she will take a mile." If you're too permissive and negotiation becomes a weekly or daily ritual, you'll become exhausted and wonder why you ever created the document in the first place.

Negotiate on specifics, but don't give in on your vision and values unless for some reason a value has changed. It does happen. Some parents are changing their views regarding the social issues of the day such as gay rights, piercings, tattoos, and gender identity. We are constantly changing as humans, and your values may reflect such a shift. This may, in turn, affect your Home Agreement.

The ultimate goal here is to use this document as a tool to get your child from one place to another. After six months or a year, if your son or daughter is a healthy, mature child who respects you, then the Home Agreement has been fully integrated into the family culture and is a success! It has done its job.

Until then, your Home Agreement will serve as an invaluable guide, a road map to where and how you want your child to live.

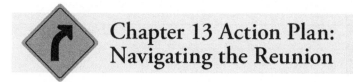

Chapter 13 Action Plan: Navigating the Reunion

(To download blank worksheets, visit www.TheRoadHomeBook.com/downloads.)

#1. The Coffee Shop Technique

Try the Coffee Shop Technique. While waiting in line, start a conversation with a stranger your child's age. Notice what you say, and his or her reaction. Now engage your child in the same type of conversation. Write about this experience.

_____

_____

_____

_____

_____

_____

_____

#2. Communication Skills

Have you learned healthy communication skills? Do you know how to reflect? How to de-escalate? If not, re-read Chapter Six on TLC and some of this chapter. Maybe get coached or read some of the books I've recommended. Take a moment to write down the communication skill you want to improve.

_____

_____

_____

_____

_____

_____

Now try it out. Don't worry about messing up. Do your best at improving communication with your child

#3. Triggers

Write the answers to the following questions:

a. Identify the triggers that led you into parenting you're not proud of. What are your parental triggers around arguments? Rescuing? Begging? Babying your child? Talking down? Communication?

_____

_____

_____

_____

b. What triggers led to your child's regression?

_____

_____

_____

_____

c. Can you identify triggers that led to regression for both you and your child?

_____

_____

_____

d. How are you going to deal with these triggers? Talk to your partner, your child, his treatment therapist, and your own therapist if you need help with coping techniques. Transfer the above triggers into the chart at right and also write in how you will manage these triggers.

Trigger	Parent	Child	Coping Technique
Hanging with red-light friends	✓	✓	Check in with my expectation and honor it
When I yell	✓	✓	When my family asks me to calm down, I'll take the time and room to do so
Alcohol in the house	✓	✓	Maintain a dry house
When I hear her in the bathroom late and get anxious	✓		Have a TLC discussion about why I feel this way and discuss with my therapist
When my son puffs up and yells	✓		TLC discussion with my son and also do more healing work around my abusive stepfather

Trigger	Parent	Child	Coping Technique

Trigger	Parent	Child	Coping Technique

14

Growing Your Child's Inner Adult

In working with my young clients, I've noticed that maturity is the savior. And yet too many teens and young adults are afraid to grow up. They unconsciously—or sometimes intentionally—sabotage their own maturation. This might be because, to them, holding down a job, obtaining a driver's license, or going to college signifies the death of their childhood.

You might, yourself, have lost your childhood early and feel that you grew up too fast. If you have been dealing with these feelings, perhaps you've been counseled to get in touch with your wounded inner child. In treatment, your son or daughter might have done the same type of work. I believe in the merits of this process, and in fact would like to introduce a similar idea.

Your child who has returned from treatment now needs to culti-
vate his inner adult. People in the process of maturing need to give up
their childish ways, not their childlike spirit. I always say to my young
clients, in essence: "Never give up your childlike spirit of wonder-
ment, creativity, joy, feeling, and being.
Please *do* give up your childish ways of
tantrums, selfishness, irresponsibility,
and manipulation."

> People in the process of maturing need to give up their childish ways, not their childlike spirit.

As one enters the mid-to-late teens,
it is time to acknowledge that childhood is over. Many teens who have
been in treatment, or need treatment,
dread doing this. Many wish to be treated like an adult, but want to
get away with murder, like a kid who doesn't know any better. For
these teens and young adults, saying goodbye to childhood is painful
and frightening. This is why treatment programs tackle the idea of
maturity head on. They help kids regain their childlike true self while
shedding immaturity.

Before treatment, your child lost his innocence; his childlike spirit
became increasingly jaded and selfish. Now he's back to health and
hope, and is able to pursue goals. He has been given solid skills for
moving toward maturity. It might be a struggle, but maturity is what
your child needs to keep himself driving safely on the right side of
the road.

In treatment programs, we organize teams into age-specific
groups. We tend to divide the age ranges like this: 1) 12 and younger,

2) 13 through 17, and 3) 18 to 28. Each group has its fundamental differences in the developmental tasks that need completing. For the purposes of this book, we're focusing on the two older groups, as most kids in treatment are age 13 and up.

The 13-to-17-Year-Old

Much of the work we have done so far concerning the Home Agreement has been directed to this age group, and many of the nuts-and-bolts, how-to aspects have already been covered. The tricky thing about this group is that it's hard to know exactly when a teen has become a young adult psychologically.

Your daughter who is early to mature physically might look like a young woman at 12, but you know that emotionally she's still a girl. It's much trickier to know what's really happening inside your 13-to-17-year-old. TLC can help you discern this.

What I can share with you that might help is this: Kids who have gone to treatment have often grown up too fast and developed a jaded perspective on life, due to their experiences prior to treatment. Treatment became the safe house, a place to grow and heal. And yet part of that healing process was being exposed to peers with even more serious stuff to assimilate and try to understand. Stuff that most of us have no desire to confront or even hear about. Unless you work in the mental health field, or a hospital, or were once a troubled youth yourself, it's unlikely that you've been exposed to the level of hardship that your child has witnessed.

My father can't believe the trauma I work with or the downright evil, criminal crap that happens to kids. Much of what our youth confronts seems inconceivable. But frightening things do happen, and your child already knows something about the dark side of life. You can't turn back the clock. What's happened has happened. But you can protect the innocence your child still possesses.

> You can't turn back the clock. What's happened has happened. But you can protect the innocence your child still possesses.

Before treatment, your child was probably drinking, doing drugs, or having inappropriate sexual relations. She was too often brooding and unhappy . . . "disturbed" is how some parents describe it. As is true in many long-term treatment programs, she learned to play again. Play was encouraged, as was authenticity, and she has learned how to free herself from her demons.

Upon your child's return, do your best to protect her from the dark side of life that manifests as violence, aggression, negativity, addictions, and toxic human relationships. Your kid has been around the block, but a teen doesn't need more exposure to life's underbelly to grow up—just the opposite. Your teen needs to feel safe knowing you have things under control, so she can continue to grow into a healthy young adult. Safe, but not controlled.

The human spirit is wired to be free, and teens crave their freedom. If you attempt to control a person they might resist simply because they feel their freedom of choice is being taken away. I often say to my young clients, "No one can make you do anything. It's up to you." I emphasize this freedom to decide one's fate, as it tends to put the responsibility squarely on the teen's shoulders, where it belongs. Most often when someone bears this weight of responsibility, he or she makes more responsible choices.

The nitty-gritty is that you can no more control your child than any of us could in treatment, but you can show him the road to maturity and set up guardrails to keep him traveling in the right direction.

Returning to High School

Regarding your child's return to high school, be aware of these two common issues:

1. Finding the right fit.

2. Capturing credits accurately from school to school.

The chances are that your child's former school is no longer an appropriate place for your son or daughter. Do some research to discover what other local schools might be a better fit and offer a fresh start. Unique alternative schooling is available in most communities, such as private schools with small classes, independent study programs, junior college alternatives to high school, homeschooling, tutors, and learning centers. Boarding school is another option not to be overlooked.

As for capturing credits, make sure you receive a formal transcript from your child's former school as well as the program he is exiting. Many programs, especially therapeutic boarding schools, have a staff member who is on top of this. Also check with your child's wilderness program, as he might have acquired credits during his time in wilderness. It's also probable that your child accrued community service hours while in treatment, so be sure to obtain verification of that.

Young Adults and Rites of Passage

Legally and within treatment modalities, the age of 18 carries a lot of significance. It's the agreed-upon age for separating the men from the boys, so to speak. A young adult is just that—an adult who is still young in years. For the sake of simplicity and congruency with the treatment programs, we can define this as ages 18 to 28. I encourage you, however, to define the term based on your family culture and beliefs. When do *you* think a child becomes an adult? What milestones signify this passage for *you*?

Please don't rely on me or any other professional to tell you when or what the rites of passage to adulthood should be. You are the sage of your family system, whether or not you believe yourself to be. When did your family acknowledge you as an adult, and what did they expect of you? Do you agree with how you were raised to be an adult, and were there markers to indicate this process? Often religion and ethnicity speak to when we become a man or woman. If your child doesn't know what it means to be a man or a woman, or even when that happens, confusion as to when he or she is a grownup might prevail and be passed on from generation to generation.

I ask parents to put serious intention and work into this one question: What does it mean to be a man or woman in your family? This is different than using the more objective term *adult*, because there might well be different rites of passage when a girl becomes a woman than when a boy becomes a man. Communicate what womanhood and manhood looks like in your family.

Most young men want their father's approval and blessing. Most people have a problem admitting this at any age. The need for acceptance by the father is a mythological truth, an unspoken desire and hunger within each man. So talk about what it means to be a man. In my family, a Jimenez man is expected to work hard, not whine, be strong, respect women, and not take any crap. We were taught in word and deed to be proud of our name and not back down from what we believe in. I knew this at age five, and throughout my youth it was demonstrated or talked about almost daily.

In your family, when does a girl become a woman? Let your daughter know what benchmarks are ahead of her, how women relate to men, what it means to be a mother, and the like. I can't speak to this firsthand, but a friend has told me that she first felt like a woman when she was allowed to stay in the kitchen while all the aunts were visiting with her mother. That she wasn't shooed from the room, as the children were, signaled to her that she had been accepted into the sisterhood of women. Events like this can be especially joyous milestones of maturity.

When Is a Young Adult Mature?

Behavior and measurable benchmarks are the best indicators of your child's growth. In determining if your child has made it to adulthood, and is therefore ready to fly from the nest, look for signs of self-reliance and psychological health.

A mature young adult takes responsibility for the full gamut of life, from fitness, hygiene, finances, work, and help around the house to car, gas, insurance, education, and intimacy. Observe your daughter in action. Is she managing her own money, taking an extra shift at work without moaning, buying things she used to expect you to buy, and getting good grades in school with no monitoring from you? If your child is sober, choosing appropriate friends, and driving safely and responsibly, if she has of her own volition gotten a job to pay for extra expenses and is studying for the SAT to get into the college of her choice, she's well on the road to becoming a woman.

> In determining if your child has made it to adulthood, and is therefore ready to fly from the nest, look for signs of self-reliance and psychological health.

She also needs to know how to manage her emotional and physical health. Signs to look for are emotional stability; sobriety (if addiction is an issue); solid friendships and romantic relationships; low levels of defiance toward you (yes, I mean peaceful relations); physical self-care, such as eating well and getting regular sleep and exercise; a budding spirituality or philosophical curiosity; an ability to ground herself in the midst of challenges; and, most importantly, the know-how to manage thorny problems by reaching out for help.

When a young adult is effectively managing his psychological state, he monitors and evaluates daily what is going on for him and what he needs. He is now capable of accessing resources, such as your wisdom, going to a counselor or therapist when he needs to, or to a psychiatrist to manage any needed meds, or choosing from a plethora of resource options to cope with mental distress, from group therapy, spiritual practices, naturopathic doctors, and addiction support groups to yoga, exercise, body work, and meditation. The bottom line is that a mature adult of any age takes responsibility for his mental well-being, in addition to the physical, emotional and practical, and these are daily activities he expects and realizes are lifelong.

The road to young adulthood traverses hills and valleys, and can present blind curves or be riddled with potholes. To navigate such terrain, a young person must possess enough confidence and self-esteem to muster courage, resiliency, and inner resourcefulness. He can start out on this road as early as 15, and continue until his mid-thirties. But the earlier this passage is completed, the better for surviving our John Wayne culture. We, a nation of rugged individualists regardless of political bent, tend to launch our kids early. The downside to this philosophy and practice is that we lose some connection with them.

This early eviction from the nest works best if it's balanced with a deep and abiding connection to family on the part of the young adult. Interdependence, not codependence, is beneficial for the entire family. Your child might need your assistance for many things, from financial support for college to successive treatment. She might need you to be there during a transitional period when she bites off certain developmental tasks that are not easily swallowed.

It's a good thing to watch each other's backs and provide a safety net, but to step in only when your help is truly needed. Don't misconstrue interdependence as giving your child everything he or she needs. The boundaries are still meant to be there, and spoiling is still to be avoided. The idea is for your child to know that you're there, and vice versa. The long-term benefit of maintaining a functional interdependence is that you might not feel so empty after the kids leave the nest.

Paying for Maturity

You might find that your fledgling young adult wants privileges that are inherent in adulthood but doesn't want to pay for them, metaphorically or practically. Too many young adults just expect their parents to pay for everything, from three-dollar coffees to clothes, outings, entertainment, and technology. They might want the respect due a mature, self-reliant adult and yet be unwilling to do the honest work it takes to earn true self-reliance.

Don't underestimate the importance of this issue. Young teens are much easier to parent than young adults who aren't prepared to pay the full price of independence. With younger teens you have more legal and economic power. Young adults are in a challenging transition, *and* they're trying to separate from you. This time is complicated for parents, as your child's developmental tasks, psychological processes, and economic self-sufficiency are all developing simultaneously. Consider this: Your child is trying to separate from you in order to be his own autonomous person, while in fact still being utterly dependent on you. This sets up a tense environment, ripe for arguments and communication breakdowns.

If ever your child needed a parent, it is at this point in his life. So set the pace, the tone, the expectations, and the rules. You create the benchmarks and develop the rites of passage. This might mean your child lives at home but gets a job and pays for his clothes, phone, gas, car insurance, and entertainment. It might mean staying at home and going to junior college while helping to care for younger siblings. It might mean managing his own meds and attending Marijuana Anonymous meetings while working part-time and paying you a little rent.

The expectations created depend on your family culture and your child's needs. If you are passive, peers and pop culture will create the road markers for your child. Taking the lead and shedding light on the right way assists young adults in knowing when they've made it—when he has become a man or she has become a woman.

Failure to Launch

Children who are delaying their journey to adulthood are paying a heavy price, and so are their parents. In our culture, the trend is to do for our kids much of what we were expected to do for ourselves when we were young. This is done with the best of intentions. After all, you don't want your child to struggle as you did when you were 18, do you? Well, I'm here to tell you that struggle is necessary and good. When a 25-year-old still needs items ranging from rent to toothpaste paid for by her parents, dependency is well entrenched. I have yet to see this dependency yield healthy results. This is failure to launch.

I see struggling as a natural part of the transition to adulthood, and I believe that experiencing it is imperative for the mental health of those sons and daughters who go to treatment. Your child needs to be challenged to be more authentic, practical, and objective about his life. He won't attain his optimal state when coddled by loving parents or allowed to regress to childish patterns.

> When a 25-year-old still needs items ranging from rent to toothpaste paid for by her parents, dependency is well entrenched.

But how can you, as the parent, help him grow? By encouraging his "inner adult" to show up. Most teens and young adults are much more capable than we think. Expect him to be mature in his thinking, dialogue, and behavior. Expect her to behave like an adult, and show surprise if she behaves like a child.

Don't dignify childish behavior. For example, when you enforce a consequence your child might resort to acting outraged. Calmly remind him that he needs to behave like an adult, and engage him only when he can approach you in a mature way. "When you can talk to me calmly, adult to adult, we can continue this discussion." "When you're ready to talk in a mature way, come back to the dinner table."

Remember, back in Chapter 4, the discussion about how the voice in which we speak to ourselves is a blend of our own voice and those integrated from our past? We borrow ideas from our parents, coaches, teachers, siblings, godparents, and aunts and uncles, and this accumulation of voices gets integrated into our self-talk. As we move into adulthood we begin to live by that collective voice, and if we do so in a beneficial way we integrate the positive messages and lose the negative.

In treatment, your child heard a lot of healthy talk from solid peers and role models. When she comes home, keep her in the presence of mature, positive people so her own inner voice can mature. This is a golden opportunity to impart to your child your vision, your values, and your voice.

Four factors can interfere with your wish to help your child grow up. These are fear, guilt, pleasing your child, and rescuing behavior. Therapists, case managers, and team leaders don't act out of fear or guilt, and they have no need to please or rescue your child. Because of their caring nonattachment, these professionals aren't disturbed when kids make mistakes, for they know that this is how humans learn.

When your child comes home, greet her with the expectation that she is capable of healthy behavior. It's not in your job description as parent to be pleasing, indulgent, and entertaining every time your child is bored, brooding, or acting out. Nor is there any need to overpraise or to hand out too many rewards. And it's not at all advantageous for you to rescue her from sticky situations she's created. When your child has to extricate herself from a mess she's gotten herself into, she gains empowerment to change her life.

If you find yourself trying to save your child from reality by giving him things just because you feel bad for him, wanting him to always be comfortable and happy, or micromanaging his life because you're afraid he'll fail, please hold back your impulses to act in such ways. Give your son space to live and not always be doted on. Let him experience the mundane, boring, uncomfortable, and sometimes embarrassing consequences of his behavior. When you let your child fail by his own hand and correct by his own hand, you're helping him develop the tools he needs to thrive.

I endeavor to empower my young clients to live in the world of reality. I don't save them from the challenges of growing up. Most kids mature greatly by dealing with the natural consequences of the wilderness; that's why that modality works. Now that your child is in the wilderness of life outside treatment, allow her to experience its reality and natural consequences: budgeting her money, developing healthy passions, driving a car responsibly, maintaining friendships that are true, the balancing act of staying sober, the nervousness of looking for a job, meeting the expectations for her school grades, communicating with her parents in a mature way, not getting lost in addictive habits like gaming, and planning for college, tech school, or a job to pay for her future life as an adult.

This is the stuff of life with which we must all learn to contend. There's no cheating or taking a shortcut. Help your child develop insight and judgment. To do so, she must exercise choice and experience the natural consequences of doing so. Don't, in the attempt to be loving parents, save her from growing up.

Leaving the Nest

Good treatment teaches kids how to fly from the nest, but this doesn't mean they're ready. Although they might have learned the life skills necessary for a successful launch, their wings might still need more feathers. In nature, when a fledgling leaves the nest too early, a parent bird will watch and care for the young one until it has the strength and know-how to fly away. When your bird comes back home from treatment, he'll need your continuing supervision and care. Depending on his age and mental health, it might be a while before he's able to leave the nest, but start immediately to let that day become a reality.

For the Jay Family, it is time for Junior to leave the nest.

Each time your son goes out with true friends or goes to work, it's an exercise in spreading his wings. Let him stretch and flap those wings. When he does so, he's heading closer to maturation and your engagement in his life needs to become less. As your son continues to mature, he'll practice more self-reliant activities. Don't interfere; if you prevent him from flying you might create an enmeshment that can cause psychological issues. Bear in mind that children don't resent parents who raise them to be their own person and to cope with life as an adult.

> Bear in mind that children don't resent parents who raise them to be their own person and to cope with life as an adult.

The day your child realized she could change just one thing in her life is the day she first experienced responsibility. Some kids have heard the word *responsibility* so much that the word has a negative connotation. Whatever we call it—maturity, accountability, acceptance of what one has set into motion—responsibility is good. If your child continues to shirk the opportunity of responsibility, she's really saying that she feels ambivalent about growing up. Whether she's afraid she lacks what it takes or simply doesn't want to leave the comfort of the childhood nest, she's saying, *Don't make me grow up!*

In response, focus on ways to increase her self-confidence and desire to mature. Teach her that it's worth being an adult by showing her the freedoms and privileges adulthood affords. Parents who maintain an adult child's dependency upon them lose out, along with their child, on the richness of life. Plainly stated, the 27-year-old who is still dependent on his parents will blame and resent those parents. Let him go as soon as he is capable, and from a distance watch him thrive. He will then come back and visit of his own volition.

Living Away from Home

When your young adult moves out on her own, I highly recommend that she move into a structured living arrangement for the first phase of her out-of-the-nest experience. If she's heading off to college, consider dormitory life for her. If not, a group-living situation is ideal. Not only will your young adult have the support of peers (who are positive influences, one hopes), but she will not encounter the loneliness that often sets in for those who first go out on their own. This is where guidance from you, through TLC, is invaluable to your child. Do you remember how exciting and scary moving out was? If you can talk to your child about her choices and guide her lovingly, her move will be an even more rewarding experience.

From the day your child leaves your home, it's important to tease out how resourceful she is becoming. In other words, stay in touch. When roadblocks loom, observe how she maneuvers around them. Be slow to rescue and solve her problems. This is a great temptation, but waiting and watching with your finger on the rescue button is great policy.

Be genuinely curious about your child's latest problem, and actively listen and reflect back her experiences, but don't solve the problem.

*Mrs. Johnson just got wind that their child was
getting a "D" in pre-Calc.*

Watch to see her master the situation on her own, and then reinforce her success with legitimate praise.

Be aware that not all issues are dealt with in treatment, so when your child stumbles a bit, be there to discern the nature of the issue and your child's resilience and resourcefulness. If she begins to party too much, is an addiction developing? Is your son able to pull out of his depression after a breakup? Can your daughter hold down a job and also earn satisfactory grades? Watch, communicate, watch, analyze, watch, support, watch . . . and only when your child's health is at risk, rescue.

One last comment about young adults. It's a funny thing—they can take quantum leaps in a matter of months. Once the lightbulb goes on and they experience the fun and self-esteem of owning one's own life, they can blossom like the time-lapse film of a tulip. Your child can become the person you dreamed she would be . . . not necessarily overnight, but faster than you might have believed possible.

Education Beyond High School

If secondary education is on the table, whether a university, junior college, military academy, technical college, or apprenticeship in the trades, your child will need a fair amount of help beyond financial support. Also, he or she should be given a strong voice in the decision. But here's the rub. From my vantage point as a life coach, I see teens and young adults floundering with post-high school preparation. Many of my clients think something will magically fall into place, and therefore they're not seeking out professional support. As a parent you do need to stay on top of this issue, or else your child will graduate from high school and potentially wander aimlessly or sit in your nest. I find when I discuss with my teen and young adult clients their possible educational future, they are sponges hungry for options. Hear me and believe me when I say that they don't know all the available options, even if they pretend they do.

Some parents hire an educational consultant who specializes in the college application process to get the right student-school fit. For some, this option is not affordable. I am not an expert here, but I do know that other parents have gone to their child's current high school to see if a college counselor is available. Also, discuss this with your child's treatment program as they often have career counselors. Books, relatives who have been in your shoes, other college kids, the Web—there are tons of resources out there.

If your young adult returns home for a short stint and then leaves for secondary education, develop a Home Agreement for home and then a College Agreement (sample at the end of Chapter 11) that will be specific to your child's education and personal-development goals away from home. The process of creating such a document is much the same as for a Home Agreement, but because the child is a young adult, it's wise to approach it as a *very* collaborative process.

College Agreements are different from Home Agreements. Because you will most likely be far away from your child, you will not be able to know what is truly going on. And that's the way it should be. The goal is to create boundaries that give your child freedom and then have faith that she will manage it well.

An effective College Agreement addresses issues and factors regarding launching a young adult: work, food cards, car usage, an allowance, potential legal issues, healthy and responsible behavior, potential drug or alcohol issues, academic performance standards, and respect. Choose the most important issues for your family and then set up expectations, monitoring systems, and consequences.

If sobriety is the key concern, make it a stipulation that your child get drug tested. Many parents have drug test results sent to them by the college's health center. In the College Agreement, spell out what the consequences to a dirty drug test might be. With young adults they are often supportive (drug counseling) and sometimes restrictive (less allowance or loss of the car). You can also insist that you have access to grades and debit/credit card usage online. Monitor and follow through with consequences if rules are broken.

Safeguards such as these allow you to keep a finger on the pulse, but the day-to-day is really up to your child. If she gets a parking ticket or a speeding ticket or drinks to excess one night, you will not know (at least not immediately). If your child is maturing, she may handle these issues all on her own. If she is not able to, eventually you will find out. That's when transparent and loving communication and follow-through on consequences come into play big time.

When your child leaves the nest but is still under your financial wing, you have some clout. During this transitional time, TLC is the ticket. Keep lines of communication and trust wide open. You are always a phone call or text away. Don't expect your child to tell you everything, and don't expert her to like the rules. Do expect her to make some mistakes. Your job with a College Agreement is to set up an agreed-upon way to track what you can, and still give her freedom to explore her world. Get out of the way and use this time to establish a new and different relationship with your child. Enjoy what she chooses to share and who she's becoming.

The Fulfillment of a Life Vision

I observe that this generation of parents clearly and admirably believe that children should realize dreams of the child's own choosing.

Encourage those dreams. By this I mean his real goals—the ones that take years of planning and execution, not offhand wishes or flights of fancy. A wish is a teen saying he wants to be a rock star, or the next Bill Gates or Kobe Bryant, yet he doesn't mean it enough to work at the trade. Many of the kids who come to treatment are almost delusional about the actual blood and sweat it takes to accomplish dreams. If your treatment program has done good work, your child knows there is no easy way to attain one's goals. He has learned to dream and work, not wish and pine.

A young person will experience great happiness pursuing a dream stemming from a genuine passion, especially if the journey includes struggle and delayed gratification. He'll come to realize that the journey was and is the joy. For example, a child with a dream to be a teacher must put in years of studying well in high school in order to get into college. Then it takes four years minimum to be qualified for a teaching credential. The time spent studying and learning, the jobs worked while in school, the student loans to be repaid, and eventually the wearisome grading of papers are all part of realizing his dream.

Parents today don't project onto their children nearly as much as parents of past generations did. To keep this spirit alive, encourage your child to individuate and create his own vision for his life. Try not to project onto your child your own lost dreams. It's challenging enough to pursue one's own vision, let alone try to retrieve a parent's lost passion.

To obtain his dreams of a career, lifestyle, home, and family, your child will need to keep his eye on the ball and not falter too much. This is how life works. Travails can befall any of us on our way:

addiction, depression, divorce, recessions, bankruptcy . . . a multitude of distractions can sidetrack our dreams.

I like the quote "A goal is a dream with a deadline," by the American writer Napoleon Hill. Dreams, goals, visions, and passions translate into reality when we're willing to apply steady hard work, without giving up. If your child can do this, and can accept some delayed gratification, he'll become a master at what he wants. And eventually someone won't think twice about paying him well for what he has mastered.

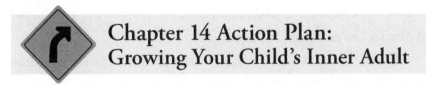

Chapter 14 Action Plan: Growing Your Child's Inner Adult

(To download blank worksheets, visit www.TheRoadHomeBook.com/downloads.)

#1. Rites of Passage

Reflect back on your own coming of age, and make a list of what you see as the markers (Bar or bat mitzvah? Driving and working?) for becoming a young a man or woman. Why not share these mile markers with your child?

_____

_____

_____

_____

_____

_____

_____

#2. Leaving the Nest

How does your child measure up in ways you consider necessary for independent young adulthood? Are there areas where you know she needs work? Is he unable or unwilling to find a job? Does your daughter have no clue about how to manage money? Can your children do laundry? Cook for himself or herself? Make a list of areas where you feel the need to better guide your child toward becoming a young adult.

_____

_____

_____

_____

_____

_____

_____

_____

_____

_____

_____

_____

_____

_____

_____

_____

_____

_____

#3. Action Step

Take action to fulfill one practical skill on the list you just created in step #2 as soon as you possibly can. For example, *I will help my child to write a resumé and help her role-play job interviewing.* Make your way through the list or find mentors and family members to take over some of these tasks. It does take a village.

#4. Education

Do you know your child's future regarding education? How about her ability to live on her own? Do you know what dreams of his are achievable? Spend some time with this issue. Talk to your child's therapist, educational consultant, and mentors. Talk to your child, then start making a plan that fits in with your vision and values around education. Jot down a few education possibilities here.

_____

_____

_____

_____

_____

_____

#5. Fostering Independence

Can you think of ways you might be holding back your child? How can you be more lovingly nonattached? Write a few changes you could make here. Example:

I will stop buying my daughter expensive clothes, because that's not something that teaches her to be responsible for her own life.

_____

_____

_____

_____

_____

_____

_____

_____

_____

_____

_____

_____

_____

_____

_____

#6. A Life Vision

Do you know your child's dreams for the future? Have the two of you ever discussed them? Why not ask and find out? Write them down so you know something about where the road away from home is going.

_____

_____

_____

_____

_____

_____

15

Dealing with Regression

Regression is one of those frequently batted-about treatment words, especially as your child's return home becomes imminent. It's not a clinical term per se, but a concept used in the treatment world to describe serious setbacks. Regression is the opposite of progression.

Your child making some mistakes and pushing a few rules is not regression. Regression is when your child resorts to earlier, less mature, dysfunctional behavior that doesn't further his well-being. It's not one or two steps back. It's five steps back. It's not a slip, but a relapse.

To use our metaphor of the road, regression is turning around and heading the other way. It's choosing to take a dangerous back alley. It's driving so far in the wrong direction that parents can no longer see their original, authentic child. Instead they see only red taillights!

Knowing what behaviors signal regression is extremely useful in creating the Home Agreement. Your Agreement can then help you monitor your child's progress and possibly predict regression. Rules give you the ability to determine if what you're experiencing on the part of your child is regression or growth. Is he falling into old, maladaptive patterns or trying new ways to be an adult? Is she manipulating in ways that led to dysfunctional behavior or attempting to communicate a new point of view?

> Rules give you the ability to determine if what you're experiencing on the part of your child is regression or growth.

If occasionally she argues to have rules changed, or breaks a rule out of defiance, you might be dealing with a young adult who is pushing for more freedom. But if rules are being consistently broken, that's regression. How do you discern which is which? You talk, listen, and watch.

I say again that TLC is the mortar that will keep your relationship and Home Agreement intact. You might find yourself having the same conversation a few times. That's okay, as long as you keep enforcing the rules. When you do, your child should eventually correct. If he doesn't, then the regression is severe. It's then that you will need to seek more help. The type of help will depend on the form of regression.

Clinical concerns regarding your child might or might not have been fully resolved in treatment. So before your child is on your doorstep, discuss with her therapist and with her what regression would look like. Let your child's treatment counselor help you determine what kind and degree of behaviors on the part of your child would be considered regression. Because her reentry to life outside of treatment will stress her and test her coping skills and mental resiliency, part of your job in this next year or so will be watchful for clinical issues to arise. Ensure that your Home Agreement contains consequences to support your child (and you) if depression, addictive behavior, pronounced anxiety, or any other pathology returns.

Stress, which can trigger dysfunction, rises steeply when we're not prepared with adequate coping skills or not resilient enough to handle the trials of life. The possibility exists that, despite treatment and the coping skills gained, your child might still reach a breaking point. The first year or so home will be a test, and you must be able to gather information and assess whether the mental health issues and dysfunctional behaviors that emerge daily, weekly, or monthly are manageable. To do this, it helps to have already determined which actions or behaviors on the part of your child will be considered "misdemeanors" and which will be "felonies." We can define these problem behaviors in terms of a color continuum:

COLOR CODE BEHAVIOR

GREEN ↔ YELLOW ↔ ORANGE ↔ RED

Green behaviors do not pose a problem—all systems are go. Your child is making healthy choices and following the road map you've set before him. Yellow and orange behaviors send out a cautionary warning. You can probably handle these by enforcing the Home Agreement, creating stiffer consequences, and maybe calling for some local backup. Red behaviors signal a code red situation of immediate danger. Emergency measures must be taken, because your child's actions are showing a blatant disregard for your values, the rules, and his safety.

Creating a color codification of behaviors will help you determine which dysfunctional ones warrant the greatest concern. Perhaps smoking weed once is yellow. Smoking weed now and then, hanging around with red-light friends, but exhibiting honest regret might be orange. Erratic mood swings, combined with proof that someone is regularly abusing weed and prescription meds, would be code red.

If you're watching and color coding your child's behavior, as he sends out more and more orange behaviors, you should get very proactive so as not to have to declare code red. An orange behavior is where you want to push for more TLC and get a bit more heavy-handed on consequences. Orange behaviors might be cutting, a dirty drug test, a psychotic break, not coming home all night, aggressive communication, or a refusal to take mood-stabilizing meds.

Holding the Line

If parents hold the line during regression by following through on consequences and backup plans, the backward movement can be checked. The two exceptions to this are when mental health issues are more than you and your child can effectively deal with and when your child has resolved to be defiant and refuses to engage in TLC. In both these cases, there is little you can do. You can't change pathology singlehandedly, and you can't change someone's mind if they don't want it changed.

Otherwise, holding the line is important—not just to show your child "who's in charge" but also to provide him with the support he needs to get back on track. Your son or daughter needs to stay on the right side of the road to mature and heal. It's up to you to clearly demarcate the lines on the road and enforce them. This helps keep your child on the straight and narrow and away from a disastrous collision. Draw the line and then hold the line. It's simple but effective advice.

Stepping into Regression

Regression, if it happens, usually occurs in a succession of small steps, and not all regression in these incremental steps is serious. If your daughter is taking five steps forward and only one or two back, then life is good.

If she exhibits some of the same behaviors that prompted you to send her to treatment, then she is most likely regressing. Regression is most accurately spotted not in what your child says, but what she does. So it's her actions to which you should hold her most accountable, not what she says in a fit of anger or fear.

> Regression is most accurately spotted not in what your child says, but what she does.

Sometimes parents become worn down over time and have trouble discerning bad behavior on the part of their kids. When in the thick of it, parents can be blinded by hope. That's why color coding ahead of time is helpful. You can most likely tolerate a few yellow infractions, but if your kid is blazing with code red rule breaking and behavior, it's time to bring out the fire extinguisher.

It behooves parents to consistently assess the regressive actions to see if they're increasing in either number or severity. If you have slight suspicions because (1) your son is complaining of being sick and staying home from school a bit too often, (2) you're missing cash, or (3) your daughter is skipping family meals and wants to be alone in her room, then it's time to confront the idea that something might very well be amiss.

Don't justify these behaviors by deciding it's a nasty flu season, or you must have spent more cash than you thought, or she's tired and needs some personal time. If you see rule breaking (no matter what the excuse) or behavior or circumstances that challenge the Home Agreement on a daily or weekly basis, look closely at these transgressions to gauge how significant they are.

In the following examples of regression, most of the behaviors are code red while some are orange and some yellow, depending on frequency. You need to be the discerning adult here. Keep emotion out of it, put some distance between yourself and your child, and aim to see your child's behavior for what it truly is.

Some examples of regression are:

- A relapse into substance abuse or another addiction

- Blatant disrespect, with lying, aggressive language, or violent threats

- Blowing off curfew for a week

- Refusing to go to school or dropping out

- Frequent sneaking out after midnight to go sleep with the boyfriend

- Forging checks or stealing your jewelry and pawning it

- Felonious activity such as drunk driving, dealing drugs, or assault

- Hanging out repeatedly with red-light friends

- Disregarding many of the Home Agreement rules

- Disregard for your property, seen as punching holes in walls, breaking items on purpose, or crashing the car and not caring

- Alienation from the family

- Excessive moodiness, defiance, or anger

- A refusal to take mood-stabilizing medications

Issues that might be of lesser concern in determining whether regression is happening (more orange and yellow light) are skipping chores, inadequate hygiene, slight educational slips, small amounts of defiance, one slip into smoking pot or drinking, a disrespectful episode or fit, a one-or-two-night curfew offense, or stealing twenty bucks—once.

All breakdowns regarding the Home Agreement need to be looked at carefully and discussed in a TLC moment. Addressing all offenses against the Agreement is important because it will let your child know you're being vigilant. And, with TLC, you can then determine whether it's regression or simply a child finding her way in the world.

This process of two steps forward, one back, can go on for some time. The time will be shorter if you send your child a very clear message that this whole Home Agreement deal is real and that you absolutely expect her to live accordingly.

Sometimes you might notice the same issue, such as refusal to get a job, reoccurring and not being corrected through support or consequences. While talking with your child about it, it might become apparent to you that this subject is her Achilles' heel. Perhaps this obstacle—in this case, obtaining a job—is her greatest fear. It is an area where she must still grow. A good course of action would be to accept this fear, this area of potential regression, and allow some time for working through the issue with your child.

Help her take baby steps until she can overcome the obstacle. Do this by problem solving with her, listening and reflecting what she's going through. Walk with her through this life experience with compassion, and in the timeframe she needs.

The F#@k-It!s

If regression takes hold in your child, the degradation of his actions and character can seem to happen overnight. He might be getting overwhelmed, and feeling like being home and playing by the rules is just too hard. He wants to simply give up. This can result in his developing "the f#@k-it!s."

This is a scary time for parents, and a moment of truth for the entire family. Why? Because this moment of regression is when your child breaks not one rule, but three or four. He's not just refusing to get a job; he's also skipping school, smoking pot, hanging out with all the wrong friends, and getting verbally abusive. He's having a total verbal meltdown, and his actions are frightening and disruptive for all—code red beyond a doubt.

This behavior will test the best of your parenting. It's important to be the leader here, and create a sense that you're in charge and are going to take care of your kid while not tolerating his antics.

At this crucial juncture, find a quiet place to read and review your Home Agreement either on your own or with your partner. Breathe. Then, with new resolve, follow through on every aspect of it. Employ consequences 100 percent. This is your best shot at settling your child, asserting your parental authority, and keeping the rest of the family safe.

This is what professionals do in treatment. We follow through with steadfast leadership. We don't get reactive. Your troublemaker needs to know that you're going to be solid and consistent, that you can't be manipulated. It's time to hold the line. If your child has the f#@k-it!s for a week or longer, even with you following through on consequences, this is clearly code red behavior—a sign that he needs more help.

Parental Regression

When a parent regresses, it's different than it is with the child. For instance, it's unlikely that anyone will send a parent back to treatment! When a parent can't or hasn't dedicated the past month to two years to personal growth, it can be problematic, because it's up to the adult to provide leadership.

It's of course best if all the adults important to your child lead with personal awareness. To do this takes practice. Parents are often unaware of how their actions trigger arguments and promote family dysfunction. Therapists work diligently to manage their own triggers, and parents need to as well.

If you're falling into less-than-optimal behavior, check to see which of the following reactions to your child might be occurring:

- Allowing him to control the conversation by badgering you until you give in

- Not holding yourself to the rules and consequences in your Home Agreement

- Lecturing, preaching, and giving advice instead of listening and validating your child

- Being overly trustful or overly distrustful of your child

- Avoiding necessary confrontations (being intimidated by her tantrums)

- Fearing to be assertive with your child

- Feeling afraid to insist on drug testing

- Failing to lead the family into productive meetings when there are problems to work out

- Failing to use TLC and other therapeutic communication skills

- Feeling overwhelmed and ineffective to parent your child

- Allowing your own old issues and patterns to interfere with confident parenting

As a therapist, I've seen that when a child nears the age at which a parent had a developmental struggle, the relationship between the two becomes tense. Often the parent will encounter mental health issues he or she thought had been put to bed. If a parent suffered a huge life event (illness, a death, bankruptcy, abandonment) at age 14, the trauma can leave a subconscious fear that comes back when he parents children of his own. His own history of regression or developmental arrest gets layered on top of his child's.

To provide a more specific example, if a parent was steadily abused in his teen years by his father, and at the age of 14 the abuse led to his being removed to foster care, when he is a parent and his son nears 14, unconscious projection might begin. The father could become neurotically over-protective of his son. This is unhealthy for both the son and the dad. In such a case, the father can benefit from discussing this with his therapist, and so can the whole family.

When I bring up this phenomenon, parents will readily admit that they fear their child will suffer as they did. Unaddressed, this can result in both the parent and child becoming over-anxious in their relationship, and this will subsequently spill over into other areas of their lives. Awareness of this issue allows the parent to revisit his "demons" through therapy and heal his old wounds. This brings relief and allows the child to be free of the parent's projections. The child can now deal squarely with his own issues without also contending with the parent's.

To stop parental regression, the first step is awareness that it exists. If you have a partner, ask him or her to help you identify your weaknesses: What triggers you into regressive actions? Do the same in turn. Identify how things can be handled more advantageously. Once you're aware of your triggers and areas of challenge, problem-solve how to handle them better. For instance, if you're not good at validating your child and find yourself preaching to the wall as she rolls her eyes, you can improve your reflective listening by reading about it and practicing. Don't be reluctant to "practice" on your child.

The Zen of Regression

In treatment and at home, the ebb and flow or regression and progression of your child's life is a natural occurrence. Expect regression, and don't be thrown off by it. Most of the time a regression is minimal, especially if you hold to the Home Agreement and manage strife with TLC. Coming home is all about seeing how well your child can thrive outside of treatment. He'll need to practice. He'll need to learn. He is likely to take four steps forward on Monday and two steps back on Tuesday.

If regression is yellow to orange, you can work with this. If he tailspins and nosedives (code red), you'll catch him and help him move to the next supportive process he needs. During this back-and-forth, acknowledge those old feelings of fear, guilt, and failure, but don't allow them to own you. Be present in the here and now, and lead to the best of your ability. The very fact that you're taking the time to read this book proves you're not a ne'er-do-well parent. You've taken on a role that calls for diligence and perseverance. You haven't taken the easy way out; quite the contrary.

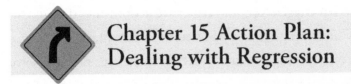

Chapter 15 Action Plan: Dealing with Regression

(To download blank worksheets, visit www.TheRoadHomeBook.com/downloads.)

#1. Signs of Regression

Review the issues that you see as key to your child's growth and maturity. What are the actions he or she might take that you would consider regression? Let these examples help you make a list:

smoking weed, hanging out with red-light boyfriends, cutting when she's stressed, lying to us about key values

_____

_____

_____

_____

#2. Code Behaviors

Now codify the behaviors you've listed as yellow, orange, or code red regression. Here's an example to get you started.

Behavior	Yellow	Orange	Code Red
Aggression	*Yells at Mom once only*	*Becomes verbally abusive more regularly*	*Verbally abusive, punches Dad, and punches holes in the kitchen wall*

Behavior	Yellow	Orange	Code Red

#3. Home Agreement

Read again through the first draft of your Home Agreement. Did you include consequences for these areas where regression might occur? Do you have a good backup plan? If not, go back and revise your current draft.

#4. Parental Regression

Look at your own behavior. Do you see possible parental regression? Make a list here; for example:

projecting my own childhood onto my daughter, my temper flaring up and halting communication, avoiding conflict because I'm afraid

_____

_____

_____

_____

_____

_____

_____

_____

_____

_____

_____

_____

#5. Parental Triggers

What could trigger these regressions for you? Make a list here. Work on recognizing and dealing with these triggers. Keep handy the list you developed for step #4, along with this one. Remember that awareness of your own foibles and triggers is the first step to handling them. Here are a few examples:

when my son yells me at, when I hear from friends that my son was at a drinking and/or drug party, when my son sleeps until noon and doesn't get up and do his chores or exercise

16

Surviving a Transition in Trouble

When the road to "normal" life starts to seem longer and more arduous than ever for you and your child, it might mean that something more than growing pains or adjustment angst is behind your child's behavior. Perhaps regression is your child's less-than-desirable way to prove that he's an adult and wants to leave the nest. Regression might stem from clinical or pathological issues, and sometimes things don't work out because your child is choosing options for his life that sharply differ from what you've laid out as being the best for him.

Issues that would have more of a downward-spiral effect on your child and family are harm to self, school truancy, addiction relapse, illegal behavior, full-blown defiance, aggressive communication, withdrawal from day-to-day life, and regular disregard for your values. These behaviors signal that it's time to rely on your backup plan and support network. I would classify continuous infractions of this sort as code red, and go into decisive action.

When major regression occurs, the decline can be rapid. I hear parents say, "What happened? He was doing great, and then he went downhill in a couple of weeks!"

It can happen that you wake up one day and all the ugly pieces of the puzzle fall into place. You see that your son has returned to smoking pot daily and is missing school, not holding down a job, and hanging out with the old red-light friends. And the money on your dresser is gone. In your gut you know it's just a matter of time before he does something illegal like dealing for cash and more drugs. Listen to your inner wisdom, and don't deny that this regression is real.

Another key indicator of a transition in trouble is a breakdown in TLC. When you can no longer effectively communicate with your child, your ability to influence her, and hear her, is lost. When healthy, open communication is no longer viable in your home, and life with your child seems unbearable, it's time to evoke the "If Things Don't Work Out" clause of the Home Agreement.

Please don't procrastinate. I've seen parents avoid this step, sometimes out of wishful thinking. Living with such an anxiety-provoking unknown *(Is she or isn't she in a bad enough place that we have to take major action?)* is just as disconcerting as taking that monumental step to get assistance. If your child chooses code red behavior and needs more help than the home environment (including your city, schools, hospitals, and local professionals) can provide, then reach outside for help.

Most parents instinctively know when things aren't going well and it's time to call the game—time to say, "We all gave it our best shot. She needs more help." Grief and relief will accompany this decision, just like it did when you first sent her to treatment. You might consider it to be your own fault. Be slow to judge. Upon reflection, and with hindsight, you'll most likely see that you and your child both did the best you could.

From a clinical standpoint, the capabilities of a family system are limited when it comes to managing mental health. Even the best parenting can't keep addiction, bipolar disorder, schizophrenia, panic attacks, or chronic depression contained. The ability to heal these issues is not in your hands. It takes wisdom and perspective to know when your child needs professional care and to send her away from home to find a better path to health and maturity. You did this once before; you can do it again. And, yes, this is sad. You have a right to feel that way and it is appropriate. Don't hesitate to get all the outside help you may need in this instance: pastoral, therapeutic, or logistical.

> It takes wisdom and perspective to know when your child needs professional care and to send her away from home to find a better path to health and maturity.

Continuing the Healing Elsewhere

If you have exhausted your Home Agreement options and cannot find an alternative form of care for your child, enlist or rehire a therapeutic educational consultant. These professionals are worth the money they charge, as they study and track programs nationwide and even internationally. An educational consultant should be able to help you plot the next course for your child. You can locate one near you through the Independent Educational Consultants Association or IECA *(iecaonline.com)*, the National Association of Therapeutic Schools and Programs *(natsap.org)*, and *strugglingteens.com*.

Therapeutic programs tend to have savvy websites and good admissions personnel who might say the right things on the phone, but in fact a particular program might be a poor fit for your child. An experienced ed consultant can help you discern which program will be the most effective and suitable. Consultants often know what great therapist just left a program, or what treatment center just took a nosedive in quality—information that websites won't disclose. Consultants can also help match the ever-shifting population in specific treatment centers to your child.

For instance, maybe last month a certain wilderness program would have been a good match for your 14-year-old, but now all the 14-year-olds have graduated and a great number of 18-year-olds remain. Consultants spend hundreds of hours visiting programs and monitoring firsthand the nuances that do matter. They cost money, but they can better ensure that the money you'll be spending on treatment will get positive results.

You might also find that a transitional coach, local therapist, or therapist from your child's past program can help you determine if she'll do better leaving home to heal elsewhere. They might be able to help with the new placement as well. If your child has become a young adult since her first treatment placement, the best options this time around might be different. Each situation is unique, and getting the right fit is what counts. Check with your insurer to see what programs are covered by your plan. You may even check back with a therapeutic program previously attended by your child to see if you can get a scholarship or a second placement for your child.

Respect your child's autonomy by working with her on this next phase of life outside home. If possible, maintain TLC and figure out with her, and any professionals, what the next step will be. Empower her. Let her know she's responsible for her past choices and for this present one that will affect her future. She might not like the prospect of leaving home again, and yet in retrospect she might really appreciate it. The chances of her doing well in a new program are better when she has helped formulate the plan. Six months in, when she's struggling with the same issues she ran into at home, she'll know that she is responsible for where she is, not her parents.

Treatment Options Besides Home

Troubled teenagers of today have many options. If your son isn't doing well in the local high school, and his attitude tends toward defiance and disrespect, he might transition into a boarding school beautifully. Maybe he only needs to get away from unwholesome influences, and doesn't need that much therapy. He might even choose the school on his own and go eagerly. Or maybe working on Uncle Rex's ranch in Texas over the summer, or some other vigorous outdoor program, will be the ticket for your defiant, weed-smoking son. Sometimes a change of scenery is all that's needed.

If you can afford it, consider wilderness, either for the first or second time. Many teens return to a previously attended wilderness program. I suggest, though, that you take some time to research other programs, too. There are many out there, and an alternative might better suit your child at this point in his journey. The structured assistance of a therapeutic boarding school might be what he needs to address his continuing therapeutic needs so he can graduate from high school. In some cases psychiatric care is needed for serious mental health crises such as mania, psychosis, suicide attempts, deep depression, or debilitating anxiety. For addiction, you might enroll your child in a local inpatient clinic that takes your insurance and offers follow-up outpatient care, or something in another county or state might be the best bet.

Young adults can choose a transitional program, such as a group home that teaches independent living skills from cooking to budgeting, while they attend college or tech school or work at a job. Adventure programs instill confidence, along with teamwork and healthy recreation. Gap programs offer young adults the opportunity to take a year off to mature and see the world. Or maybe your child will choose to study in France, Japan, or Costa Rica for a year with a study-abroad program. Even working on a commercial fishing vessel in Alaska might help your child "get his head on straight."

Some of my buddies tell me that when they were 20 years old and up to no good, their parents walked them down to the recruiter's office, and the military service they then entered turned them into adults.

The armed services offer years of structure and no-nonsense environments that develop maturity and integrity—just as a treatment program might, except that your child gets paid. Much of the world uses the military system as a rite of initiation and to help instill responsibility in young adults. German, Swedish, and Israeli youths are obligated to give back. If you're concerned about your child fighting in armed conflict, consider a more peaceful service such as the Coast Guard.

I've seen all these options bring success. The idea is to be creative and take into account who your child is.

Young adults have one other obvious option: maybe it's simply time for your child to move out on his own. The 23-year-old who has bombed out of college four times and refuses to work might never grow up until you release him to get an honest dose of reality. More than a few young adults have confided to me that they're holding out for a trust-fund lifestyle. They also admit, though, that the best thing for them would be for their parents to withhold all financial support, forcing them to deal with their psychological and functional issues.

Many of us choose to hold on to immature patterns until life itself denies us our fantasies. If your child won't get on board with your Home Agreement, and he's making your life difficult, put an end to his fantasy. Reality, instead of another therapist, can be the best therapy. Doing this isn't unkind; just the opposite. Over time, life's "school of hard knocks" will bring any true clinical issues to the surface to be worked out.

> Reality, instead of another therapist, can be the best therapy.

Failure Is Not the Operative Word

The parents with whom I work often struggle with serious feelings of doubt, guilt, and regret about how they parented. It doesn't necessarily work to tell a parent to not feel guilty. You just do sometimes. When I discuss these emotions with parents, I find I hold up the mirror. "Yes, your son is making poor choices and has hurt many people." "Your daughter is an addict who struggles with keeping a job. She is choosing a tough road, and you can not control her." "It's hard watching this, isn't it?" "So you do know, deep down, that you've done the best you knew how at the time and are continuing to do so?"

> Inevitably the healing comes when the parent recognizes his or her true part in the story of their child's life and allows their child to own and have her story.

Acknowledging guilt and other feelings is part of your work. In doing it, be honest with yourself about how you parented, but also be honest in letting your child bear the decisions and consequences he has made. Let him own who he is. You did not put the cocaine in his face. He did. You did not invent bipolar depression. It just happens. Inevitably the healing comes when the parent recognizes his or her true part in the story of their child's life and allows their child to own and have her story.

Dealing with your feelings and being open and honest allows you to create your story of this journey with your child. Let it be a realistic story, a human story. This will give you the ammo you need when well-intentioned acquaintances, friends, or family say something that triggers shame or guilt. Have a story you can tell the world that lets you and your child have dignity. An honest reckoning can help stop unnecessary guilt and provide a hefty amount of emotional relief.

When a teen or young adult needs more support, it doesn't mean that he or you have failed. Serious regression doesn't necessarily mean it was a poor decision to bring your child home, although some parents later admit that they knew in their hearts it wasn't the right time. Major regression can mean he isn't resilient enough to cope with the home environment at this point in his life, and needs to move on to heal and mature. Sometimes a family has reached its limits in the help it can give. Occasionally the child isn't trying his hardest and chooses a far-less-than-optimal path. The few times a transition home has *not* succeeded, I have always heard the parents say, "We did all we could." And then they were able to plot Plan C for their child's future with an open heart.

So I invite you to look at a road away from home as possibly being a necessary part of your child's journey. If you hadn't brought her home, she might never have gotten certain emotional needs met that could have plagued her for life. She needed to come home and experience fuddy-duddy reality to realize that her addiction is still strong or that immaturity is still ruling her decision-making. Yes, even when the transition home is bumpy, messy, and ultimately unsuccessful, it's still an important part of your child's life story. She came home, and now it's time for her to embark on her own heroine's journey.

Try not to get lost in this snapshot in time. Long-term, and sometimes not even that very long, I see and believe that most kids turn out much like their parents. The teen and young adult years are rife with separating from parents and dissention, and yet, much of the time, all those seeds planted through a lifetime of growing up with you are still here. Leaving home for more treatment or living on one's own and working, going off to college, or backpacking in Europe just might be the watering and fertilizing your child needs. Not all is gotten at home anymore, but the basics *were* planted. It's time now to let your child's roots sink into the earth and the branches grow and spread into the world.

Chapter 16 Action Plan: Surviving a Transition in Trouble

(To download blank worksheets, visit www.TheRoadHomeBook.com/downloads.)

#1. If Things Don't Work Out

Review the "If Things Don't Work Out" clause of your Home Agreement. Have you made a list of actions to take if regression occurs? If not, do so now. What will you do if your child regresses severely? Who will you turn to? For example:

increase therapy hours, call Mary the Ed Consultant, check out the outpatient rehab clinic Carol's son went to with much success, research a community service gap year in Africa

17

Paving the Road Ahead

I get up each day feeling inspired to help families succeed in a post-treatment world. Why? Because I see the love and the undying "never-give-up" mentality of parents. I began this work with a passion for helping teens and young adults, and it blossomed into a greater passion for the parents and their work. I love parents, and I have found that, when I work with them, I get more done for their kids.

If this book has given you hope for the future that you'll share with your child, I have fulfilled my intent. And I'm not referring to elusive hope based on wanting your child to be "fixed" in treatment, but real, practical hope based on preparation. *The Road Home* asks that you do a lot of upfront work: to sort out what type of parent you want and dream to be, to have confidence in yourself and what you hold dear, and to spell out to yourself and your child what it means to be a member of your family.

Most importantly, it asks you to follow through on what you put in your Home Agreement. Don't forget: you can always change ineffective agreement specifics such as curfew or a rule about cars or chores, but the vision and values rarely change. A huge chunk of this process, your work, is about standing behind who you are—when you can be that loving traffic cop, when you can be clear on what you expect and set up boundaries with consequences. When you stand by your Home Agreement as if it's the law of the land, you'll find that one day you have a healthy, mature, and independent child, capable of going out on his or her own.

What's Left for You to Do?

In your process of reading *The Road Home*, your child's homecoming success has been your main preoccupation. What else is left to do? Live! Live the life you spelled out for your child in the Home Agreement, the life based on who you are and the legacy you want to leave for future generations. You've paved a road home for your child, educated yourself on his clinical nuances, and given him a road map with which to navigate the future.

You should feel proud, accomplished, and ready. But if you need any further encouragement, let it be this: I created this model because it works. The great majority of the families I coach succeed at helping their child adjust to life back home after treatment. Whether your child's treatment lasted 28 days or two years, you'll be feeling anxious

THE ROAD HOME

HEALTHY MATURE CHILD

A person, whether an adolescent or young adult, who takes responsibility for his or her own physical and mental health, chooses to be functional in daily life, and reaches for his or her potential.

HOME AGREEMENT

CONSEQUENCES

RULES OF THE ROAD

EXPECTATIONS

PARENTAL VISION

FAMILY VALUES

POSSIBLE ISSUES

Communication & Attitude   Dishonesty   Laziness & Lack of Motivation
Hygiene, Exercise, Diet & Sleep   Piercing & Tattoos   Smoking, Drinking or Drug Use
Cutting   Eating Disorders   Peers   Dating, Love & Sex   Curfew   Money
Counseling, Therapy & Medication   Spirituality & Faith   Chores & Work Ethic
Education & Academics   Technology   Pornography   Video Gaming   Cars & Driving

about her success back at home. You'll face trying days, complicated days, and days that are confusing, saddening, or maybe even dark.

For whatever reason, maybe a full moon, there will be days when your child pushes against too many boundaries or goes through some gut-wrenching struggles. Expect those days. Expect two steps back and three steps forward. This will sometimes prove difficult, and feel like a relentless test. But the bold truth is that the journey of raising a child, especially one who has gone to treatment, starts and ends with your parenting. Life with your child won't be all raindrops on roses and whiskers on kittens, but you can make the most of life with your child by adhering to the values and structure in your Home Agreement.

> Live the life you spelled out for your child in the Home Agreement, the life based on who you are and the legacy you want to leave for future generations.

You may feel exhausted some days, and without answers, if your child chooses to challenge who you are and what you believe in. I have no greater words of wisdom to offer than "Hang in there." Trust yourself. You can get through the moment-to-moment deliberations of daily parenting. When you're feeling vulnerable and weak, drop into TLC and don't back down from what matters most to your soul. Because you took the time to create your Home Agreement and to engage in healthy communication patterns, you can weather the storms.

I withstand such storms daily with my clients. I show flexibility and reasonableness when the child has a workable or better idea, but ultimately success occurs when I stand firmly as an individual who is responsible for guiding this young person into maturation. Your child needs your wise guidance. She needs to know with every sinew and nerve that you've got her back and you are not going to falter.

Keeping the Doors Open

When you're living day to day and are stressed, tired, worried about work, and facing life's many challenges, it's easy to forget about the Home Agreement and parenting from the middle of the road. For those days when your patience, your parenting skills, and maybe even your core beliefs are tested, you'll need a communication process with which to wade through the morass with your child and partner. Families don't just *survive* on authenticity and mature relating, they *thrive*. No matter what happens to your child, no matter what he or she chooses, keep the doors open for transparent and loving communication—TLC.

If you have the foundation of an honest relationship based on trust, not judgment, which comes from consistent boundaries and consequences, you'll be able to work things out. At the very least, you'll understand one another. You might not agree, but you'll understand. Your child, especially as a young adult, must make her own choices—based on your guidance. It's her life. Setting up a viable structure with the Home Agreement provides your child an opportunity to live authentically. And a lifestyle should be authentic by the young adult's own definition as well as yours. As your child makes choices, let her fail. Don't be quick to rescue. Have the faith in her to know that, with the roadside assistance you provide only when she really needs and requests it, she can navigate this next phase of life's road on her own.

I can think of no more selfless or honorable thing to do in life than to be a parent. The love, patience, energy, empathy, and integrity that a parent puts forth to grow a child is extraordinary. Sometimes the support you offer is scorned, ignored, or rebuked, and still you continue to love.

You're a parent, and you'll never be otherwise. It's who you are. You have chosen this path, and it's leading you somewhere. Don't give up, and yet don't work harder than your child at his life. Let him self-determine. Let him figure out how to fly from your nest and then let him do it.

My intention is that someday you will see an aspect of your vision and values alive in your child. It won't be exactly how you dreamed it would be, but it might be even better. Once your child leaves, you might not see him for days, months, or longer, but sometime in the future your two roads will merge, and your child will say, "Hey, can I walk with you?"

That's when you'll know you've done your job.

You're a parent, and you'll never be otherwise. It's who you are.

Acknowledgments

I can honestly say that this book would not have happened without the leadership of Heide Boyden. Her incredible passion, dogged determination, and organizational skills encouraged me in making this dream come true. Thank you, Heide!

Thank you to Marco Morelli and your wonderfully creative wife, Kayla. You get me. You have listened to me for years and made me look presentable to the world. Thank you for creating the cover, formatting this book, and creating the "look." I love working with you guys, and hope to do so for many years to come.

Thank you to the art director, Joseph J Jolton, and the artist, Greer Haines Nelson, who did "drawings and stuff." You two nailed the cartoon graphics. So glad a teacher-student team, in step with youth, created the mirth this book needed.

Much appreciation to those who reviewed and judiciously critiqued the manuscript: Anne Lewis, Hallie Rosen, Jacque Connor, Trudie Town, Dave Boyden, and Heide Boyden. Your comments made all the difference. Each bit of feedback was digested and contemplated, and each affected the outcome of the final draft. That 10 percent of change made 100 percent of the difference. Your time is precious, and I am so grateful that you gave some to this book.

Thank you, Sonia Nordenson, for doing the copyediting. Your attention to detail smoothed out my voice. You made me sound good. Cheers to you.

To my parents: You took the time to parent me, and I am eternally grateful. Your spirit and personality are alive in this book, and I hope I have honored you. Forever I am grateful to have you as parents for life.

To my sibs—Matt, Felicia, Mike, and Cece—thank you for believing in me, giving me useful feedback for the book, and, most importantly, helping me laugh when I got too serious.

Thank you to a few dear friends who were particularly encouraging when I felt doubtful: Joshua Cluff, Jade Wimberly, LeeAnne Heinbaugh, Peter Milhado, Vania Matheus, Michael Wilson, Katie McHugh, John Adams, Orlando Pablo Eguez Gutierrez, John Cohen, Lori Schmidt, Mary Maranville, Jean Grose, and my cousin Tom Batey.

I am grateful for my community in Meiners Oaks ("Mo Town") and Ojai, California. My little "Mayberry" gave me the hope and inspiration that I, too, am a writer. Without your holding my hand I would never have dared to explore my literary creativity or given myself permission to write. Hey, Jon at Coffee Connection, thanks for creating a space where I could think, contemplate, and dare to type my first word.

To conclude, I am more deeply aware, and grateful beyond words, because of the moms, dads, teens, young adults, siblings, and even dogs and cats who welcome me to their families, the most sacred of all tribes. It is in their living rooms that I have learned so much of the stuff of life.

Made in the USA
Monee, IL
29 October 2022

16801541R00256